Comfort & Joy

Comfort & Joy

Nine Stories
for Christmas

Kirk H. Neely

illustrations by June Neely Kern

Spartanburg • 2006

Second printing, December 2006

Front cover and title page watercolors—June Neely Kern
Back cover photograph—Mark Olencki
Cover & book design—Mark Olencki
Project editor—Deno Trakas
Copy editing—Beth Ely, Kathy Green, Clare Neely, Emily L. Smith, Tina Smith, Betsy Teter
Scanning—Mark Olencki & Christina Smith
Printed by Electric City Printing in Anderson, South Carolina

Library of Congress Cataloging-in-Publication Data

Neely, Kirk H.
  Comfort & joy : nine stories for Christmas / by Kirk H. Neely ; illustrations by June Neely Kern.
    p. cm.
  ISBN 1-891885-49-9 (pbk. : alk. paper)—ISBN 1-891885-50-2 (hardback : alk. paper)
  1. Christmas stories, American. I. Kern, June Neely, 1974-ill. II. Title. III. Title: Comfort and joy.
  PS3614.E35C66 2006
  813'.6—dc22
                20060165

Hub City Writers Project
Post Office Box 8421
Spartanburg, South Carolina 29305
(864) 577-9349 • fax (864) 577-0188 • www.hubcity.org

Table of Contents

Introduction…**ix**

Publication of *Comfort & Joy* is made possible through the generous contributions of :

Mr. Roger Milliken
The Phifer/Johnson Foundation
The South Carolina Arts Commission

Mr. and Mrs. Callis J. Anderson, Jr.
Greg and Lisa Atkins
Valerie and Bill Barnet
Mr. and Mrs. Dean Anderson
Mrs. John Anderson
Mr. and Mrs. James Ballew
Mr. and Mrs. Robert Caldwell
Cleveland-White Realtors
Dr. and Mrs. Paul Cook
Mr. and Mrs. John Faris
Donald L. Fowler

Mrs. Harry Gibson
Stewart and Ann Johnson
The Hon. Bruce Littlejohn
Ed and Gail Medlin
Mr. and Mrs. Ken Neely
Dwight and Liz Patterson
Mr. and Mrs. Robert V. Pinson
Jerry Richardson
Mr. and Mrs. F.A. Smith
Mr. and Mrs. William Turrentine
Bette Wakefield
Mr. and Mrs. John B. White, Sr.

Arkwright Foundation
Barnet LLC
Carol and Jim Bradof
Mellnee G. Buchheit
Harrison Chapman
Sally and Jerry Cogan, Jr.
Colonial Trust Co.
Nancy Rainey Crowley
Dave and Sandy Edwards

John and Nora Beth Featherston
Marsha and Jimmy Gibbs
Marianna and Roger Habisreutinger
Dr. and Mrs. Bob Haas
Dr. and Mrs. Hugh Hayes
Dr. Carol and Charles Ketchen
Olencki Graphics, Inc.
Mr. and Mrs. Milton Smith
Spartanburg County Foundation

Dr. and Mrs. Mitchell H. Allen
Margaret Allen
Patty and Mack Amick
Tom and Ceci Arthur
Ryan and Kim Atchley
Mr. and Mrs. Robert Atkins
Nancy Babb
Lamar and Kimberly Baehr
Brion Bahnmuller
Mr. and Mrs. Thomas Bartram
Charles and Christi Bebko
Philip and Kelly Belcher
Ann Bishop
Clarke and Martha Blackman
Shirley Blaes
June and Glen Boggs II
Carl and Carol Anne Bostick
Ann Brown
Faye Brown
Linda R. Brown
Paul and Cathy Burnett
William and Katherine Burns
Katherine and Marvin Cann
Terry and Janis Cash
Ruth L. Cate
John and Lisa Chapman
Martha Chapman
Lora Chisholm
Nan and Tim Cleveland
Robert and Janeen Cochran
Marcy and Lester Collins
Mr. and Mrs. Richard L. Conner
Austin Connors,
   in memory of Doris Connors
Mr. and Mrs. Justin A. Converse
The Hon. and Mrs. Gordon Cooper
Mike and Nancy Corbin
Jim and Jan Couch
Tom Moore Craig
John and Kirsten Cribb
Mr. and Mrs. Wade Crow
Garrow and Chris Crowley
Debra Daniel
Mr. and Mrs. H. Lee Davis Jr.
Wilhelmina S. Dearybury

Fredrick B. Dent
Georgie and Bill Dickerson
Bob and Doris Dinning
Judy Dodd
Chris and Alice Dorrance
Dr. and Mrs. William C. Elston
The Rev. Beth Wickenberg Ely
Virginia Elwell
Andy and Lynne Falatok
Mr. and Mrs. John Faris
Sharon Fields-McCormick
Elsie Finkelstein
Marilyn Fisher
Vivian Fisher
Anne and Larry Flynn
Liz and Will Fort
Caleb and Cordelia Fort
Dr. and Mrs. J. Sidney Fulmer
Mr. and Mrs. T. Lyell Garland
Lee and Patricia Gaskins
Barney and Elaine Gosnell
Mr. and Mrs. Will Gramling
Mr. and Mrs. Charles Gray
Margaret and Chip Green
Maribelle Green
Mr. and Mrs. Tom Grier
Lucy Grier
Jim and Kay Gross
Lt. Col. C. L. Guthrie Jr.
Dr. and Mrs. Magdy Habib
Lee and Kitty Hagglund
Benjamin and Tanya Hamm
Mr. and Mrs. Robert Hammett
Mr. and Mrs. Robert Harbison III
Karen P. Harris
Eaddy Williams Hayes
Kirk Hedden
Mike and Nancy Henderson
Rick and Coby Hennecy
Lisa Dinning Henningsen
The Rev. and Mrs. Mike Hensley
Mr. and Mrs. Michael Henthorn
Marie High
Hot Eye Photography
Doug and Marilyn Hubbell

Erin M. Hubbell
Mr. and Mrs. Kenneth R. Huckaby
Jim and Patsy Hudgens
Margaret W. Hudson
Barry and Susan Huey
Woodrow Hughes
Max Hyde
David and Harriet Ike
Sadie Jackson
Bill James
Dr. and Mrs. Vernon Jeffords
William Jeffords
Thomas L. Johnson
Lottie H. Johnston
Mr. and Mrs. Albert Jolly
Mr. and Mrs. Charles W. Jones
Frannie Jordan
Jim Joyner
Mr. and Mrs. Daniel Kahrs
Charles and Peggy Kay
Ann J. Kelly
Bennett and Karla King
Mr. and Mrs. R. Kugler
Jack W. Lawrence
Wood and Janice Lay
Chris and Christy Ledford
Francie and Lindsay Little
Wayne Loudermilk
Brownlee and Julie Lowry
Robert and Nancy Lyon
Dr. and Mrs. Nathaniel Magruder
James Maguire
Honor Marks
Mr. and Mrs. Harold T. Marshall
George and Agnes Martin
Zerno E. Martin Jr.
Gaines H. Mason
Dan and Kit Maultsby
Jill and John McBurney
Dr. and Mrs. Dean McKinney
Jerry and Janet McLeskey
Bob McMichael
Boyce and Carole Miller
David and Angie Mims
Whit and Jackie Mims

Chip and Peggy Mims
Karen and Bob Mitchell
Eileen and James Mitchell
Sam and Dennis Mitchell
Lewis and Dolly Mitchell
Mr. and Mrs. Walter Montgomery, Jr.
Nancy and Lawrence Moore
Daniel Moore
George D. Mullinax
Woody Needham
Bob Neely
Emily and Kam Neely
Kirk and Ruth Neely
Rena G. Neely
Virginia New
John Newcome
Jim Norris
Corry and Amy Oakes
Janice Pack
Geneva F. Padgett
Mr. and Mrs. W. Keith Parris
Carolyn Pennell
Mr. and Mrs. Edward P. Perrin
Mickey and Nancy Pierce
Andrew Poliakoff
John and Lynne Poole
Harold P. Powell
Mr. and Mrs. L. Perrin Powell
W.O. and Elizabeth Pressley

Mr. and Mrs. Clinton Pruitt
Mr. and Mrs. Norman Pulliam
Phil and Frances Racine
Eileen N. Rampey
Karen Randall
Allison and John Ratterree
Mr. and Mrs. Richard Rhodes
Ricky and Betsy Richardson
Elisabeth Robe
Dr. and Mrs. Thomas L. Roberts
Martial and Amy Robichaud
Ann Weaver Rogers
Ronald and Peggy Romine
Donna Long Roper
Steve and Elena Rush
S & ME, Inc.
Muffet and Olin Sansbury
John and Sue Scott
Maribel Sharkoff
Tony and Flonnie Shaw
Rep. Doug Smith
Dot Smith
Betty B. Snow
Harold and Jo Sosbee
B.G and Sandra Stephens
Eliot and Michel Stone
Dr. and Mrs. James Story
Mamie Suits
Christine and Bob Swager
Allene and Jess Taylor

John Lane and Betsy Teter
Ray Thompson
Rachael Deal Thompson
Rolin Tillie
Bob and Cheryl Tillotson
Tim and Diane Timmons
Nick Trainor
Michael and Janna Trammell
Mark and Pat Voelker
Mr. and Mrs. J.W. Wakefield
Charles Reback and Melissa Walker
Mary and Bill Walter
Mr. and Mrs. John Wardlaw
Dr. and Mrs. Lawrence Warren
Mr. and Mrs. Wofford Webb
Billy and Lindsay Webster
David and Kathy Weir
Dave and Linda Whisnant
David and Jana White
John B. White, Jr.
Neila R. Whitlock
Mary K. Wilborn
Alanna and Don Wildman
Mary G. Willis
Bob and Carolyn Wynn
Julia B. Young
Young Office Supply
Suzanne and Jon Zoole
Mr. and Mrs. Kurt Zimmerli

Introduction

The season of Advent presents two challenges to a pastor. The first is to tell the old story to people who have heard it over and over again as well as to those who are only vaguely familiar with it. The preaching task is to retain and restore the mystery and wonder of the original story, liberating Mary and Joseph, the shepherds and the magi from imprisonment as stained glass icons, freeing them to be real people again.

The second challenge is to remember that Christmas is a time of sharp emotional contrasts. Many people are happy and have little difficulty finding joy in the season, but December brings sadness to others. For those who are hurting, the coming of Christmas may be filled with dread, despair, bitterness, and anger. Some are freshly wounded; others carry deep scars from years gone by. For them, Christmas is anything but "the season to be jolly." They suffer while others celebrate.

In forty years of pastoral ministry, I have learned that there is no better way to present the message of hope and love that is at the heart of Christmas than through stories that parallel and perhaps merge with the original story.

In my first year as pastor at Morningside Baptist Church in Spartanburg, South Carolina, I told a Christmas story as a part of the sermon on the last Sunday in Advent. I recounted the time I played the part of Joseph in a children's Christmas play at Croft Baptist Church. The Morningside congregation was delighted with the change in format. Several friends encouraged me to present a new story every Christmas. In the years since, on the Sunday a week or so before December 25, we have removed the pulpit from the sanctuary and replaced with an easy chair where I sit and tell an original Christmas story, written as my gift to the congregation.

Each of the stories in this collection started life as a sermon. In their original forms they included a neatly crafted homiletic conclusion and a traditional Baptist altar call. Some were printed in the Spartanburg *Herald-Journal*. I have rewritten them for this book, editing them for a wider readership. Some are much longer than the original versions. All have significant changes, new characters or new twists. If you have heard or read one of these nine stories before, I encourage you to read it again. Now they are different and, I believe, improved.

I am often asked, "Where do you find your stories?" The stories come from life events, most from my own personal experiences. Following her mother's death, for example, my wife, Clare, found in her mother's possessions a gold charm bracelet with a silver bell attached. Then there was the hot August afternoon when I ascended the disappearing stairway into my mother-in-law's attic where I discovered an old tattered quilt, half-eaten by mice. The Christmas following our son Erik's death, we placed a Fraser fir tree on his grave and prepared ourselves for the possibility that it might be stolen. Another story emerged when my sister's snow globe collection disintegrated in the heat of her attic. An unemployed textile plant manager provided inspiration when he shared with me his struggle to provide for his family. On a visit to the ancient Angel Oak, I was surprised to learn that there were no published stories about the tree. So I wrote one. I was invited to speak to our local chapter of the Blue Star Mothers, and I decided their stories needed to be told, too.

A well-written piece of fiction seems real because it conveys truth about life. The people in these stories were birthed in my own imagination. Their thoughts, words, and actions are my own creation. If you think you see yourself or people you know in these stories, it is completely unintentional, but it is also just as it should be.

The stories are written for adults, but most of them—maybe all of them—are suitable for teenagers and children. I can imagine a family reading these stories aloud together. The responsibility for deciding whether they are appropriate, I leave to the parents, who always know best.

Clare and I have experienced both the joy and the sorrow that Christmas can bring. Our oldest child, Mike, was born on Christmas Day 1970. As we awaited his birth, the season of Advent was filled with anticipation and hope. The uncertainty and apprehension of becoming new parents was part of our emotional mix. Christmas was a day of fulfillment for us. Thirty years later, our second son, Erik, died two weeks before Thanksgiving. Christmas that year was a season of deep grief for us. Still, we were able to find a measure of peace and joy mingled with our tears.

Erik's widow, June, has always been like a daughter to us. She has allowed us to share the journey of grief and the joy of life with her. June's beautiful watercolor illustrations enhance these stories beyond measure. Together we have dedicated this book to the memory of Erik. He would have enjoyed the stories. He would have loved the art. Erik would have been so excited to see this book in print!

I know of a home where the decorated Christmas tree remains in the living room throughout the year. The tree is, of course, artificial, but the life situation that prompted the custom is real. At the beginning of the Christmas season, after they had put up their tree, the onset of a terminal illness besieged the family. At the end of the holidays, they just could not muster the energy to take the tree down. Over time, their reason for leaving their Christmas tree in place changed. "My husband got sick the first week of December and died twenty months later in August," said the widow. "The whole time he was dying we enjoyed the tree. It gave us a feeling of peace and comfort."

My hope and prayer is that these stories will bring you peace, comfort, and joy at Christmas and all through the year.

—Faithfully,
Kirk H. Neely

The Angel Tree

Sara Williams sat in a lawn chair beside Highway 17 North, seven miles up the road from Mount Pleasant, South Carolina. She had positioned the chair to take full advantage of the lengthening shade of the palmetto tree that stood next to Gertrude Hawkins' roadside stand. Even in late November, in the Lowcountry, the midday temperatures could reach into the 80s. The three-sided structure was made from weathered gray slats, as were most of the other basket stands along the highway. Gertrude had graciously offered Sara the use of the stand on the weekends, since Gertrude sold her baskets at the Old Market in Charleston on Saturdays and Sundays.

Weekend traffic along Route 17 was always heavy, but on this Saturday afternoon after Thanksgiving there were even more cars than usual. Most of the travelers were in a hurry, hurtling from wherever they had been for the holiday, returning to wherever they were going. Though she had been working at the stand for nearly seven hours, Sara had sold only two of her baskets.

Sara's nimble fingers worked on a newly begun basket. She had learned the craft years ago from Granny Lucy, regarded as one of the finest makers of sweetgrass baskets in all of Charleston County. Many people credited Granny Lucy's mother with saving the art of sweetgrass basketry from extinction after World War I. The younger women, even Granny Lucy's own sisters, had not been interested in learning to make baskets. Granny Lucy's mother was the first woman to open a roadside stand on Highway 17 North. She encouraged women who still knew the craft to set up roadside stands as well. Before long, tourists were buying baskets, and older women were teaching younger women to sew sweetgrass, bulrushes, and pine needles into coiled baskets, using thin strips of palmetto leaves.

Sara's hands moved at a steady pace. "Not too fast, not too slow." She could almost hear Granny Lucy's thin voice cracking as she spoke to her. Sara inserted a small bundle of pine needles into the sweetgrass, blending the dark brown needles in with the lighter strands of grass. She pressed the nailbone through the previous coil as she sewed, stacking a new coil in place and pulling the palm strip tightly. She wore Band-Aids on the thumb and the index finger of her right hand to keep the thin palmetto strip from cutting or blistering her fingers. Granny Lucy would never have used Band-Aids because her hands were calloused and tough from years of sewing with palmetto strips.

A sharp awl-like nailbone and scissors were Sara's only tools. A nailbone was usually made from the bone of an animal or a steel nail. It was sharpened to a point and used to open a hole between the sweetgrass coils so the palmetto strip could be sewed, binding the coils tightly together. Upon her grandmother's death, Sara had inherited Granny Lucy's nailbone, a fine silver spoon handle that had been sharpened on a grinding stone by Sara's grandfather.

Sara thought of Gertrude at the Old Market in Charleston. Baskets were probably selling well there. At the market tourists were on foot. They seemed to have more leisure and more money than those who stopped at the stands beside the highway to Georgetown. Customers at the Old Market didn't haggle as much over the price. They seemed to understand that these baskets were folk art, remnants of an ancient African culture from three centuries back in time and half a world away.

Earlier in the afternoon a couple driving north in a silver Lexus with Pennsylvania tags had stopped to look. "Why do they call them sweetgrass baskets?" the blonde woman asked, smelling the one she was holding. "It doesn't smell sweet."

Sara explained that sweetgrass smells like freshly mown hay when it is first gathered. "As the grass dries, the fragrance is fainter."

"Did you weave all of these?" the bald man asked, pointing with one hand to the array of baskets in the stand while swatting black gnats with the other hand.

"The baskets are not woven; they are sewn," Sara quietly explained. "You can judge the quality of a basket by holding it up to the light. You should not be able to see any light shining through."

The woman seemed enchanted by Sara's voice. "What language are you speaking? I mean, what is that accent?"

Sara smiled, "I speak English but with a Gullah accent."

"Where did you learn to speak it?"

"From my parents and grandparents, who learned from my ancestors all the way back to the West Coast of Africa."

"So, did you make all of these baskets?" the man asked again, holding one up to the sunlight as he continued to fight the gnats.

"Yes, I made all of these."

"Must not take very long. What kind of job do you have?"

"This is my main job," said Sara. "I also have another job in Charleston."

The man was not listening. "Just making grass baskets? That's it?"

"What kind of job do you have?" Sara asked.

"I am a land developer," answered the man, swatting to no avail the black gnats swarming around his sweating bald head and hooded eyes. "How do you stand these bugs?" he asked in frustration. "I don't see you swatting."

"Those are no-see-ums," Sara explained. "You'll wear yourself out swiping at them. We just puff them away." She demonstrated the technique by protruding her lower lip and blowing several short breaths directed up toward her nose and eyes.

The bald man tried unsuccessfully to puff the gnats away but made himself even more attractive to the pests by drooling down his double chin.

The blonde woman selected one of the larger baskets. She handed it to her husband and asked him to purchase it as a gift for her mother. When he looked at the price, he had a red-faced fit. "One hundred and fifty bucks for a bunch of grass, pine needles, and palm leaves! No way! Especially not for my mother-in-law! How long did it take you to make that thing?"

"Not counting gathering the materials, about a week to sew it," replied Sara in her quiet manner. With that, the couple left, arguing over issues that went far deeper than the fair market price of sweetgrass baskets. The silver automobile roared away, heading north without a basket.

Sara returned to her basket making, welcoming the solitude. Land developers were not her favorite people. In Granny Lucy's day Daniel Island was one of the best places to gather sweetgrass. The expansion of the city of Mount Pleasant and the development of Daniel Island had made sweetgrass scarce. In the old days men and boys gathered the materials for the baskets. Granny Lucy used to say that she had never even set foot in the marsh.

"I couldn't navigate the pluff mud," she would say with a chuckle, referring to the deep, gooey muck that reeked of decaying shellfish.

Her husband, Papa Sam, used to say, "You can just about lose a good-sized dog in marsh mud at low tide." Papa Sam used to bring back sweetgrass and bulrushes after every fishing trip. He never came home empty-handed, even when the fish weren't biting. Now Sara had to go by boat to Deweese Island and slog through knee-deep, smelly pluff mud to gather sweetgrass. She had never lost a dog in the marsh, but once the pluff mud sucked off and swallowed the shoe from her left foot.

A flock of geese flew into the low sun that hung just above the Wando River to the west. Sara carefully packed her baskets into the rusty trunk of her 1983 Toyota, the car her father had given her. Jim Williams had worked hard to make a living for his family. His oft-stated motto was, "You gotta scrabble hard to make life more better." His regular job was driving a logging truck for a timber company. His side job was cutting cypress knees and making them into lamps, tables, stools, and other knickknacks that tourists might buy. He used to display them in the roadside stand where his wife, Ma Janie, sold her baskets. Big Jim, as the other loggers called him, gave Sara the used Toyota as an early graduation present when she was still a junior in high school, and it was still running now twenty years later. She needed transportation for her part-time job as a waitress back then, so he gave her the car early. But Sara never graduated.

Most of the cars on Highway 17 had turned on their headlights as Sara drove into traffic. She stopped at the Piggly Wiggly for a few groceries. Sara selected the items she needed and went through the express line. J.T., the store manager, spoke to her. "Hello, Sara. Did you find everything you were looking for?"

"Hey, J.T., I found it all."

"How's the basket business?"

"A little slow today."

"Even on the busiest retail weekend of the year?"

"Afraid so. I sold a few. Looks like business at The Pig is booming."

"People have to eat," J.T. laughed as Sara paid for her groceries.

"I'll see you tomorrow, I guess," Sara said, pushing her cart toward the door.

"I have to work tomorrow, too. My assistant manager is gone for the weekend. But be sure to stop by and see Tamara. She'll be at the Angel Tree just outside the Fellowship Hall. Tell Tamara you want an angel for Christmas."

Sara nodded as she turned to the door. Sara remembered when the three of them were students at Wando High in the class of 1986. J.T. had been sweet on her before she quit school in the eleventh grade. She enjoyed high school, but after she got pregnant, she had to drop out. It was the rule back then. It was Sara's first, but far from her last, big mistake. J.T. has done well for himself, she thought. He and Tamara had two children and a nice home. Tamara worked as a paralegal in Charleston.

Janie Williams had told her daughter Sara that she must never think of the pregnancy as a mistake. When Sara's baby was born, Ma Janie brought her granddaughter's name following an old African-American tradition. The naming of a child is the prerogative of the baby's grandmother or another matriarchal figure. The practice is called bringing the name. She said, "Your name is Anna. Anna, the Lord God has a plan for you." Turning to Sara, Ma Janie had said, "Your baby is not an accident. The Lord God has a plan for your child, and He has a plan for you." Still, Sara knew that she had made a mistake. Her mother knew it, too.

In an unguarded moment, Ma Janie had said, "I am just glad Gullah Jack and Mama Sallie, and Papa Sam and Granny Lucy are already in heaven. This would have been very hard for them." Sara knew it was the truth. Her mistake was hard for everybody.

She had been so foolish. She was working as a weekend waitress in a Charleston restaurant. From the first weekend on the job, she had waited on his table. He and his college friends were regular late-night customers, usually coming in about ten o'clock. A hamburger, fries, and a Coke were his usual fare. He tipped well, probably to impress her. He treated her as if she were one of them, teasing her, amused by her accent, and insisting she call him by his first name. Though Sara had dated others boys, this college boy was different, mannerly and handsome. When Sara dressed to go to work, she dressed for him.

One night after he and his friends left, he came back to the restaurant about midnight, an hour before closing. There were no other customers. He said he just wanted to be alone with her. He asked her to sit in a booth with him. They each had a Coke while they talked. He did most of the talking. When closing time came, he walked with her to her car.

Over the next three months their talks until closing became frequent. Even when he came with his friends, he would say, "I'll see you after while." If there were no customers, they would sit together in the last booth and talk. He talked about his future. He wanted to be a lawyer and a politician. His ambition was part of her attraction to him. After closing he would walk with Sara to her car, occasionally asking if they could go somewhere together. The first few times he tried to hold her, Sara resisted. She knew it would never work for the two of them to be together though it was what she dreamed about. When she finally allowed him to embrace her, her dreams became more erotic.

One warm fall night after work, her car would not start and he offered to take her home. She was reluctant, but she needed a ride. He took her instead to Sullivan's Island to a beach house owned by his fraternity. He said he had admired her and dreamed about making love to her. She was flattered and foolish. He was persistent, and she gave in.

Sara saw him only twice more at the restaurant. Once, she was called in to work on a Thursday night. He seemed surprised to see her and hardly spoke. Sara was confused and bewildered. Was he embarrassed? Was he ashamed? Was he just using her as a part of a fraternity game? Sara would never know.

The last time she saw him was after she started having morning sickness. She was not working but drove to the restaurant hoping to see him. When she told him she was pregnant, he couldn't get away fast enough. He denied that the baby was his. She still remembered his parting words, "You're not going to blame me for your Geechie baby!" Sara was deeply hurt.

When he found out what had happened, her daddy, Big Jim, wanted to find the boy and talk some sense into him. "He needs to do right by you. He should marry you." But Sara and Ma Janie knew that was impossible. It was 1984 in Charleston, South Carolina. Even the perennial senator Strom Thurmond went to his grave keeping a similar secret. The baby's father was a student at The College of Charleston, and he was white. Sara didn't know it at the time, but he was already engaged to be married to a beauty queen from Columbia. The following June, about two weeks after her baby girl was born, she read the announcement in the Charleston *Post and Courier* Sunday newspaper. Sara's hurt became anger. The frat boy and his Snow White bride were married in Columbia. He was from a prominent Charleston family; she was the daughter of an attorney. After a honeymoon in Jamaica he would enter the University of South Carolina Law School.

Sara returned to the present from her painful memories at the same time she arrived at her home. She took her grocery bags inside to spend another evening alone. She fixed a simple supper, a toasted cheese sandwich and a cup of coffee. Sitting at her kitchen table, she thought again about J.T. and Tamara. She thought about them celebrating Christmas as a family. They had done well for themselves. She remembered her daddy's words, "You gotta scrabble hard to make life more better." Sara had not done so well, but she was doing better. She looked around at the place she had called home most of her life. She felt fortunate to have a home at all after everything that had happened.

On September 21, 1989, on Sara's twenty-first birthday, Hurricane Hugo struck with a vengeance. Big Jim said it was Sara's coming-of-age party. Half of the house, the basket stand, and much of Charleston County were blown away. Ma Janie lost some of her baskets, but many were safe in the trunk of the Toyota, some of the few possessions that escaped Hugo's wrath. Much of the rest was washed away.

The family had to live for the better part of a year on John's Island in the vacant house where Ma Janie's parents had lived before they died. The home was as it had always been with no electricity, no running water, and no indoor plumbing. Through the winter months the old house was heated with the same wood stove used for cooking. Every day the Williams family drove from John's Island, across Charleston, over the Cooper River Bridge. Every day they witnessed the widespread destruction left by Hugo's fury. Trees were twisted and broken. Big boats were washed up and grounded far from the water. Buildings, large and small, were demolished. Big Jim rebuilt the roadside stand out of scrap lumber from the house. Even before electrical power was restored, Sara and Ma Janie were stationed at the new roadside stand, making and selling baskets and taking care of four-year-old Anna. Sara saw what her daddy meant by scrabbling hard to make life more better. Big Jim hauled timber and managed to work on the house for a few hours each day. Finally, a generous church group from Indiana volunteered to help them complete the rebuilding of their home.

The thought of John's Island brought back pleasant memories for Sara. Her granddaddy had been a legend on John's Island. Everyone knew him as Gullah Jack. He and Mama Sallie lived on a small farm on Hoopstick Road near Bohicket Creek. Gullah Jack grew the best vegetables: squash, corn, cabbage, okra, tomatoes, green beans, butter beans, and black-eyed peas. He raised pigs and had a yard full of chickens, ducks, and guinea hens. He grew cantaloupes and watermelons to sell along Maybank Road out of the back of his mule-drawn wagon.

Gullah Jack was also one of the best fishermen on Bohicket Creek. He used only a hand line and a cast net as he fished from his *bateau*, a flat-bottom, wooden boat with a square stern and bow. As a girl Sara frequently went fishing with Gullah Jack on Bohicket Creek in his homemade boat. She recalled a time in particular when she and Gullah Jack brought the *bateau* back loaded to the gunnels with creek shrimp.

As Sara washed her plate and cup, dried them, and put them away, her cell phone rang and she answered. "Hello...Yes, this is Sara Williams...Yes, I'm at home for the night...Yes, I'm going to church tomorrow. No problems, at all...Good-bye."

The call was from her parole officer. Though the calls could be annoying, Sara was glad to comply with the terms of her parole, which was scheduled to come to an end the week after Christmas. She had made significant changes in her life. She was a free woman, and she wanted to stay that way. The only thing she still wanted to change was her relationship with her daughter, Anna. Sara had not seen Anna in ten years, since her daughter was eleven years old. Sara had heard that Anna had lived with a foster family in North Charleston for seven years and then had joined the Army. She was convinced that in time, her relationship with Anna would be better, too. With that thought in mind, Sara showered, said her prayers, got into bed, and slept soundly.

✳   ✳   ✳

On Sunday morning, Sara went to church, not because it pleased her probation officer, but because church was where she wanted to be. The congregation of Olive Branch African Methodist Episcopal Church had stood by her through deep water. When her mother and father died, the members brought food. When she was too strung out and too ashamed to attend, the people refused to give up on her, try though she might to avoid them. When she was arrested, the pastor visited her in jail. When the Department of Social Services took Anna away from her, the church was her support system. Her church was her family now.

As she had promised J.T., Sara went by the Fellowship Hall to find Tamara and the Angel Tree. "Hey, Sara! J.T. said I would see you, girl. He wants you to have an angel from the Angel Tree."

"Hey, Tamara. Tell me how this works."

"The Angel Tree is supposed to help children who otherwise won't have much Christmas. You see all of these paper angel ornaments? Each one has written on it a child's name, age, sizes, and a toy they've requested. You just choose a name. Buy two or three gifts for that child. Wrap the presents. Either we'll deliver them or, if you like, you can deliver them to the child before Christmas. Most of the children on our Angel Tree are the children of prisoners."

For a moment, Sara could not speak. Tears welled up in her eyes. When she was able to speak, she said, "I'll be glad to take an angel."

"Thank you, Sara. Just choose the angel you want. I know you'll help a child have a merry Christmas."

Sara selected just one of the thirty or more paper angels hanging on the small artificial tree. Her eyes still moist, she put the small paper angel in her purse without even looking at it.

On the last Sunday of November, The Hanging of the Green was the morning worship service at Olive Branch A.M.E. Church. When Sara was a little girl, her daddy, Big Jim, joked about the service. "We're gonna have a hanging at church. Some fellow named Green."

Sara corrected him, "No, Daddy, it's the hanging of greens!"

"Oh," he teased. "We're hanging up turnip greens and collard greens."

The Hanging of the Green service was the way they began the Christmas season. The idea was borrowed from a white congregation some time back. Sara remembered her daddy saying, "White folks just don't have as much religion as black folks." The members of Olive Branch gave the Hanging of the Green service their own touch. The choir and congregation broke out Christmas carols that had been lying dormant for a year. Scriptures from the Old Testament prophets were read. Mixed into all the singing, the swaying, the clapping, and the amens, the congregation decorated the sanctuary with wreaths and garlands, ribbons and bows. The finishing touch was the trimming of the Chrismon tree with ornaments made by the children of the church. Their ornaments, depicting Christian symbols, were hung on the tree as the choir sang "O Come, All Ye Faithful."

Following the service, Sara drove the old Toyota past the church cemetery where Papa Sam and Granny Lucy, Big Jim and Ma Janie were all buried. Making her way through the construction zone on Route 17, she drove to work at the borrowed stand of Gertrude Hawkins. She stopped at the drive-in window of a local fast-food restaurant. She ordered a chicken sandwich combo and proceeded to Gertrude's stand, just across the highway from the entrance to Boone Hall Plantation. Sara parked her car beside the stand nestled close to the palmetto tree.

Taking her lawn chair from the back seat of the car, Sara set about the task of arranging her basket display. Once the baskets were all set in place, she sat down to enjoy her lunch and wait for customers. On this Sunday afternoon, there was more waiting than customers. The up side was that a slow day gave Sara time to work on the basket she had begun the day before. Most of all, she needed time to think.

Christmas was coming, and Sara faced the prospect of celebrating Christmas alone. Christmas had always been a happy time for Sara and her family. Each year they drove to John's Island the weekend before Christmas. Her grandparents put up a red cedar Christmas tree in the front room and decorated it with homemade ornaments. Gullah Jack always told the story about how electricity came to John's Island way back in 1948 when Ma Janie was just two years old. But, he declared proudly, he and Mama Sallie had never needed electrical power. Then he would add that Bohicket Road was paved the same year Ma Janie was born.

Christmastime for Gullah Jack was hog-killing time. The weather was cold enough, and the family looked forward to fresh ham, bacon, and pork chops. Mama Sallie cooked the Christmas meal on a wood-burning stove. The smell of wood smoke was one of the pleasant aromas Sara associated with Christmas.

Sara remembered that one year a hurricane had destroyed most of the crops. Gullah Jack had to sell his Christmas hog to make enough money to get by. The family was sadly resigned to the fact that they would have no Christmas ham that year.

But Gullah Jack promised, "My folks ain't gonna chew no dry bones for Christmas." He took his homemade *bateau* to the creek and fished all night long, using a gig, by the light of a kerosene lantern. After a night of striking, he had two hundred and eight sea trout. He hitched his mule and wagon and drove all the way to Carroll's Fish Market on East Bay Street in Charleston to sell the fish. With the money he got for the fish, he bought all the fixings for Christmas, including a cured ham to replace the Christmas hog he had to sell that year.

Always a part of Christmas on John's Island was the traditional pilgrimage to the ancient Angel Oak. Every year, Mama Sallie, Ma Janie, and Sara went to the towering live oak tree. Mama Sallie told them the story of how, as far back as the Gullah people had been living on the island, the women had gone to visit the tree before Christmas. Sara vividly remembered the annual trek to the tree. Mama Sallie held Sara on her hip with her right arm. She placed her weathered left hand on the tree. Ma Janie stood close by with a hand on each of them. Mama Sallie repeated the words, exactly the same way every year.

> *Child, this is the Tree of Life.*
> *This is where the angels come.*
> *And, if the Lord God can take care of this tree, as old as it is,*
> *God's sure gonna take care of you and me.*

The Angel Oak was a symbol of strength to these women. More importantly, it was a symbol of hope. And so, a few days before Christmas every year, the Gullah women made a pilgrimage to the massive oak tree.

✳   ✳   ✳

Sara remembered the Christmas after Mama Sallie died, when Granny Lucy went with them to the Angel Oak. Because Granny Lucy was the oldest woman, Ma Janie had insisted that she say the words, but Granny Lucy didn't know the words. Though Lucy had heard of the tree and the tradition, she had never before seen the oak or been a part of the pilgrimage. That year, Granny Lucy held Sara's hand and placed her gnarled left hand on the bark of the even more gnarled live oak. Her daughter-in-law, Ma Janie, said the words before her, like an old timey song leader lining out the words to a hymn, pausing between each line so Granny Lucy could say the words.

After Anna was born, Ma Janie found time each year, just before Christmas, to take her daughter and granddaughter to John's Island to the Angel Oak. "Why is it always before Christmas?" Sara asked one year.

"It just is," answered Ma Janie. "It's like picking a cantaloupe. There's just a right time to do it,

...if the Lord God can take care of this tree, as old as it is, God's sure gonna' take care of you and me.

and Christmastime is the right time."

Sara suspected that there was a better reason, but it was part of the tradition that had been lost. Still, Christmas did seem like a good time to be reminded that the Lord intended to take care of His children. At times, Sara wondered if God had forgotten, like the Christmas right after Hugo hit or the Christmas two years after that when she and Ma Janie were trying to understand why Big Jim had been killed. His logging truck hit a ditch, and the impact threw him out the driver's side door. The truck, loaded with pine logs, turned over on top of him, crushing him to death. Sara's daddy was only forty-seven years old when he died. In hard times the Williams women went down to John's Island to the tree as always. Ma Janie would pick Anna up in her arms and put a hand on the Angel Oak. As Sara put her arms around both of them, Ma Janie would repeat the words,

> *Child, this is the Tree of Life.*
> *This is where the angels come.*
> *And if the Lord God can take care of this tree, as old as it is,*
> *God's sure gonna to take care of you and me.*

In 1995, when Ma Janie died of cancer, Sara did not take Anna to the Angel Oak. Sara had not been back to John's Island since.

Sara's thoughts were interrupted when a car with a North Carolina tag stopped at the roadside stand. Two women got out of the car to look at the baskets. One was using a walker, and the other, the driver, assisted the older woman. Slowly they made their way to the stand. The older woman spoke pleasantly, "Are you related to Gertrude Hawkins?"

"No, ma'am. She's a friend who sometimes lets me use her stand."

The woman picked up Sara's finest basket, a large fanner, the kind used in plantation days to winnow rice. She held it up to the late afternoon sun. No light came through.

After examining the basket, she said, "I have made it a practice to purchase one basket each time I come this way. I was hoping to buy another of Gertrude's baskets, but I see she didn't make this one."

"No, ma'am, these are all my baskets."

"May I ask your name?"

"Yes, ma'am, I'm Sara."

"Sara, who taught you to make sweetgrass baskets?"

"My grandmother, Granny Lucy, taught me. And my mother, Ma Janie."

"You are a Williams."

"Yes, ma'am, Sara Williams."

"Sara, do you have a business card?"

"Not yet, I have really just gotten back into basket making. I was away from it for a while."

"Sara, you must never stop making baskets," she said, looking carefully at several more. "Please, may I have your name, address, and phone number?"

Then she said to Sara, "I see you are using your grandmother's nailbone."

"Yes, ma'am, how did you know?"

"Because that sterling silver spoon handle is my wedding pattern. I set the spoon down on a hot stove and melted the bowl right off. I gave the handle to your grandmother, Lucy."

Sara, somewhat taken aback, gave the elderly woman the information she requested. The woman bought two of the baskets, the large fanner, priced at three hundred dollars, and a breadbasket, priced at one hundred and twenty-five dollars. The elderly woman said to the younger woman, "I want you to have the breadbasket. I have been buying at least one basket a year for fifty years, and these are the finest I have seen since Sara's mother and grandmother died."

She handed Sara five one-hundred-dollar bills, adding, "I don't need change, Sara. You need to charge more for your baskets. They really are fine pieces of art."

As she used the walker to move back to the car, the woman said, "My name is Essie Messervy. I am originally from Charleston. I'll be in touch. In the meantime you need your own basket stand. And let me know where it is. I want to buy all of my baskets from you from now on."

As the car drove away, Sara sat down, hardly able to believe what had happened. She looked at the five crisp one hundred dollar bills in her hand. What a surprise to meet a woman who remembered Granny Lucy and Ma Janie. It was a pleasant and profitable ending to what started out as a slow weekend. There was a refreshing chill in the air. A purple and pink sunset streaked the sky over Charleston. Sara Williams packed her baskets and her lawn chair into the Toyota and drove back home.

When J.T. had mentioned the Angel Tree to Sara at the grocery store on Saturday, she, of course, thought of the Angel Oak. Lost in her memories of John's Island and the massive live oak, Sara had completely forgotten about the paper angel she had selected from the Angel Tree at church. Just before saying her prayers and turning in for the night, she took the small paper angel from her purse. When she opened the folded angel, Sara read for the first time the name of the child she had chosen. The child was a five-year-old girl who lived on John's Island. The little girl's name was Anna, Anna Lopez.

* * *

Monday morning started early for Sara. She dressed and fixed a bowl of cereal for breakfast. She had to be at her other job by eight o'clock. Driving into Charleston took about twice as long during rush hour, so Sara gave herself plenty of time, usually leaving her home by seven.

While she ate her Wheaties, Sara looked again at the folded paper angel from the Angel Tree at church. Five-year-old Anna Lopez wanted a baby doll for Christmas. Sara tried to remember what it was like to have a five-year-old daughter. When her daughter, Anna, was five at Christmas, it was one of the happiest times of Sara's life. It was the year after Hurricane Hugo hit and the year before Big Jim died. They were living in this same house, so recently rebuilt by the church group from Indiana.

Ma Janie had talked about how blessed they were. Anna was in a Headstart program so Sara had time to make baskets with her mother. That was the year when she really became a much better basket maker. The sweetgrass basket business had been good, as had the logging business. After Hugo, so many of the pine trees had been twisted by the hurricane that almost all of the timber had to be used for pulpwood. Big Jim had also built many pieces of cypress knee furniture to be sold at the basket stand.

On one of his excursions into the swamp, Big Jim had found an unusual cypress knee. He brought it home to show Ma Janie, Sara, and Anna.

"It looks just like Mary holding sweet little Jesus boy," he declared. It was hard to see the resemblance until Big Jim had stripped away the bark and polished the cypress wood. Then, it really did look like Mother Mary holding the Christ child. The cypress knee Madonna became the permanent centerpiece on the kitchen table in the Williams' home.

Sara touched the cypress likeness of mother and child, thinking about her own child and remembering what it was like to hold her so long ago. For her five-year-old Christmas, Anna Williams had gotten her first baby doll, a Cabbage Patch Doll from Wal-Mart. Anna Lopez would certainly have to have a baby doll for Christmas this year.

Sara placed her dishes in the kitchen sink, put on her sweater, and drove toward Charleston. The new bridge over the Cooper River made the drive into town easier. Sara was glad when the bridge opened and even happier that the old bridges were being dismantled. Charleston, she thought, is a good place to live and work, at least for most people. For Sara, though, there had been several years when Charleston had been a living hell. Whenever she came across the river, especially on the old bridge, she thought about those terrible times living and working on Shand Street on the northeast side of the city. That time in her life was like a nightmare. She just wanted to forget about it.

Sara drove to the Circular Congregational Church where she was employed as a custodian. It was a good place for Sara to work. She had gotten the job just before Christmas two years earlier while she was still a resident at Magdalene House. She was grateful to have a job. The historic downtown church had given her a chance when other employers would not. When she arrived, she parked in the lot where the church had reserved a place for her. The parking space was only one of several benefits provided by the church. Sara went to the church office and started the morning coffee.

She recalled the events that brought her to this job. After Ma Janie died, Sara felt bitter and alone. She would catch herself singing or humming, "Sometimes I Feel Like A Motherless Child." She had Anna, but Anna was only ten years old. Sara was twenty-seven. One Saturday she was selling sweetgrass baskets at the Old Market with several older women, including Gertrude Hawkins. A handsome man wearing black leather and lots of bling came along and asked Sara about the baskets. She knew intuitively that he had no interest in her baskets. He was interested in her. He would walk away for a while, and then come back to talk some more. Gertrude warned her, "Sara, he is a bad man! Look at him wearing all that gold and diamonds! He's up to no good!"

After the other women had packed up and gone, the man returned. Sara was loading her car, and he offered to help. "You say these baskets are made out of sweetgrass?"

"Yes," Sara said. "It's getting harder and harder to find."

"I know where there is some sweet grass," he said. "I'll show you."

"I don't even know your name," said Sara.

"James is the name, and you?"

"Sara."

"Sara, let's go find the sweet grass. We'll take my car."

Sara knew better, but she was terribly lonely and grieving deeply. Ma Janie had been her best friend and her strength. After she died, Sara had only Anna. Maybe Anna should have been enough, but being a single mother was exhausting. There was no relief, no one to help, other than friends from the church and that never seemed to be enough.

James paid attention to her, making her vulnerable and responsive against her better judgment. The gold chain around the license plate on his gold SUV should have been a warning sign. She had been told that the gold chain around a car tag was the symbol for black unity. For Sara it became a sign of bondage. The fact that his golden chariot, as he called it, was parked in front of the Old Slave Market was an evil omen.

James knew where to find sweet grass, all right. He had a bag of it under the front seat of the chariot. But it was not for making baskets. At age twenty-seven Sara had her first experience with marijuana. James wanted her to stay with him for the night, but Sara refused to sleep with him, insisting she must go home to Anna. She did agree to meet him after work at the restaurant on Monday. Again, they smoked grass in Charleston, while a neighbor kept an eye on Anna in Mount Pleasant. James' company and his kind of sweet grass seemed to ease the pain of loneliness and grief in Sara's heart.

After work one Friday night, Sara met James at his place on Nassau Street. They had always smoked marijuana in a water pipe. On that night James offered Sara the pipe as usual. But it was not just marijuana; it was laced with crack cocaine. One time was all it took, and Sara was hooked. Over the next several weeks, James gave her all the crack she wanted. Still she resisted his sexual advances. By then she was leaving Anna at home alone all night. The neighbor confronted her, and Sara agreed to pay the neighbor to keep Anna and take her to school each morning.

One night Sara met James, expecting to have her fix of crack, but he was different. He was harsh with her. "Baby, if you want more crack, you going to have to start paying for it." By then Sara couldn't do without it. She was missing work at the restaurant, neglecting her bills, and, worst of all, neglecting Anna. She paid for her crack habit by doing whatever James wanted her to do. He became abusive mentally and physically. His words were demeaning; his hitting was brutal. In her more lucid moments, she knew that her life was completely out of control. When she lost her job, James offered her a room on Shand Street and a job on King Street. Sara Williams became a King Street hooker.

Sara's mind shifted from her painful memories back to her work at the church. As Sara cleaned the sanctuary of the Circular Congregational Church, she read the sermon title in one of the discarded bulletins: "A New Beginning." Her mind drifted back in time. She thought about how her life had changed over the last three years. Shand Street had been a bottomless pit. She was abused by James, she was addicted to crack cocaine, and she was a streetwalker. She was arrested on multiple counts of prostitution and possession of drugs with intent to distribute.

One night while she was still in jail, she prayed for help. That night she dreamed that she was standing at the Angel Oak with Mama Sallie, Granny Lucy, Ma Janie, and Anna. She heard the voice of a woman she did not recognize speaking in a thick Gullah accent.

> *Child, this is the Tree of Life.*
> *This is where the angels come.*
> *And if the Lord God can take care of this tree, as old as it is,*
> *God's sure gonna to take care of you and me.*

✳ ✳ ✳

It was that night, in the Charleston County Jail, that Sara knew her life was going be better. It was the next day that the pastor from Olive Branch A.M.E. Church came to visit her. Two days later, she met Trina, a social worker from Magdalene House. Things had been looking up ever since. Sara had gotten the job at Circular Church with Trina's help.

Magdalene House, modeled on a similar ministry in Nashville, Tennessee, offered residential housing and a recovery program for women with a history of prostitution and drugs. Sara qualified in every way. For two years Magdalene House had provided just the help she needed to escape the bondage of Shand Street. As much as she wanted to forget that time in her life, Trina and the other women in recovery had insisted that Sara face her past. It was not easy to face. She was able to complete the GED and get the job at Circular Church. There at Magdalene House, she recovered her dignity and her integrity. With the help of Gertrude Hawkins, she started making sweetgrass baskets again. Gertrude, a longtime friend of Janie, had been a steady source of encouragement to Sara.

In the hallway outside of the sanctuary of the Circular Church, Sara saw something she recognized immediately. It was an Angel Tree. A few of the paper angels remained. A poster explained that the names of children of prisoners had been placed on the tree. This was an opportunity for church members to help needy children have a blessed Christmas. Sara wondered if anyone had helped her daughter, Anna, while Sara was enslaved to crack cocaine.

The pain of Shand Street was greatest when Sara thought about Anna. Sara's daughter had been eleven years old when the Department of Social Services removed her from Sara's care. A neighbor had been caring for Anna for eight months, but the neighbor had problems of her own, including poor health. When Sara could no longer pay, the neighbor reported the case to DSS. It was just as well, Sara thought, because the neighbor moved to a nursing home within a year.

Anna Williams lived with foster parents in North Charleston for seven years until she graduated with honors from Stratford High School. While Sara was at Magdalene House, she found out that Anna had joined the Army and was stationed at Fort Bragg, North Carolina. Reunification with family members is one of the goals of Magdalene House. Anna was Sara's only living family member. Trina had tried contacting Anna, but to no avail. Sara wondered if Anna had decided she wanted nothing more to do with her mother. As her mother, Sara was the one person in Anna's life she should have been able to count on, and Sara had abandoned her. She tried to understand the hurt her child had experienced and imagined the hostility and bitterness Anna must have for her.

Returning again from her memories, Sara picked up a few pieces of paper around the bottom of the Angel Tree. She went back into the sanctuary and sat on the back pew. She prayed for Anna Lopez, and she prayed for Anna Williams.

*   *   *

December was a busy month for almost everybody. Both Olive Branch A.M.E. Church and the Circular Congregational Church had a full calendar. But for Sara December was a lonely month. She had only the gifts to buy for little Anna Lopez, and she took care of that at Wal-Mart late one afternoon after work. She stopped by Magdalene House one day to visit the staff and to go to lunch with Trina. She baked a cake to thank Gertrude Hawkins for letting her use the roadside stand. Sara went on an early December outing to Deweese Island to gather more sweetgrass. She spread the grass out to dry on pieces of plywood in her backyard. She also received two unwanted telephone calls, both from James. When she heard his voice, she quickly snapped shut her cell phone.

On December 15 Sara received a surprising letter. The letter, from the director of the Avery Research Center at the College of Charleston, read:

Dear Ms. Williams,

The Museum of African-American History and Culture has received a generous endowment from Miss Essie Messervy, a patron of our museum. Miss Messervy is a native Charlestonian with a lifelong interest in African-American Art. Her special interest is the Gullah craft of basket making.

Miss Messervy has a fine personal collection of sweetgrass baskets, which she has bequeathed to our museum. One of your baskets, a fanner, is her most recent addition. The collection includes baskets made by your mother, your grandmother, and your great-grandmother. This fine collection will be presented to the museum on January 15, Dr. Martin Luther King's birthday. An exhibit of sweetgrass baskets will open on that day and continue through April 15.

Miss Messervy has requested that you be our Artist in Residence during the exhibit. The Artist in Residence will have an area in the museum devoted to the pursuit of her work. We would expect the Artist in Residence to offer classes to students and members of the community at large as a way to perpetuate the art form. We want you to set up an authentic working roadside basket stand inside our museum where you will produce and display your baskets for three months. We agree to provide all of your materials, including sweetgrass. In addition, you may sell your baskets here or wherever else you choose.

This letter is your official invitation from our Board. I would like to meet with you immediately after the first of January to discuss the salary and other arrangements. Please call me for an appointment.

Miss Messervy was quite taken with your baskets and very impressed with you.
I look forward, with pleasure, to meeting you.

Sincerely,
Jeslyn Haynsworth

Sara was overwhelmed. She hardly knew what to think. Her mind immediately flashed to the age-old question, "What will I wear on this special occasion?" This was a frock opportunity, and Sara would make a new dress for the event. Her life was getting much better. Her parole would be over soon, and she was going to set up her own roadside stand inside a building in downtown

Charleston. At least for a while, she would not have to slog through pluff mud to gather sweetgrass, and she would not have to worry about "chewing no dry bones." She could do what she did best, make sweetgrass baskets.

* * *

On Saturday, a week before Christmas, Sara drove the Toyota to John's Island for the first time in eleven years. She was to meet Anna Lopez and deliver her Christmas gifts. She had called the cell phone number printed on the paper angel, but the person who answered spoke only Spanish and did not understand English, especially not English spoken with a Gullah accent. The address was 2014 River Road, John's Island. Sara decided she would just have to find it on her own.

The Lopez home was not easy to find. River Road follows the Stono River all the way from Limehouse Bridge down to the community of Cocked Hat. Sara felt as if she were traveling back in time as she drove beneath the live oak trees draped with Spanish moss. She drove slowly looking for the number of the Lopez home but also enjoying being back on John's Island, the place associated with so many happy memories. Sara finally narrowed her search for the Lopez address to a trailer park just past Burden Creek. Even then, she found that several of the families in the trailer park were named Lopez.

Anna Lopez was a precious little girl with brown skin, dark black eyes, and a beautiful smile. Anna's mother spoke English well, and the two women enjoyed visiting while Anna played with her new baby doll. Mrs. Lopez explained that her husband was in the Central Correctional Institution in Columbia. He had been convicted of armed robbery. His daughter was less than one year old when he was sentenced. Following a pleasant visit, Sara said her good-byes and little Anna gave her a hug. It had been years since a child had hugged Sara.

The old Toyota moved north on River Road. Sara decided to cross to the other side of the island. She turned left on Plowground Road. As she drove, she thought about how much John's Island had changed. Ever since the time the Williams family had lived here for a few months after Hurricane Hugo, the island was different. Back then, the only Hispanics were migrant workers who came to harvest strawberries in the early spring and returned to pick tomatoes in the summer. Now, the sizable Hispanic community was no longer itinerant. St. John's Episcopal Church, founded before the Revolutionary War, offered a worship service in Spanish every Sunday. Sidewalk signs at the Piggly Wiggly were printed in both English and Spanish. Three grocery stores specialized in Latino foods.

As she came to the intersection with Bohicket Road, Sara thought of her grandparents. Gullah Jack, who remembered when there was no electricity and when there were no paved roads on the island, wouldn't recognize Bohicket Road. Development of the barrier islands had brought in new

businesses. McDonald's golden arches and the face of Colonel Sanders were prominent at the corner of Maybank Highway and Bohicket Road. Grocery stores and service stations were readily accessible.

Sara continued across the highway onto Hoopstick Road. It was the continuation of Plowground Road, but here it became a sandy scrub-board track. The old Toyota bounced its way to the end of the road.

Just ahead was the burned-out shell of her grandparents' home. Sara wished it had not changed. She thought back to so many happy Christmas memories: the ham, the vegetables, and the smell of wood smoke. She thought of the stories and the teasing between Gullah Jack and Big Jim. And she thought of Mama Sallie and Ma Janie working in the kitchen as they prepared Christmas supper. She remembered the sounds of laughter. Behind the burned house, Sara saw the remains of an old boat, the one built by Gullah Jack, now destroyed by termites. She remembered fishing and shrimping with him in Bohicket Creek.

Sara looked around at several large fire ant hills and the field of weeds that was once a garden. Many things had changed, including Sara. And then she remembered one thing that had probably not changed very much at all. She got back in her car, turned it around in what used to be a yard full of chickens and guineas, and bumped back down the sandy track to Bohicket Road.

Heavy traffic both to and from Kiawah and Seabrook Islands had turned Bohicket Road into a major thoroughfare. The development of the barrier island was the biggest change of all. When the traffic finally cleared, Sara made a left turn. Just before Haut Gap she turned left again onto another sandy road, this one scraped smooth by the county. The road led just a short distance to the Angel Oak.

No one knows for certain just how old the Angel Oak actually is, but it has been estimated to be fourteen hundred years old. The massive tree is rumored to be the oldest living thing east of the Mississippi River. Some say the Bohicket, Kiawah, and Edisto Indians knew of the tree and conducted sacred ceremonies beneath it. Others say the name Angel refers to the huge limbs that droop to the ground, giving the appearance of a large angel, especially at night. Historians say the name came from Justin Angel who owned the land inherited by his wife, Martha Waight, after they were married in 1810. None of those stories really mattered to Sara Williams. She knew what the Angel Oak meant to the women in her family as far back as anyone could remember.

Sara stopped at the small gift shop. Several sweetgrass baskets were for sale, a large number of books, and even more souvenirs. She overheard a conversation between the woman operating the cash register and a tourist.

"I'd like a book about the folklore and legends surrounding the Angel Oak," the tourist said.

"I'm sorry, there is no such book because there are no stories and legends."

"How can that be?" the man asked incredulously. "Surely, there are stories."

"I've lived on John's Island all my life, and I've never heard of any stories about the tree."

"No ghost stories, no war stories, no pirate stories?"

"The Angel Oak was sold to the city of Charleston in 1991. That's about the only story I know."

"Somebody ought to make up a good story."

"Maybe somebody will," replied the clerk.

Sara knew a story. She knew that just before Christmas every year the Gullah women she knew came to the Angel Oak with their own ritual, a prayer of sorts. It was a simple reminder that God was watching over all living things, including His children, through the good times and the bad.

Sara walked onto the porch of the gift shop, the screen door slapping closed behind her. She walked slowly to the massive oak tree. It was one thing that had not changed, though the tree was even larger than she remembered. She had not been to this place for eleven years. She was standing alone at the Angel Oak for the first time in her thirty-seven years. Even alone, she still sensed the presence of Mama Sallie, Granny Lucy, Ma Janie, and her daughter, Anna. She moved almost reverently beneath the large, moss-draped limbs hanging above her like sheltering angel wings. Sara had no one to touch and no one to touch her, but she reached out with her left hand and touched the bark of the Angel Oak. The words came to her mind and she repeated them silently.

> *Child, this is the Tree of Life.*
> *This is where the angels come.*
> *And, if the Lord God can take care of this tree, as old as it is,*
> *God's sure gonna take care of you and me.*

The same disgruntled tourist was standing behind Sara, still complaining that there were no stories about the tree. Sara walked away, wanting to savor this moment for a while. It might be the best part of Christmas for her this year, even better than the job offer from the museum. She sat down at a picnic table some distance from the tree and thought about the people in her life who had been strong and good. She had certainly made her share of mistakes, but she could draw deep strength in this place.

As the afternoon was fading, a few visitors lingered around the tree. A young woman sat at another picnic table with sketchpad and pencils, trying to fit the Angel Oak onto one piece of paper. A couple who seemed to be on their honeymoon walked arm in arm around the tree. A younger woman carrying an infant stood at a distance. An elderly man who seemed to be grieving took photos with a digital camera that was obviously new to him. The disgruntled tourist talked loudly on his cell phone.

Gradually the visitors drifted out to the parking area, allowing Sara to enjoy the peaceful return of solitude. As she watched the sun setting beyond the Angel Oak toward Bohicket Creek, she became aware that the young woman carrying the small child had walked closer to the tree.

She remembered bringing little Anna here when she was barely six months old. Sara was startled to see the young mother reach out and touch the Angel Oak with her left hand. Sara moved to the tree, away from the picnic table. She heard the soft voice of the young woman speaking the last lines of that familiar refrain.

> *"And, if the Lord God can take care of this tree, as old as it is,*
> *God's sure gonna to take care of you and me."*

Sara's heart was racing. She could hardly speak. Finally, she said, "Anna?"

The young woman turned to face her. Those dark eyes were unmistakable. "Mama?"

Neither woman knew what to say. Both were so unsure of themselves. After what seemed an eternity of silence, Sara said, "I am so glad to see you."

"You, too, Mama."

Sara wanted to rush forward and embrace her daughter, but she knew it was not the thing to do. "What are you doing here?"

"I always try to come before Christmas. I kept thinking that one of these Christmases I might see you."

"I'm so sorry, Anna, I'm so sorry."

Anna didn't say anything for a few moments. She held her baby close and turned her back to Sara, walking several steps away. Finally, she turned around and said, "Mama, you remember after Ma Janie died, you used to sing 'Sometimes I Feel Like A Motherless Child?' Well, that's the way I've felt all this time. It was like I just wasn't important to you."

The words cut Sara deeply, but she knew they were true. "I'm so sorry. I hope some day you can forgive me. I know it won't be easy."

"Right now, I'm just glad to see you. I just kept praying that you'd get better."

"Thank you, Anna. I am better. I've been praying, too."

There was another moment of awkward silence. Again, Sara wanted to hug her daughter, but she did not. Finally Anna took a few steps toward her mother. Sara broke the silence by changing the subject. "Tell me about your baby."

"Well, I joined the Army and was sent to Fort Bragg. I met a great guy, Michael. We got married June a year ago. This is our baby. She was born in August. Michael is in Iraq now, but he'll be back soon. We both have less than a year left in the Army, and then we're going to settle down. Michael wants us to come back to Charleston. Right now I'm working a desk job and taking care of this little girl."

"What is your baby's name?"

"I didn't have you to bring the name, so I did the best I could. Mama, meet your grandchild,

Sara Jane."

    With that, Anna handed the infant to her weeping mother. Highlighted by the fading sunlight, Sara, holding her granddaughter, looked for all the world like the cypress knee Madonna.

    With her grandchild in her arms and her daughter by her side, Sara walked to the Angel Oak. She reached out her left hand as Anna held tightly to her arm. And Sara Williams said the words that were as old as the first sweetgrass basket, words that were the message of Christmas for generation after generation of Gullah women,

> *Child, this is the Tree of Life.*
> *This is where the angels come.*
> *And if the Lord God can take care of this tree, as old as it is,*
> *God's sure gonna take care of you and me.*

Joe's Tree

Standing at the workbench in his garage on the Friday after Thanksgiving, Steve O'Neil placed two pine 1 x 6's side by side. They were exactly the same length, just right for the cross he was building. He was not a carpenter. He was a banker, the first in his family to finish college. His dad and his granddad were proud of Steve's college education, but they teased him, saying he went to Presbyterian College because he didn't like to get his hands dirty. Steve's usual retort was, "If you get enough education, you get to work in the shade." His grandfather, father, and brother were carpenters, and Steve knew they had always wanted him to learn the family trade. He had learned a little, at least enough to build a cross for his son, Joe.

When Joe was born Steve and Wanda thought their son should have at least one family name. In Wanda's family all of the suitable family names had been used for her eleven nieces and nephews. In Steve's family, only one name had been used for male children. His grandfather was Benjamin Earl O'Neil. His father was Benjamin Earl O'Neil, Jr. His brother was Benjamin Earl O'Neil III. When Steve was born, his mother decided on Stephen, the name of the first deacon mentioned in the Bible.

Steve and Wanda named their son Stephen Joseph O'Neil. Stephen was, of course, for Steve, and Joseph was for the biblical carpenter. Wanda had gotten extra credit in-law points for coming up with her son's name, points she would surely need in the future.

The tree idea also originated with Wanda: "I'd like to have a Christmas tree on Joe's grave." The moment Steve heard it, he liked it. As Steve put the finishing touches on the cross, he thought about his son, his only child. Steve drilled a half-inch hole through the center of the wooden cross, which was to become the Christmas tree stand.

Christmas had been Joe's favorite time of year. He especially loved having a Christmas tree. The O'Neil family made the Friday after Thanksgiving their Christmas tree day. They would drive up to the North Carolina mountains to one of the tree farms near Linville. The Fraser fir was selected from the field where it was still growing. Wanda always had to look at several before she made up her mind. The tree was cut, bundled with twine, and tied on top of the Toyota 4Runner for the trip home. On the way back the family stopped near Marion at Granny's Pancake House for supper. It had become a Christmas tradition, and Joe loved every minute of it. He called the restaurant Granny's Fanny House.

When the fir tree was brought into the house, Joe could hardly wait to lie down on the floor under the tree and pretend he was camping in the woods. He would run to his bedroom to get his Christmas bear, a brown teddy bear wearing a Santa cap. Then Joe curled up under the tree. He loved the feel and the fragrance of the Fraser fir, and he enjoyed decorating the tree with Steve. He would hang his favorite ornaments on the bottom half of the tree while Steve decorated the top half. Then, Steve would lift Joe up on his shoulders so that Joe could put the shiny brass star in place. When they finished decorating the tree, Steve and Joe would have popcorn and hot chocolate with Wanda. Then they all would go camping on a quilt under the tree. Snuggled together with Joe's Christmas bear, they would gaze up through the branches, mesmerized by the lights as if the tiny bulbs were stars in the sky.

There would be no trip to the North Carolina mountains this year. Earlier in the morning, just as traffic from the Christmas parade was thinning out, Steve purchased a small Fraser fir from the local Ruritan tree lot. Steve put the finishing touches on the simple pine cross, the stand for Joe's Christmas tree. Along the edge of one of the boards, he printed in small letters using indelible ink, "Joe's Tree."

Steve walked into the kitchen from the garage. "I finished the tree stand," he announced.

"Good," Wanda said. "Lunch is ready. We'll be able to get the tree in place before dark."

"Okay," said Steve. "Just let me wash up."

Steve understood that Wanda did not like to be at the cemetery when there was even a hint of darkness. The O'Neils had received friends prior to Joe's funeral at the church. But so many people went to the committal service at the cemetery that a second spontaneous receiving line had formed. Steve and Wanda had remained at the grave until they had spoken to everyone. It was dusk when they finally left Joe's grave. "I don't ever want to be there in that dismal darkness again," Wanda insisted.

As Steve and Wanda ate lunch together, hardly a word was spoken between them. Ever since they had dated at Presbyterian College, they had loved each other dearly but had always had difficulty communicating. Even before Joe's death, they had sought marriage counseling, not so much because they had a troubled marriage, but because they were aware of the stress Joe's illness placed on their relationship. They were advised that nothing should be unspeakable between them, but sometimes talking to each other was just too hard. Steve was often mad, and Wanda was usually sad.

As Joe's disease progressed, they knew that his death was imminent. Their counselor had warned them that following the death of a child, two out of three marriages end in divorce. Both Steve and

Wanda were determined that the loss of their child would not lead to the loss of their marriage. But then Sly Sutton had reentered their life. He was in the class ahead of them at Presbyterian. He was captain of the golf team and president of his fraternity, the ultimate frat boy. His real name was Christian Sutton, but his nickname, Sly, suited him far better. Always dapper, he looked as if he had stepped out of the pages of *Gentleman's Quarterly*. Sly majored in wine, women, and golf. By the time he graduated, he had dated his way through most of the senior and junior women on campus. Wanda went out with him when she was a freshman, before she met Steve. Steve had never liked Sly.

On the day of Joe's funeral, Sly showed up in the unplanned receiving line that formed at the cemetery. Both Steve and Wanda were surprised. Sly greeted Steve with a firm handshake. He gave Wanda a prolonged embrace. He explained that he had recently divorced and moved from Hilton Head to become the golf pro at the local country club.

"We'll have to get together soon," he said. Glancing at Steve, then staring at Wanda, he added, "You're as pretty as ever. You haven't aged at all."

Even in her bereavement, Wanda blushed at the compliment, and Steve noticed. Steve felt the hair rising on the back of his neck. His old adversary had returned and on the very day their son was buried.

Following lunch, Steve and Wanda got into the 4Runner with the Christmas tree tied on top and made their way through the heavy Friday afternoon traffic to the cemetery. Steve could hardly believe they were going to be without Joe this Christmas. He remembered the excitement he and Wanda shared when they knew they were expecting a baby. They had been through the disappointment of a previous miscarriage. They had been so happy, so hopeful, when they learned Joe was on the way. The pregnancy and birth were rich experiences for Steve and Wanda. They enjoyed preparing the nursery and attending childbirth classes together. Steve was in the delivery room with Wanda when Joe was born.

When Joe arrived, he immediately became the center of their lives. He brought so much joy to them and to others. On the day he was baptized, the infant Joe grabbed the pastor's moustache and wouldn't let go. The whole congregation at Clearwater got a chuckle out of that. Grandpa Ben said it served the pastor right for having a moustache in the first place. He was proud that an O'Neil had the gumption to do something about it. Several weeks later, the pastor preached a sermon entitled "*Carpe Diem*, Seize the Day" and used the moustache grabbing as an illustration. His point was that we should make the most of every day. Every day was special to Joe, and he made each day special to others. No wonder the comedian Jerry Lewis always made such a big deal over children like Joe, especially during his annual Labor Day television telethon for muscular dystrophy. Joe was one of Jerry's kids all right. By disposition and by disease, Joe was one of Jerry's kids.

Steve and Wanda first noticed something different about Joe when he was still an infant. Their pediatrician attributed their concerns to first-time parents' anxiety. But, as their child grew, it be-

came more obvious that something really was wrong with their son. Joe had been a little late learning to walk, but he managed to ride a bicycle by the time he was in the second grade. And he could throw a baseball, even if his Uncle Trip said he threw like a girl.

But when Joe was in the fourth grade, things changed dramatically. Steve and Wanda thought Joe's problems were behavioral at first. He complained of being tired and seemed uninterested in school. Getting homework done required a major effort every day. Earl said Joe was just lazy, blaming Steve for not teaching his son how to work, and that made Steve mad. Steve's mother blamed Wanda for working outside the home instead of staying home where she belonged, and that made Wanda mad. Even though those in-law criticisms made them angry, they still blamed themselves for whatever was wrong with Joe.

When Joe started stumbling and falling in the fifth grade, the pediatrician suggested that they be patient and see how things developed. Both Steve and Wanda became angry and agreed to change physicians, taking Joe to a neurologist. Steve's parents thought that was throwing good money after bad. But by the sixth grade, they had a diagnosis: a progressive neuromuscular disease, the neurologist called it, in an attempt to soften the blow. "Why should a disease be called progressive when it is only going to become worse?" Wanda asked.

"In fact, it is a degenerative neuromuscular disease," explained the physician. Joe had muscular dystrophy, and Joe wasn't going to get better.

But Joe did get better, in a sense. It was as if the more limited he became physically, the more joy he brought to others. He cracked jokes, enjoyed his friends and their accomplishments, and always seemed to have a twinkle in his eye and a smile on his face. Steve and Wanda took delight in their son, but all the while they were grieving as they anticipated his death.

When Steve and Wanda arrived at the cemetery to place the tree on their son's grave, the air was crisp and the day was sunny. A committal service was being conducted on a hill near the entrance to the cemetery. Joggers and walkers were getting their daily exercise. A car marked STUDENT DRIVER slowly circled the cemetery, weaving along the paved road around the perimeter.

"Joe never learned to drive," Steve said to Wanda, "but this does seem like a good place to learn. There's not much chance of hurting anybody. Most of the people here are already dead." Steve was embarrassed by his lame attempt at humor. It was one of the ways he tried to deal with his hurt. Sometimes it helped, sometimes it didn't.

"The worse you feel, the more you joke," Wanda sighed.

Stopping the 4Runner near Joe's grave, Steve removed the fir tree from the roof. He took a six-inch lag bolt out of his jacket pocket and put it through the hole in the center of the pine cross. As he tightened the bolt, attaching the stand to the trunk of the tree, Wanda walked to Joe's grave. It had been a March day very much like this cold, sunny December day when Joe's body was laid to rest in this place. The summer months had enabled the grass to grow, creating a soft green mat over the grave. Despite her deep sadness, Wanda found comfort in thinking of her son enjoying heaven. She knew heaven was enjoying Joe. She smiled as she thought about Joe running and jumping again. Some of her friends were disturbed by her vivid images of heaven. Still, she thought of Joe playing baseball or football in heaven though she was not at all sure sporting equipment was available in the hereafter. Sometimes she thought of him breaking into a spontaneous dance as he so often did as a lighthearted little child.

Steve and Wanda had learned that men and women often mourn differently when their child dies. The grief of a mother comes from deep within—their counselor had called it womb grief. Wanda felt a confusing mixture of anger and sadness. Her tears often flowed unbidden, sometimes welling up as uncontrollable sobs. Wanda had given up wearing mascara, even the waterproof kind. Steve, on the other hand, had channeled much of his grief into his work. "Stay busy and try not to think about it." Wanda had the feeling that Steve didn't love Joe as much as she did because she saw no outward evidence of his grief. Both Wanda and the counselor had encouraged Steve to grieve with Wanda rather than trying to be strong and stoic, but it was difficult for him.

Steve placed the tree on the grave. He remarked that Joe always looked forward to sleeping under the Christmas tree. Together the husband and wife smiled. From her pocket Wanda took the freshly polished brass star, which she knew would soon be tarnished. Steve fastened it to the top of the tree with thin wire. The couple quietly clung to each in the cold air, arm in arm, admiring Joe's tree. Wanda cried, but Steve did not.

✳   ✳   ✳

Since Joe's funeral, Steve had not seen Sly Sutton. But like a farmer that suspects that the fox is lurking somewhere near the hen house, Steve had been vigilant. He had seen two calls from the country club on the caller ID in early May. He noticed that the first lasted for less than one minute, the other less than three minutes. He considered asking Wanda about the calls, but decided against it. If she wanted him to know anything, she could tell him.

Then, September 9th on what would have been Joe's sixteenth birthday, Steve found an e-mail on the computer. It was on the screen as if Wanda had intended for him to see it. Sly had written to Wanda, "I know this is a difficult day for you, and I just wanted to express my condolences. If you ever need to talk to an old friend, just give me a call. Love always, Sly." With the e-mail, he left his cell phone number.

Steve was furious. He said to Wanda, "I saw the e-mail from Sly."

"I wanted you to see it," she said.

"As if Joe's death was not hard enough, that creep has to make it worse! What a lowlife!"

"It would be nice to have somebody to talk to," Wanda snapped.

Steve had no answer. He knew his wife was vulnerable, but he did not know what to say. He had wanted to do something for Wanda to mark Joe's birthday. They put flowers on Joe's grave, but did nothing else. Wanda went to bed early, retreating alone to Joe's room where she cried herself to sleep.

Steve went back to the computer and responded to the e-mail from Sly. "Thank you for your concern. Do not contact us again." Steve could not even think of going to sleep. He was too mad, too hurt, and too afraid. He stayed up until long after midnight playing cyber solitaire. When he finally went to their bedroom, Wanda was not there. He found her sleeping in Joe's room, hugging the Christmas bear. Steve pulled a quilt over his wife before sleeping alone in their king-sized bed.

Friends and relatives noticed the tree on Joe's grave. Several commented on how much they liked the idea. Steve's dad and granddad thought it was a waste of good money. Still, Joe's mom and dad felt that they had done the very thing that would have pleased their son.

Just one week after Steve and Wanda had placed the Fraser fir on the grave, they visited the cemetery. Much to their dismay, Joe's Christmas tree was gone. Both Steve and Wanda were upset by the tree's disappearance. Wanda was hurt. She looked at Steve in disbelief. "Why?" she cried. Leaning against her husband's chest, she wept, trembling with each sobbing breath.

Steve held his heartbroken wife in his arms. His face flushed with rage at the pain inflicted on his wife by whoever took the tree. He realized that he would never find the culprit. "Whoever stole it had better hope I never find him!" he said, seething. Then, trying to reassure his wife, he said, "I'll get another tree."

"What's the use?" asked Wanda.

As they were leaving, Steve noticed something in the grass on Joe's grave. He stooped down and picked up it up.

"Our thief left a clue," showing his wife a blue golf tee.

The national charter of the Sigma Alpha Epsilon fraternity at Mitchell College had been suspended. Though officially the fraternity was on probation and could still use the SAE name, the members had formed a social club under a new name, Sigma Omicron Sigma. It was the ne'er-do-well group of male students on campus who were most like the fraternity in the movie "Animal House." Their numbers had dwindled, and they were in serious financial trouble. The brothers had been told that if they did not get their act together by the end of the semester, they faced the death penalty. The national fraternity would disband them, causing them to lose all social privileges as a campus organization. They had not gotten their act together. Their composite grade point average was 1.8. Their fraternity president had been expelled for reasons known only to him and to the administration. The Christmas party on Friday night would almost certainly be their last.

The SOS Club had only three new pledges: Arthur, Thomas, and Ted, affectionately referred to as AT&T by the brothers. Because the fraternity had no money and no Christmas tree for the party, the Pledge Master put the responsibility on the pledges. He demanded, "Get us a Christmas tree. Have it here, decorated, by Friday night."

AT&T, true to form, started their search late on Thursday afternoon. Flamboyant procrastination was their standard. "If it weren't for the last minute, we'd never get anything done," was their motto. Fitting into Ted's old Mazda truck was a tight squeeze for the three pledges. They drove from one tree lot to another, looking for a suitable tree. The man at the Optimist Club lot offered them a tree at half price, but they were looking for a better bargain. They might have actually been given a misshapen tree at the Methodist Church lot if they hadn't had the poor taste to introduce themselves as "the three wise men looking for a virgin." Their humor went unappreciated by the gray-headed men of the Methodist Brotherhood, though after AT&T departed, the old men got a good laugh out of it.

The search for a tree was going nowhere until they drove past the cemetery. Ted saw it first, a beautiful little Christmas tree that stood on one of the graves. Arthur suggested the plan, and Thomas was selected by his fellow pledges to carry out the heist. After all, it was Christmas, and Thomas was the only one of the three named for a saint. Nobody had ever heard of Saint Arthur or Saint Ted, but St. Thomas was a great place to go for spring break. Thomas had his doubts, serious doubts about whether the three pledges could pull off this theft without getting caught. Besides that...well, it just didn't seem right.

They waited until dusk and watched as the joggers and walkers completed their rounds. Ted commented on how ironic it was that people exercising for their health would choose to do so in a cemetery. Arthur claimed the graveyard offered the best kind of motivation for staying fit. Thomas sat quietly, trying to justify in his own mind what he was about to do, as the cemetery cleared and darkness fell. Ted drove the truck. He parked behind a hedge, hiding the truck from the view of passing cars. Arthur was the lookout, though by his own admission, he had forgotten his glasses. Thomas, disguised as a night jogger, made a run, looping around the graveyard. By the time he got back to the scene of the crime, Thomas, the night jogger, was nearly a night crawler. He grabbed the little Fraser fir, as Ted wheeled the truck to the rendezvous point. Thomas threw the tree, stand, star, and all, into the back of the Mazda pickup, and away they went. The plan went off without a hitch.

Sigma Omicron Sigma didn't have enough money to have a fraternity house. Instead, they had the SOS hall, half of the first floor of a dorm. The Mitchell College Student Affairs Office had housed a group of unaffiliated students on the other half of the hall, hoping they would have a good influence on the fraternity brothers. Peer pressure is a powerful force among college students, but on the SOS hall, peer pressure had worked in reverse. The Nerd Herd, as the unaffiliated students were called, became *ad hoc* members of the fraternity.

Decorating the tree became a project for the entire hall. One frat brother had been stringing together all of the pop-tops from aluminum cans accumulated during his entire college career. He thought the impressive twenty-foot chain, a trophy for him, should be in the *Guinness Book of World Records.*

"You can save a lot of pop-tops in six years," he would say when questioned about his accomplishment. When questioned about his six-year college experience, he explained, "You can stay in college for a long time if you go on academic probation every other semester."

The legendary pop-top chain became a garland for the SOS Christmas tree. One of the Nerds offered a pair of Christmas underwear to the cause. They had been a gift to him by the expelled fraternity president. After cutting the bright red underwear into ribbon-width strips, the pledges tied them into bows on the branches of the tree.

Another Nerd, an art student, boasted that he could make an angel from an aluminum can. After one of the brothers found an empty Coors Lite can under a pile of dirty laundry, the Silver Bullet Angel was completed with just a few scissors snips here and there. The Nerd took the tarnished brass star off the top of the tree and secured it in the hands of the shiny aluminum Angel with a twist-tie from a loaf of moldy bread. Then the Silver Bullet Angel holding the brass star was attached to the top of the little Fraser fir.

Thomas was in trouble with the Pledge Master. Each pledge was required to have certain things on his person at all times for the convenience of the brothers. Spot checks were frequent and random. Required items were a black pen, a can of snuff, a supply of breath mints, a pack of chewing gum, a cell phone, and a golf tee. Thomas had lost his golf tee. "I think I lost it when I got the tree," he explained. His penance was to gather more ornaments for the Christmas tree. As he passed by the nicely decorated trees in the Dining Hall and the Library foyer, he slipped several ornaments into his pockets and his book bag.

As they were placing the swiped decorations on the tree, Arthur noticed writing on the stand. "Joe's Tree," it read.

"Who is Joe?" he asked.

"That's St. Joseph," Ted explained. "You know. He's the guy named for the aspirin."

❊   ❊   ❊

Maggie Tucker hated this part of her job most. It was December 14. All the students at Mitchell College had deserted campus for Christmas vacation, leaving behind piles of pizza boxes, assorted aluminum cans, and trashcans filled with the things college students don't want their parents to see or know about. As a member of the housekeeping staff of the college, Maggie enjoyed her work, most of the time. A single mother of three children, she depended on the income, and she was thankful for steady employment. Even when others were being laid off, the college still had to be cleaned. But cleaning up after the Sigma Omicron Sigma brothers and the Nerds should have warranted combat pay. She knew that the end of semester exams was not the time to expect students to clean up after themselves, but she could not imagine young men who were supposed to be educated being content to live in such filth. The squalor on the SOS hall was disgusting. It had taken Maggie most of the day to clean just that one area.

As Maggie cleaned the hall, she hummed Christmas carols. Even cleaning up after SOS and the Nerd Herd could not dampen her Christmas spirit. She always wished that she could do more for others, especially for her children. She managed well on a tight budget, and this year she was giving her children a trip to visit their grandmother in Washington, D.C. This was also a gift to herself. For the first Christmas in four years, she was able to afford a visit with her mother.

As she took a large bag of trash out to the dumpster behind the dormitory, she hummed the melody to "Silent Night." When she rounded the corner, she saw the tree, a beautiful little Fraser fir, complete with stand and decorations, discarded beside the dumpster. She felt lucky that the garbage truck had not already picked it up. Maggie had decided not to buy a tree this year since she and the children were going to be in Washington for Christmas. Besides, she needed to save as much money as she could for the trip.

Students leaving school for Christmas break or summer vacation often left treasures by the dumpster. Those left-behind items were fair game on a first come, first served basis. Maggie had previously been the beneficiary of this method of recycling. She had already acquired a kitchen table and a perfectly good television set.

This Fraser fir was a godsend. Her children would love it. It must have been used for a party on one of the halls, she thought. Maybe that's why there were tree needles all over the floor on the SOS hall. The tree looked lonely. All that the tree needed was a good home, and Maggie knew just the place.

She called a member of campus security who often gave her a ride in his truck when the weather was bad. Maggie didn't like to drive in a heavy frost, much less ice and snow. The security officer agreed to give the newfound tree a lift to her home. He said, however, that some Christmas decorations had been missing from various locations on campus. Some of them, maybe all of them, appeared to be on Maggie's dumpster tree. She gladly returned them to the campus police officer. The shiny Coors angel, holding the tarnished brass star, she allowed to remain attached to the top of the little tree.

When Maggie and her tree arrived at her modest home, her three children were every bit as excited as she had hoped they would be.

"Who is Joe?" her oldest asked, noticing the name on the wooden stand.

"I don't know," answered Maggie. "Must be one of the college students."

"Well, it's our tree now," her daughter squealed. "Let's decorate it!"

The tree was already partially decorated with ribbons tied to the branches and a shiny metal angel holding a brass star attached to the top.

"Look, Mama!" said one of the children. "That angel is made out of a beer can!"

"It's okay," said Maggie. "There are all kinds of angels."

Maggie took a cardboard box from the closet and gave it to the children. The box contained Christmas ornaments the children had made over the years in kindergarten and in Sunday school. She served warm cookies and cold milk to her children for their surprise Christmas party.

Later that night when the children were in bed, Maggie sat next to the tree, thinking about her family. She propped her feet on the coffee table and relaxed all the way to her toes as she absorbed the peace and quiet. She was thankful for the tree and the Christmas joy it added to her home.

✳   ✳   ✳

On the Sunday morning before Christmas, Maggie Tucker and her children went to the Mount Calvary Methodist Church just as they usually did. Following the morning service, Pastor Davis reminded the congregation that Sunday night was the children's Christmas program. When the pastor made a special appeal for a Christmas tree, Maggie did not hesitate to offer the little Fraser fir she had in her living room because, after all, her three children were in the program. Since she and her children were leaving for Washington early on Monday, she had thought about getting the tree out of her house anyway. The last thing she wanted was to be greeted by a floor carpeted with fir needles when she returned from her trip on New Year's Day. Thanking Sister Tucker for her generosity, the pastor said he would have Brother Jones pick up the tree about three o'clock that afternoon.

When Brother Jones arrived at the church, Pastor Davis was there to meet him and the small but beautiful tree.

"This tree might be too short," Brother Jones apologized. "It's only about five feet high."

"Better to be five feet high than six feet under," the pastor quipped. Pastor Davis had arranged for the Altar Guild to decorate the Christmas tree with Chrismons, symbols of Christianity through the centuries. There were crosses of various types and symbols of the sacraments lovingly crafted by the women of the church.

The first order of business was to remove the decorations that remained on the tree. There weren't that many, but the Altar Guild agreed that those stringy red ribbons had to go. It seemed so unlike Sister Tucker to have those tacky pieces of cloth on her Christmas tree. As Pastor Davis helped to remove the red strips of cloth, he discovered something disconcerting. Attached to the back of one of the cloth strips was a label from a pair of men's underwear. "JOCKEY," it read. Pastor Davis quietly tucked the strip of cloth into his pocket. Why would Sister Tucker decorate her Christmas tree with ripped up men's underwear? And who was Joe anyway? And why was his name

"christmas is for everybody"

on her Christmas tree stand? Did Sister Tucker have a secret life? No doubt, these questions would remain unanswered.

The Altar Guild asked the pastor about the angel holding the brass star on top of the tree. "Pastor," one woman said in disgust, "that angel is made from a beer can, and the brass star is tarnished. What kind of woman is that Maggie Tucker?"

"It must be a honky-tonk angel," replied the pastor. "We've got some of those in the choir. And that star is not the only thing in this church that is tarnished."

The Altar Guild decided the angel holding the tarnished star could stay.

The children's musical went well. The tree, which seemed too small at first, turned out to be perfect. The sight of all of the children gathered around the tree singing carols was a special moment for the members of Mount Calvary. The pastor had arranged for four children to stand in front of the congregation, each holding a piece of cardboard on which one large letter was printed. The plan was to spell out the word STAR, with each letter serving as a reminder of Jesus. The S was for savior. The T stood for teacher. The A was for authority, and the R stood for redeemer. It would have worked well, but when the children turned to face the congregation, they were standing in reverse order. Instead of spelling the word STAR, they spelled RATS. The congregation and the children enjoyed a good laugh together. All agreed, it was a wonderful Christmas program.

That night Pastor Davis was asked two questions. Brother Jones wondered if he might take the Christmas tree to the Children's Shelter. He knew that though Christmas was only two days away the shelter still did not have a tree. Pastor Davis agreed and told Brother Jones, "Please take the Chrismons off and return them to the Altar Guild. Just leave the angel holding the star on top of the tree."

Pastor Davis' wife asked him the second question later that night. She was planning to take his suit to the cleaners and had checked his pockets. With one eyebrow raised, a sure sign of her displeasure, she asked her husband if he could please explain the torn strip of red Jockey underwear that she found in his coat pocket. No, he could not, at least not to her satisfaction.

❊   ❊   ❊

The workers at the Children's Shelter were delighted to receive the Christmas tree. They depended on someone giving them a tree every year, and, at the last minute, someone always came through. This tree was perfectly shaped, though a little smaller than the ones they usually received. The children were excited. While it was hard for a child to be in the shelter at Christmas, that was often the best place for them. Family violence usually increases during the holidays, especially in homes where there is alcoholism or drug abuse. For some children Christmas at the shelter was better than Christmas had ever been before. Childcare workers played Christmas music on the jam box and helped the children decorate the Fraser fir. The children had made ornaments and long paper chains for garland. Bright lights, donated of course, and that funny little angel on top holding the tarnished brass star completed the decorations on the tree. Christmas is for everybody, and these children needed Christmas more than anyone.

✳ ✳ ✳

The blue golf tee that Steve found on Joe's grave the week after Thanksgiving raised more questions than it answered. Steve immediately thought of his nemesis, Sly, the golf pro. When he mentioned it to Wanda, she asked, "Why would he do that?" Steve felt silly for even thinking the culprit might have been Sly and agreed that it seemed beneath him to steal a Christmas tree even if he were trying to agitate. But the discovery of the golf tee made Steve more alert; the tension between Steve and Wanda became more intense.

Then on the Sunday before Christmas a wedding announcement appeared in the newspaper. Christian Sutton had married a woman from a prominent local family. The bride was the daughter of a trustee of the country club. After a honeymoon in Italy, the couple would reside in Florida, where Mr. Sutton was to begin a new job at a prestigious golf club in Tampa.

Wanda found the article and showed it to Steve, commenting, "She's ten years younger than we are!"

"As far as I'm concerned, good riddance."

"I completely agree," said Wanda. "Pity the poor bride. He's nothing but trouble!"

Steve felt a wave of relief flow over him.

"I feel better," Steve said. "I thought I might lose you."

"Lose me! To Sly? Steve, I love you! I have no intention of ever leaving you, not for a jerk like Sly, not for anybody." She moved to her husband and kissed him on the cheek. "I do wish you were more responsive to me, though."

✳ ✳ ✳

In this first Christmas season since Joe's death, Steve and Wanda had followed a plan to simplify, with fewer parties and fewer decorations. They had consciously tried to reach out to others. They wanted to honor the memory of their son. They donated many of Joe's favorite toys to a camp he had attended for several summers, a camp operated by the Muscular Dystrophy Association. They made a contribution to the Jerry Lewis Foundation on what would have been Joe's sixteenth birthday. They got the name of a child from an underprivileged family and bought Christmas gifts for a little boy they didn't know.

But they had neglected their own relationship. Wanda longed for more time, time to laugh, time to cry, time for just the two of them. Steve, however, was too busy with his work at the bank.

Christmas morning dawned with a cold wind and a bright sun. This day might be very difficult for Steve and Wanda, but they had learned at Thanksgiving that the dreaded anticipation of the holiday was worse than the day itself. Steve got up before Wanda and made coffee. He took a steaming mug to Wanda, who showered and dressed while Steve fixed breakfast. They ate together, having little to say but enjoying the birds at the window feeder. Joe had loved to watch the birds, especially the goldfinch. While Steve took his shower and dressed, Wanda made chocolate chip cookies. Steve tried one. They were just the way he liked them, just the way Joe had liked them, soft and loaded with extra chocolate chips, and just the right size to dip into a glass of milk.

Preparing to leave, Steve got his coat and scarf from the closet but then could not find Wanda. He walked back toward the bedroom. Out of the corner of his eye, he saw her in Joe's room, sitting on the bed where their son had died. She was holding Joe's Christmas bear. Suddenly, painful memories flooded his mind. He remembered coming home from work, day after day, to find Wanda sitting on that very bed beside Joe's weakened body. Near the end Joe was completely helpless, his muscles rendered useless by his disease. He could not lift his head from the pillow, could not talk, and could not swallow. Wanda stayed by his side almost constantly, giving him nourishment through a feeding tube.

One afternoon, a hospice nurse called Steve to come home early from work. When he walked to the bedroom and looked in, Wanda was holding Joe's lifeless body, weeping and humming, "Jesus Loves Me."

Now on Christmas morning, seeing Wanda sitting on Joe's bed, holding the bear the way she had held her son, Steve was overcome. Wanda looked up at him, tears streaming down her face. Steve sat down by her and pulled her to him. As they embraced each other, they sank back on Joe's bed, sobbing, grieving together for the first time since their child had died. They held each other for nearly an hour.

"I love you so much," he said.

"I don't ever want to be without you."

Later, Steve and Wanda stopped by the cemetery. Huddled against the cold wind, they held each other for a moment, long enough to pray, long enough to cry together again. The disappearance of the Christmas tree was okay with them now. They had realized that the tree was more for them than for Joe. Steve and Wanda only hoped that whoever had taken it would enjoy Joe's tree.

Back in the 4Runner the O'Neils drove to a place they had never been before. They had decided that this Christmas, in Joe's memory, they wanted to be with some special children. Wanda wanted to take a batch of chocolate chip cookies to children who needed a little extra love. With a smile on their faces and sadness in their hearts, Steve and Wanda went to the Children's Shelter.

The shelter had no identifying sign out in front, allowed no unscheduled visits, no visitors except those who had been pre-approved, all for the protection of the children. Wanda had arranged the visit ahead of time. She and Steve had been screened and accepted.

"It's too bad," Steve said. "The world has become so mean that rules have to be made to protect children, but thank goodness there are places like this shelter to provide protection. We did everything we could to protect Joe, and yet he died. It makes me angry that some parents with perfectly healthy children neglect or abuse them. Why can't people just love their children?"

"I don't know," answered Wanda. "I don't know." She patted Steve's arm.

The woman at the desk greeted them, "You must be Mr. and Mrs. O'Neil. Merry Christmas."

"Thank you," said Wanda. "I brought cookies. Where should I put them?"

"I'll be glad to take them to the refreshment table. You are just in time. The children are gathering around the Christmas tree now."

Steve and Wanda took chairs toward the back of the room. Wanda looked at the way the light from the tree reflected in the eyes of the children seated around the tree.

"These children are beautiful," she whispered. There were black and white, Asian and Haitian children, Hispanic and Native American children.

Wanda thought of the song she had taught Joe: *Red and yellow, black and white, they are precious in His sight.*

"Every one of them is precious," she whispered to Steve.

The tarnished brass star the aluminum angel was holding on top of the little Fraser fir tree caught Steve's eye. And the tree, well, maybe the high ceilings just made it look small. A childcare worker read the Christmas story from Luke, and the children sang "Away in a Manger." Then each child received one brightly wrapped gift from under the tree.

Steve whispered to Wanda. "Do you see the star?"

Wanda recognized it, but not the angel. "That looks like Joe's star."

"That looks like Joe's tree!"

After the children had opened all the gifts and had gathered around the refreshment table to enjoy Wanda's chocolate chip cookies, Steve made his way to the tree. He lifted a corner of the white sheet that covered the base and saw the pine cross he had made and the words he had written, "Joe's Tree."

Wanda came up beside him, took his arm, and asked, "How do you think Joe's tree got from the cemetery to the shelter?"

"It's a mystery to me!" said Steve. "And how did that beer can angel get hold of the brass star?"

"I certainly don't know that," laughed Wanda.

"I guess all's well that ends well," Steve replied.

"I've always heard that God works in mysterious ways."

"I guess so. Again and again and again."

A Star for Christmas

Kate Wimbish left work early on Friday afternoon. Being the supervisor of nursing at the local hospital did have some advantages. It also had its disadvantages, especially when a winter flu epidemic was afflicting so many people. She had already worked fifty hours, and she still had too much to do before Christmas. Though her grocery list was short, she knew the checkout lines would be long. She still had a few gifts to buy for Jeff, and she had to get them in the mail before December 10, the postal deadline for overseas packages intended for military personnel.

With Christmas only three weeks away, she had finally decided to put up a Christmas tree, though no one would be at home with her to enjoy it. She would certainly not enjoy it. Christmas trees seemed like a lot of trouble to Kate. Whoever had the bright idea to cut down a tree and bring it in the house to shed needles everywhere, only to lug it back outside after Christmas, must have been either insane or a vacuum cleaner salesman. Still, Kate had decided to put a Christmas tree in the usual place in the living room because Jeff had requested a picture of it. Kate would put up the tree, decorate it, take a picture with the digital camera, e-mail it to Jeff, and then promptly remove the tree from her house.

Kate stopped at a tree lot just north of town. Her friend Sheila had recommended the place. "They have good trees at a reasonable price, and if you take your tree stand with you, someone there will fix it on the tree." Sheila said the man selling the trees, a friend of her family, had been unemployed for nearly a year. He decided to lease a vacant lot and sell Christmas trees to make money for the holidays. If she had to have a Christmas tree, Kate thought she might as well buy it from someone who really needed the funds.

Selecting a Christmas tree was not an easy task for Kate. All of the Fraser firs were too large. She wanted a tree that was no taller than she was, five feet, five inches. She figured that if the tree was her size and no bigger, she might be able to handle it alone.

The December air was cold, but the attendant was a patient man who helped Kate measure a dozen or more trees by standing them next to her. Finally, he offered, "Pick out the one you want, and I'll cut it just the right height. I'll only charge you for a five-foot tree."

Kate made her selection and waited. The man cranked up his chain saw and cut off a few branches and the trunk of the tree to make it fit her height requirements and her Christmas tree stand. When the screeching sound of the saw faded, Kate noticed for the first time that Elvis Presley was singing "White Christmas" from a jam box inside the camping trailer parked at the edge of the tree lot.

"Is that an Elvis CD?" Kate asked.

"No, it's a tape," he replied. "Pretty good Christmas tape, if you like Elvis." The man attached the Christmas tree stand to the shortened Fraser fir, loaded it into the trunk of Kate's car, and tied the lid securely. Elvis crooned his signature Christmas song, "Blue Christmas."

Though Kate had been an Elvis fan since her teenage years, the words of "Blue Christmas" had never before been more meaningful. She had certainly experienced difficult Christmases before this year. Eight years earlier, she had spent all night Christmas Eve with Jeff in the Emergency Room following an automobile accident. Jeff, then a college freshman, had recovered from his cuts, bruises, and a broken wrist. Kate and Jeff had since referred to that as their black and blue Christmas. Twenty-five years ago, her first Christmas without her husband, Davis, was her most difficult Christmas of all. Two-year-old Jeff had eased her grief, but she spent most of the holidays weeping for Davis. This year would be hard, too. She was separated from her only child for the first time at Christmas.

Kate stopped at a very crowded Wal-Mart to pick up several gifts for Jeff and a few groceries. She debated whether it was safe to leave her Christmas tree unattended in the trunk of her car. She decided that she really didn't care if somebody stole it. Maybe somebody else needed it more than she. She left the parked car and the exposed tree and entered the store.

Shopping was one of Kate's talents. She selected a sketchpad and a box of colored pencils, a lined notebook with sturdy binding to be used as a journal, two novels by John Grisham, and a small flashlight with extra AA batteries. Jeff's requests had been necessarily limited.

Kate pushed her cart to the hardware section of the store. She also needed light bulbs for the candle in Jeff's window. Because she kept the electric candle burning continuously, extra bulbs were always on her list. She pulled the last two packages off the rack and tossed them into her cart.

Moving on down the aisle, she paused at a display of Christmas cassette tapes. As she scanned the titles, she saw an Elvis tape, *Elvis' Christmas Album*, which she snatched up as if she had found a long-lost treasure. The title was identical to the long-playing record album she had as a teenager. The songs were the same ones she remembered hearing Elvis sing at Christmas when she was a young girl in junior high. Santa Claus had brought her the album for Christmas. She had played it every Christmas after that until the last Christmas with Davis. In one of his rages, her husband had thrown the record across the living room, shattering it to pieces. Then he had thrown the broken pieces and the cardboard album cover into the fireplace. The memory of the burning record and the burning rage were part of a recurring nightmare. Kate shuddered, took a deep breath, and put the tape into her cart.

Kate maneuvered through the crowded aisles of Wal-Mart to the Christmas decorations. Jeff always wanted multicolored blinking lights on the tree. Kate preferred all white lights that did not blink, but she would compromise for the sake of the photo—five strands of colored lights, but no blinking ones. Besides, a digital photo transmitted by e-mail would not show blinking lights anyway. She looked through the tree-trimming items. Jeff would also like glitzy garland, so Kate added a couple of packages of the gold tinsel to her cart. At a display of various tree ornaments, her eyes fell on a package of three gold stars. They were nothing unusual to most shoppers—three star-shaped pieces of thin Styrofoam, painted gold with a hint of glitter, labeled Made in China. But to Kate, these gold stars were just the decorations she needed for her tree.

Kate picked up the few groceries and added a bag of original Hershey's Kisses to include in Jeff's Christmas package. As she moved toward the checkout lines, she read the magazine and tabloid headlines, ranging from the usual array of the ridiculous to the sublime: "Santa Taken Captive by UFO," "How to Make Your Man Happy this Christmas," and "Eat All You Want and Still Lose Pounds during the Holidays." Other headlines focused on Michael Jackson and Glen Campbell and their personal problems. Then Kate saw the headline, "War in Iraq Drags On." She turned her head away. Since Jeff had left for Iraq with his unit, Kate avoided newspapers and news programs on television. She knew all too well the dangers of war. Any reminder that her child was constantly in harm's way was unwelcome. She preferred to get her informatgûn directly from Jeff in his weekly e-mails from Tikrit.

Kate jockeyed her shopping cart into position in the shortest of the twelve register lines. It was perhaps the shortest line, but it was not the quickest. Kate soon understood the reason. The clerk was a chubby, chatty, middle-aged woman. For her, this position with the royal blue apron was more than a job; it was a social opportunity, and she engaged every customer in conversation. To the young woman with the two preschoolers at the register, the clerk gave advice on marriage and childrearing. The clerk struck up a conversation with the man next in line, discussing automobile mechanics with him, specifically the heartbreak of a dead battery.

As Kate took her turn placing merchandise on the conveyor, she could read from the nametag fastened to the blue apron that Cheri was the woman's name. Chubby, chatty Cheri spoke to Kate as if they were long-lost friends.

"Oh, honey! What a nice little Christmas pin! Look at that pretty blue star!" Kate had decided two customers back that she was going to keep her comments to a minimum. "Where did you find that darling little Christmas pin?"

Kate looked down at the circular cloisonnè pin on her blazer lapel. "A friend gave it to me," she answered tersely.

"Must be *some* friend. I bet these Hershey's Kisses are for him."

"Something like that," Kate said, avoiding an explanation.

"Take care of your man, and he'll take care of you," spouted Cheri. Then she added, "Of course, my man left me."

Kate said nothing. She paid for her purchases with her debit card and hurried away into the fading light to discover that, wonder of wonders, the Christmas tree was still in the trunk of her car.

＊　　＊　　＊

As Kate pulled into her driveway, she was pleased to see that the Moravian Star on her front porch was shining brightly. She was saddened, though not surprised, to find that the electric candle in Jeff's window was dark. She felt that same chill of fear that came over her whenever the candle burned out. The Service flag, a sign of Blue Star Mothers'—with its red border, white background, and central blue star—was still visible in the light of the Moravian Star. But the light of the electric candle was important to Kate, not only because it illuminated the flag, but also because it was a symbol of hope for Jeff's safe return from Iraq.

The Wimbish home was a neat, well-kept, two-bedroom townhouse. Providing a good home for her son had been important to Kate since her husband died. She had worked long and hard as a nurse to make ends meet. She regarded the purchase of the townhouse as a major accomplishment. Of course Jeff had done his part, too. He had paid for almost all of his college expenses with scholarships. The Army R.O.T.C. scholarship had been a great blessing, but now he was paying for it. Jeff and Kate were both paying for the scholarship—Jeff with active duty, Kate with active worry.

Kate took her Wal-Mart purchases into her home. Her first task was getting past the shiver of foreboding by changing the bulb in the electric candle. She stepped back onto her porch just to be sure the flag with the blue star was clearly visible. Though she had only been a member for a few months, being a part of the Blue Star Mothers of America was important to Kate. She looked forward to the monthly meetings at the American Legion Post. Being in the company of other mothers who had children serving in the military gave her strength.

Though Kate was from a Roman Catholic family, she rarely attended a church of any kind since Davis died twenty-five years ago. Her in-laws had invited her many times to attend their Moravian fellowship, but she had never accepted. The Moravian Church, the oldest Protestant denomination, was started by John Hus nearly a century before Martin Luther's reformation. Kate had always allowed Jeff to go to church with his grandparents, and he had been baptized as a Moravian. But Kate had very little use for church of any kind, especially after Davis died. It was not until she became a Blue Star Mother that she was aware that anyone was praying for her, other than her in-laws and Jeff. Hilda, the woman who served as chaplain to the Blue Star Mothers, had been a special friend to her. Hilda seemed to have a genuine faith that Kate found comforting. With her encouragement, Kate had started praying again. Having Jeff in Iraq was a huge incentive to pray.

For her supper, Kate fixed a cup of hot tea and heated a bowl of soup in the microwave oven. Before she tackled the task of wrestling the Christmas tree into her living room, she needed nourishment. As she sipped her supper, she opened her mail, a predictable assortment of bills and holiday charitable appeals. At the bottom of the stack were two Christmas cards, one that included a pocket calendar from her automobile insurance agent, and the other from Peggy, a new friend she had met at a Blue Star meeting.

Kate paused before opening the second envelope. Less than a week earlier, Peggy and Carl Devon had received the news every Blue Star Mother dreads. Their son had been killed in Iraq when his helicopter was shot down. Slowly Kate broke the seal on the envelope. The card depicted the Magi following a bright star to Bethlehem. The printed message was "The Wise Still Seek the Prince of Peace." The handwritten note from Peggy read, "Dear Kate, I am praying for you and Jeff this Christmas. The star still leads to peace. Please pray for us. Love, Peggy." Kate was completely taken aback by the Christmas card. How could Peggy send her a Christmas card? How could she even think about peace when her son had been taken from her? How could she have any confidence in prayer when her prayers had not been answered? It was too much for Kate to ponder.

Kate rinsed her bowl and mug in the kitchen sink and then placed them in the dishwasher. As she walked into Jeff's room, she noticed the light from the electric candle that shone through the Blue Star flag. Kate paused in front of the dresser and gazed at the pictures of three generations of Wimbish men: Jefferson Davis Wimbish, Papa J.D., in his World War II Navy uniform; Jefferson Davis Wimbish, Jr., Davis, in his Marine Corps uniform in Viet Nam; Jefferson Davis Wimbish, III, Jeff, in his Army uniform. Kate fell across her son's bed, pulling a comforter over her. She hugged Jeff's pillow and cried herself to sleep.

* * *

Saturday morning was cold and rainy. Kate woke up later than usual, still exhausted from a hard week at the hospital and from constant worry. She turned on the television to the weather channel on her way to the kitchen to make hot tea. The forecast was for cold rain, possibly changing to sleet and freezing rain in the afternoon. While she waited for the water to boil, she ate a spoonful or two of cottage cheese from the container. Once the tea was made, Kate wrapped herself in an afghan and settled on the sofa to enjoy her tea. Peggy's Christmas card was still on the coffee table. Kate threw a magazine on top of the card to hide it from her line of vision and then propped her feet up on the table.

Kate usually got an e-mail from Jeff on Sunday afternoon. His e-mail schedule was predictable because he was a Captain in a signal battalion. As assignments went in Iraq, Jeff seemed to have a good one. He was located inside one of Saddam Hussein's many palace compounds in Saddam's hometown of Tikrit. Jeff had described the palace compound as being larger than the campus of his alma mater, North Carolina State University. The palace was constructed largely of Venetian marble and equipped with gold plumbing fixtures. If Kate's son had to be in Iraq, at least he was comfortable. She was glad he did not have to fly a helicopter.

Her thoughts drifted back thirty-seven years to 1966 when Davis was eighteen years old. He had been a four-letter athlete in high school. Kate was a seventeen-year-old cheerleader. They dated all through his senior year, her junior year. Kate loved Davis; Davis loved Kate. Her parents objected to their relationship because of the difference in their religion. Her mother was Catholic, and her dad was an avowed agnostic. They had agreed that Kate would be reared in the Catholic Church, but that was about all they agreed on when it came to religion. They did not want Kate to have the same strife in her future that their marriage had suffered, although the marital problems of her parents went far beyond their religious differences.

Davis had hoped to go to college on an athletic scholarship, but no scholarship was offered. When he thought that he might be drafted, he joined the Marine Corps. Kate saw him only a few times before he left for Camp Lejeune. She heard nothing more from him until he wrote to her from Viet Nam. Once their correspondence started, their love rekindled. In their letters, Davis asked Kate to wait for him to come home, and she promised to do so. Davis was a helicopter gunner, and his chopper was shot down. He somehow survived the crash but was burned badly. North Vietnamese forces captured him and held him as a prisoner of war in Hanoi for four years. Kate did not know whether he was dead or alive. Still, she waited.

In the meantime, Kate's parents were divorced. Her dad moved to Arizona, and her mom moved back to Boston to get out of the South. Kate decided to stay because she was enrolled in the local technical college and had almost completed her nursing degree. In the absence of Kate's parents, J.D. and Ruth Wimbish were like parents to her. Their son, Davis, was the man she loved. Together, the three waited in hope and uncertainty for his return.

When the war ended in 1972, Davis was released. After numerous medical exams, extensive treatments, and intelligence debriefings, Davis finally came home. Kate had hoped against hope that Davis would return. Davis had hoped Kate would keep her promise to wait. Once reunited, they could hardly wait to be married. The wedding took place only three months after Davis returned home.

Within weeks after the wedding, Kate knew she had made a mistake. Davis not only carried the scars of war on his body, but he also carried the horrors of war in his mind. For Davis, the war in Viet Nam never ended. Not only did he feel defeated, but the service he had rendered for his country seemed unappreciated. Few Blue Star flags were displayed in windows during or after Viet Nam.

Davis never participated in a Veterans' Day Parade. Worst of all, friends and family members almost never mentioned the war.

Davis was plagued by constant nightmares. Kate was plagued by his infrequent but violent fits of rage. Though he never physically hurt Kate, her emotional pain was profound. As his paranoia deepened, he became suspicious of Kate. He began accusing her of infidelity while he had been a prisoner of war. Though Kate gave no provocation, Davis suspected her of adultery after they were married. He would point his finger at his wife and mockingly shout the Marine Corps motto: "Semper Fidelis, Semper Fidelis, Semper Fidelis," which means Always Faithful.

After several years of therapy, Davis seemed better. Kate could remember his smile and a time of relative tranquility. It was then that the couple decided to have a child. Jeff was a bicentennial baby, born in 1976. His birth brought joy to the Wimbish household. Kate felt that the years of waiting and the years of heartache had been worth the happiness that she and Davis enjoyed.

Davis was a proud daddy. He carried a picture of Jeff in his wallet and showed it gladly to anyone who asked about his newborn. Just a few weeks after Jeff's birth, Davis showed the photograph to one of his buddies in the barbershop. Teasing, the friend quipped, "That boy doesn't look a thing like you, Davis. I wonder who his father really is." It was more than the fragile emotions of Davis could tolerate. In sudden rage he hit the jester in the mouth, knocking out a tooth and bloodying his face. The offhand remark brought back the old paranoia, and the accusations against Kate began again. Their happiness ended abruptly. Worst of all, Davis rejected Jeff, thinking in his twisted mind that another man had fathered his son.

Kate felt defenseless. Davis believed that his wife had turned his own parents against him. Papa J.D. and Mama Ruth tried to help. They offered their daughter-in-law and grandson a safe place to stay when Davis flew into his more and more frequent rages. Even court-ordered confinement in a psychiatric hospital did not help. It only made Davis more suspicious and resentful.

Finally, on a summer night in 1978, her husband flew into a fit of anger. When he began destroying their living room furniture, Kate scooped Jeff up and fled to her in-laws' home. Davis scribbled a note, "Semper Fi," before driving his pickup truck to the cemetery. After taping the note to the windshield, he took his own life with one of Papa J.D.'s guns. Though the name Jefferson Davis Wimbish, Jr. would never appear on the Viet Nam Memorial Wall in Washington, D.C., Kate had always regarded her husband's death as a fatality of the war.

The ringing of the telephone brought Kate back to the present. The call was from Hilda, the chaplain of the Blue Star Mothers.

"Hello, Kate. Have I called too early for a Saturday morning?"

"Not at all, Hilda. I'm glad to hear from you."

"Kate, you know Peggy Devon in our Blue Star chapter."

"Yes, I got a Christmas card from her yesterday."

"So did I. She and Carl have been waiting for Sonny's body to come home from Iraq."

"Yes, I know. Is there any word on that?"

"Yes. It was in the newspaper this morning. They have planned Sonny's funeral for tomorrow afternoon at the Presbyterian church. They'll receive friends tonight in the church Fellowship Hall."

"I haven't read the paper. Thank you for letting me know."

"Kate, since you know Peggy, I was wondering if you would go with me to the funeral tomorrow. We will present her Gold Star Flag at the cemetery following the military honors."

"I don't know, Hilda. I've never attended one of those ceremonies before."

"Well, it's not a comfortable thing to do. But it's not complicated at all. We just attend the service, and then at the graveside after everything else has been done, we will give Peggy a Gold Star flag and a hug. The funeral home will give her a letter of condolence."

Kate paused before answering. If Peggy could send her a Christmas card, she could certainly attend Sonny's funeral and give Peggy a hug. "Okay, Hilda. I'll be there."

"Thanks, Kate. I'll appreciate it, and I know Peggy will, too."

When the telephone conversation ended, Kate checked her watch. She still had on the clothes she was wearing when she had fallen asleep the night before. Outside, the cold rain had turned to sleet, and the Christmas tree was still in the trunk of her car. She was more determined than ever to get the tree inside and decorated. She put on boots, a warm coat, a stocking cap, and gloves for her wrestling match with the tree. She spread out a plastic tablecloth in the living room to protect the carpet. Within just a few minutes, Kate had positioned the tree inside the house in the customary place in front of the living room window. She filled the stand with water and added a few aspirin to keep the tree fresh.

After a hot shower and clean Saturday clothes, Kate was ready to decorate the tree. She had already moved a box of ornaments from the attic to the living room. She put the Elvis tape in the stereo and listened to songs from her youth as she placed multicolored lights on the tree. "I'll be home for Christmas," sang Elvis. Kate thought, *No, Jeff, but you may be home for Easter.*

She unwrapped the keepsake ornaments and hung them on the fir branches. Jeff had made some of these ornaments when he was in kindergarten or in Sunday school at the Moravian church. Some of the decorations even had Polaroid photographs of her son pasted in tiny frames. "Santa, bring my baby back to me," crooned the King. Kate knew in her heart of hearts that Santa could not bring her baby back. She surprised herself with the unexpected thought that only God could bring Jeff home.

She strung the tacky tinsel on the tree branches as Elvis accompanied her decorating with "O Little Town of Bethlehem." Kate heard the words, "the hopes and fears of all the years." *He got that right*, she thought, *hope and fear*.

Kate started to open the package containing the three gold Styrofoam stars she had purchased at Wal-Mart but paused and reconsidered. She really did not want gold stars, not even on her Christmas tree. She stuffed the unopened package into her pocket.

In the bottom of the box from the attic, Kate found a white star for the top of the tree. It was a smaller version of the Moravian Star on her front porch. As Kate put the star in place, Elvis sang "Silent Night," and Kate remembered Peggy's Christmas card with the words, "The star still leads to peace." On Sunday afternoon, Peggy would be presented what every Blue Star Mother dreads— the Gold Star flag. *How could Peggy possibly have peace?*

✳   ✳   ✳

As was her custom, Kate slept late on Sunday morning. The sleet had changed back to a cold rain overnight. Before she made her cup of hot tea, Kate turned on the computer to check her e-mail. As she glanced at her Internet home page, she noticed the headline, "Saddam Captured." She clicked on the link and read the incredible news of Hussein's arrest. The story said that a Special Forces Unit found the deposed dictator hiding underground in a spider hole in a small compound south of his native Tikrit. What would this mean for Jeff? Kate wondered. She checked her inbox. No word from Jeff yet. She would have to wait until after the funeral service to read Jeff's cyber news from Iraq.

By noon on Sunday, the sun was shining brightly. The air was cold, and a steady breeze was blowing. *At least Sonny Devon's funeral will not be in the rain*, thought Kate. Kate hated funerals. She was usually able to find an excuse not to attend funeral services ever since Davis died. She had, of course, flown to Arizona for her dad's funeral and to Boston when her mom died. In Kate's mind, cemeteries, mortuaries, and funerals were best avoided if possible. It was as if every funeral was her husband's funeral all over again. She wondered aloud, "Why did I tell Hilda I would do this?"

Kate arrived early for the service at the Presbyterian church, but it was already difficult to find a parking space. The large crowd surprised her. She remembered how few people had attended Davis' funeral service twenty-five years earlier. Hilda greeted her at the entrance to the Sanctuary.

"Let's sit near the back," Hilda suggested. "That way we can get ahead of the cars going to the cemetery."

"Won't we all go in a procession?" asked Kate.

"Not anymore. The city no longer allows it. It's everyone for himself."

The two women sat together on the back pew. Kate soon remembered why she disliked funerals. The atmosphere in the church was somber and oppressive. But it soon became clear to Kate that the service for Sonny Devon was going to be different. The pastor explained that Carl and Peggy had insisted that the memorial for their son be a celebration of his life. He acknowledged that various dignitaries were present for the service, but that the family had requested that public figures not be recognized. They wanted a worship service, not a political rally.

After the pastor quoted a brief scripture and offered an uplifting prayer, the entire congregation sang "Great is Thy Faithfulness." Kate did not know the hymn well, but she recalled having heard it on a recording. She found the words comforting. The eulogy was a touching memorial for Sonny. The pastor even included several humorous memories that prompted laughter in the congregation. What a pleasant surprise! Kate had never before heard laughter at a funeral.

Then came the biggest surprise of all! The service included a Moravian Love Feast. The pastor explained that Sonny loved the Christmas season and always looked forward to participating in the Moravian Love Feast hosted by the Presbyterian church. "This is a way of celebrating God's love for us," the pastor said.

Members of the Moravian Fellowship had come to serve the congregation. Kate was surprised to see her in-laws dressed in traditional Moravian attire, walking up the aisle of the church serving the traditional Love Feast rolls and mugs of coffee with cream and sugar cooked into the hot drink. Papa J.D., in a black suit, white shirt, and black tie, and Mama Ruth, wearing a starched floor-length white dress and white bonnet, were equally surprised to see their daughter-in-law in any church for any reason. Though Kate usually preferred hot tea, the sweet roll and coffee were quite tasty. As the congregation enjoyed the Love Feast, the church organist played Christmas carols.

After the benediction, Hilda suggested that they ride together to the cemetery, but Kate declined, saying she would rather go separately. Hilda did not question her. As Kate drove across town for the committal service and the presentation of the Service flag, she pondered what she had experienced. *How can Carl and Peggy celebrate God's love when their son has been taken from them?* The question begged an answer.

At the cemetery Kate and Hilda stood to one side as the committal service began. The pastor read Psalm 23, spoke words of committal, and prayed. Then a detachment from Fort Jackson, serving as an honor guard, gave Sonny Devon military honors. The American flag was lifted from the casket. Shots were fired, and "Taps" was played. Then the flag was ceremoniously folded.

A highly decorated sergeant knelt as he spoke to Peggy, "On behalf of the President of the United States and a grateful nation, I present this flag to you in appreciation for your son's service to our country." The sergeant stood and saluted. Kate was on the verge of tears.

Hilda, with Kate at her side, moved in front of Peggy. "For making the ultimate sacrifice in giving your son for our freedom, we present to you the Gold Star flag." Hilda handed the flag to Peggy. Hilda first, and then Kate, gave Peggy a hug.

Kate, with tears in her eyes, blurted out, "I'm sorry you lost your son, Peggy."

Peggy gave Kate another hug and responded. "Sonny's death is very hard, Kate, but I can't really say that I've lost him. I know exactly where he is. For us, Christmas will be different this year, but for Sonny, it will be the best Christmas he has ever had."

Kate had no response. Peggy's words seemed glib, insincere. Her answer came too easy. It seemed to Kate that Peggy was taking the death of her child too well.

"I know this is difficult for you," said Peggy. "Thank you so much for being here with us. Thank you for your prayers."

Kate was relieved to see tears in Peggy's eyes.

Kate left the grave of Sonny Devon. She got into her car and drove to the other side of the cemetery to the grave of Davis Wimbish. She stood alone before the granite headstone. The engraved words read:

JEFFERSON DAVIS WIMBISH
SEMPER FIDELIS
APRIL 6, 1948 – AUGUST 11, 1978

Kate was angry. She was still angry that Davis had taken his life and that he had left her alone to rear Jeff. She was angry that she had waited for him so long, only to have him return such a scarred person. She was angry that her country had sent the love of her life into a stupid war in Viet Nam. Now her only child was in harm's way in another senseless war in Iraq. She was angry that Peggy Devon had such quick, easy answers for such a terrible tragedy. She was angry that every day her mind was filled with fear and every night her heart was struck with terror. Kate dropped to her knees and pounded her fists in the soft grass on the grave of her husband.

When Davis died, Kate had called her priest. He was a kind man, but when he found out that Davis had committed suicide, he had little to say to Kate that was helpful. Since Davis was still a member of the Moravian Fellowship, Papa J.D. asked his Moravian pastor to conduct the service. It was a simple graveside service with scriptures, prayers, and little else. Because people did not know what to say, they either avoided Kate or mouthed empty clichés. Kate was so hurt that she became a church dropout. The terrible mixture of pain and anger, isolation and bitterness, flooded her soul, and Kate sobbed uncontrollably at the grave of Davis Wimbish.

Kate lost track of time, but as the cold December sun was setting, she rose from her knees. Her eyes were burning, her nose was running, but for the first time in a long time her heart was lighter. A burden had been lifted from her. Now that she thought about it, Peggy Devon's words were the only ones that made any sense to Kate. Whatever else might have been said about Davis, however twisted his mind had been, Davis was a believer. For the first time, Kate felt as if she knew exactly where Davis was. For the first time in a long time, she had some sense of peace.

* * *

Kate had dreaded the coming of Christmas, but the next eleven days moved more quickly than she had expected. Her work at the hospital continued to be demanding. The Emergency Room overflowed with patients, many suffering from flu-like symptoms or respiratory complications from the flu. The nursing staff took a disproportionate number of sick days, and Kate spent much of her time shuffling personnel schedules. Kate's job was something like that of a football coach, constantly substituting fresh players for those injured. Still, even for the Christmas season, she seemed to have more energy and a better outlook than usual.

She missed Jeff as much as ever, but his e-mails were upbeat and more frequent. The capture of Saddam had improved morale among his soldiers. He received the package Kate had sent. He appreciated the journal and colored pencils and enjoyed sketching scenes of Tikrit to accompany his journal entries. The John Grisham novels were already circulating through his unit. He hoped to read one soon. The Hershey's Kisses didn't last long. Jeff had enjoyed a few, but he had given most of the chocolate candy to Iraqi children. Jeff was especially glad for the digital photographs, both of the Christmas tree and his bedroom window. The Christmas tree looked larger than usual in the picture, and it was decorated just the way he liked it. In the photo of his window, he could see the reflection of the Moravian Star, as well as the Service flag illuminated by a candle.

In one e-mail Jeff wrote, "Tell Papa J.D. and Mama Ruth 'Merry Christmas.' I wish I could be there to go to a Love Feast with them. Tell Papa J.D. to eat an extra roll for me and please save some sugar cake in the freezer until I come home." Kate already had several Moravian Sugar Cakes stashed in the freezer in preparation for Jeff's homecoming, which she hoped would be before Easter.

In a more pensive moment Jeff wrote, "You know, Mom, the chaplain says that the Wise Men came this way on their journey to Bethlehem. They probably came from Iran, following the star. At night the stars are very bright over the desert."

After Kate's in-laws saw her at Sonny Devon's funeral, they invited her to visit their Moravian church for a candlelight Love Feast on the Sunday before Christmas. They also invited her to have Christmas dinner with them on Christmas Day. Kate accepted both invitations.

Kate's second Love Feast of the season was as enjoyable as the first. She again appreciated the beautiful Christmas music and enjoyed the sweet roll and Moravian coffee. During the candlelight service, each person in the congregation received a small beeswax candle decorated with a red crepe paper frill. The worshippers passed the light of their candles to one another until the entire sanctuary was aglow in candlelight. Kate could understand why this was so important to Jeff. The Love Feast was more than sweet rolls and coffee; it was a gift of peace and light. She thought of her son throughout the service and was glad to worship with Papa J.D. and Mama Ruth. As meaningful

The Love Feast was more than
sweet rolls and coffee;
it was a gift of peace and light.

as the Moravian Love Feast was for Kate, it left her longing for something more.

Ever since Sonny Devon's funeral and her meltdown at Davis' grave, Kate had realized that the absence of a practical faith in her life had left her a depleted, fretful person. Life was difficult; it was difficult for everybody. Kate had seen an inner peace and a constant hope in Peggy and Hilda that she herself did not have. She had long admired the same strengths in her in-laws. Her Christmas wish was to cease fretful worry. She was searching for joy to replace sadness and hope instead of fear.

✳   ✳   ✳

On Christmas Eve afternoon Kate did something she had not done in twenty-five years: she went to St. Mary's Catholic Church. St. Mary's was a small church building with a growing congregation. Kate had been a member of the parish with her mother as a child. St. Mary's was the church where she was baptized as an infant, confirmed as a youth, and took her first communion. But it was the congregation of St. Mary's that had all but abandoned her after Davis' death. Going back to the church was not easy, but Kate knew it was what she must do. She went to the empty church for confession. The priest was a compassionate man who affirmed her decision and offered pardon for years of bitterness. He also offered his apology for the disappointment Kate experienced twenty-five years earlier.

Later on Christmas Eve, Kate attended Mass at midnight. She arrived at St. Mary's in time to find a seat near the back of the Sanctuary. As she waited for Mass to begin, she admired the four colorful stained glass windows. Each was backlit so that even at night their beauty would be apparent. Each one of the four windows depicted an event from the life of Mary, the mother of Jesus. The first was the Annunciation, the angel Gabriel announcing the birth of Jesus. The second window presented the birth of Jesus in Bethlehem. The third window depicted the wedding in Cana where Jesus, at the prompting of his mother, performed his first miracle. The fourth window, the one above the altar, showed the crucifixion of Jesus with Mary standing at the foot of the cross, a witness to her son's death.

Kate studied each window carefully. The windows surrounded her with the sense that Mary was the kind of woman Kate longed to be. As Mass began, she prayed that God would allow her to become more like the mother of Jesus. When the congregation stood for the Gospel reading, Kate focused on the words from St. Luke, "And Mary kept all these things and pondered them in her heart." At almost exactly midnight Kate received Holy Communion for the first time in twenty-five years. On her way home from St. Mary's, Kate listened to the radio in her car. She heard a Christmas song she remembered from her youth. It was not an Elvis song, but it was sung by Johnny Mathis— "Ave Maria." A sense of peace swept over Kate.

✳   ✳   ✳

On Christmas morning Kate planned to sleep late, but her telephone rang early. "Must be a problem at the hospital," she thought. It was not a problem at all. It was Jeff, calling his mother on a satellite telephone from Tikrit. Their conversation was necessarily brief, just enough time to exchange "Merry Christmas" and "I love you." For Kate, just hearing the clear voice of her sweet child was the best Christmas gift she could have received.

Kate looked forward to Christmas dinner with Papa J.D. and Mama Ruth. This was her family. They regarded her as their daughter, and she loved them very much. As she prepared to leave her townhouse, Kate admired her little Christmas tree. She had planned to take it down before it started shedding needles. Too late. Kate was glad she had kept the tree. Over the last three weeks she had changed her mind about it. In fact, she had changed her mind about several things. As she left for her visit with her in-laws, Kate found the package containing the three gold Styrofoam stars. She took one from the package and hung it on her tree. The other two she strung on pieces of red ribbon and put them in her coat pocket.

Mama Ruth had prepared her usual Christmas dinner of turkey and ham, sweet potatoes, green beans, homemade rolls, sweet iced tea, pecan pie, and homemade Moravian Sugar Cake made with real mashed potatoes in the dough. As usual, the Wimbish family had invited a few other people to share their Christmas meal: a woman from their church spending her first Christmas alone after her husband's death and a young couple and their two children, new to town and too far away from their own parents to travel home for Christmas.

After dinner the young couple took their children outside to play on a sunny Christmas afternoon. The widow went along to enjoy the children. Papa J. D. mentioned the funeral service for Sonny Devon. Kate explained her connection to Peggy through the Blue Star Mothers. Kate was surprised to learn that Papa J. D. knew all about the organization. "I believe they got started in Michigan in the early 1940s. My mother, Jeff's great-grandmother, was a member. She kept a flag hanging in the front window the whole time my brother and I were overseas. I was in the Navy and took part in the Normandy invasion. My brother was in the Army. He served with the infantry in Italy and France." Kate had read Tom Brokaw's book, *The Greatest Generation*. Her in-laws were certainly among the greatest.

Kate asked a question that had been on her mind for weeks. "Were there any Blue Star Mothers during the war in Viet Nam?"

"You didn't hear much about that during Viet Nam. That was a different kind of war. The country was divided. Yet I suppose you could say that Ruth was a Blue Star Mother. We did not know about any organization, but Ruth tried to help as many mothers of servicemen as she could. You remember, Kate, that was a hard time."

Kate did remember, and this seemed like the perfect time to do something she had been thinking about for several weeks. "Mama Ruth, I have something I want to give you. You know, when a Blue Star Mother loses her child in military service, the other mothers give her a Gold Star flag. That's why I was at Sonny Devon's funeral, to give Peggy the Gold Star flag. I have always regarded Davis' death as a war fatality. For him, the conflict never ended. I don't have a flag to give you, but I do have a gold star." Kate took one of the gold star ornaments on a piece of red ribbon and handed it to Mama Ruth. She hugged her mother-in-law. The two women wept. Papa J.D., overcome with emotion, left the room as Kate and Mama Ruth embraced.

After sharing a good Christmas cry together, Mama Ruth said, "Kate, you are a wonderful woman. I love you so much."

"Thank you, Mama Ruth. I want to be the kind of woman you are."

Kate helped her mother-in-law clear the dishes before she left. She had one more stop to make on Christmas Day. She drove to St. Mary's Catholic Church. The church was open but empty. As Kate entered, she passed a beautiful, life-sized, white Italian marble statue of Mary. She had not remembered the statue from her youth but had seen it for the first time when she came for confession the previous afternoon. Kate entered the church reverently. She genuflected toward the altar, made the sign of the cross, and knelt near the front of the sanctuary. Once again, she admired the four stained glass windows illuminated by the Christmas afternoon sun. She prayed again that God would enable her to become a woman and a mother like Mary. She lit two votive candles, one for Jeff and one for the Devon family. She prayed for her son and for her friend Peggy.

As Kate rose to leave the sanctuary, she looked at the window depicting the birth of Jesus. Then she turned toward the window above the altar, the scene of the crucifixion. *Jeff is just a little younger than Jesus was when he died*, she thought. *There is Mary—with him in birth, with him in death.* As Kate walked out of St. Mary's into the late Christmas afternoon, she paused at the marble statue of Mary. She placed her hands tenderly on the figure and whispered, "You made the ultimate sacrifice as a mother. You gave your son for our freedom." From her coat pocket, Kate took the gold star ornament on the red ribbon and placed it gently over the head of Mary, draping it around her neck like a pendant, a badge of honor.

The Christmas Yard Sale

Frank Jenkins stopped at the grocery store on his way home from Harold's Auto Repair Shop. Grocery shopping was not what he wanted to do, but his wife, Beverly, had asked him to bring home a gallon of milk and a loaf of bread. As he entered the store, he searched his blue jeans pockets for all of the money he had to his name, four wrinkled one-dollar bills and a fistful of change. He walked past the beckoning displays of Christmas candy, through the bountiful fruit and vegetable section, and beyond the deli with its banquet of wafting aromas of cakes, pastries, pies, meats and cheeses. He had not been to the grocery store in several months. It was too depressing for a man who felt unable to provide for his family. The last time in the store had been so discouraging to him that he had requested that Bev not ask him to go anymore. Now his understanding wife had the flu, and Frank was left to do the shopping.

From somewhere behind the refrigerated cases, the voice of Burl Ives was singing, "Have a Holly, Jolly Christmas." As Frank made his way past the well-stocked meat and poultry section. He glanced at the array of steaks, pork chops, turkeys, and chickens. This time last year, he and Bev had a freezer full of meat for the holidays: smoked turkey for Thanksgiving, sugar-cured ham for Christmas, thick pork chops for New Year's. Not so this year. This had been the year of bologna sandwiches for the Jenkins family.

Frank found the milk, but he could not find the bread. The milk was more than three dollars a gallon. He picked up one plastic bottle with the best expiration date. The milk would last over a week beyond Thanksgiving. On second thought, he knew that with Chip and Tracy home for Thanksgiving, the gallon of milk would not make it beyond the weekend.

The bread display had been cleverly placed directly across the aisle from the cookies and candy. Frank tried to avert his gaze from the sweets. He found a loaf of the generic store-brand bread marked down to seventy-nine cents a loaf. He counted the money he was clutching in his left hand, four crumpled dollar bills and nearly three dollars in change. The sensible thing to do was to buy two loaves of bread at the special price. He really wanted to buy a package of Oreo cookies for Chip and Tracy, but he simply could not afford it.

In the early evening, just two days before Thanksgiving, even the express line, ten items or less, was crowded. As Frank moved to the long lines at the checkout counter, he could feel the muscles in the back of his neck tighten. Self-serve lines were available, and an eager teenage clerk invited him to step up to the automated checkout machine. Frank declined. He preferred dealing with a real cashier. The self-service lines seemed to work best with plastic money, a credit or debit card, and Frank had neither. In March he and Bev had agreed together to have plastic surgery, cutting their plastic cards to shreds.

As he waited in line, Frank read the headlines on newspapers and news magazines: "Stock Market Improving," "Job Rate Up," "Economic Forecast Hopeful." *These must be reports from China*, Frank thought. They certainly did not correspond to the reality in his own life. His eyes found the rack of Hershey candy. He selected a Special Dark Chocolate candy bar. He had just enough money to buy a little surprise for Bev. Sure, it was frivolous, but Bev had the flu, and, well, she was just Bev.

"That candy bar will spoil your appetite, rot your teeth out, and make you fat," a voice behind him warned. It was the most annoying person in the world, his neighbor Ralph. The tension in Frank's neck was becoming a headache.

"Hi, Ralph," Frank replied. "Does your wife have you doing the shopping, too?"

"You got that right. I'm the one with the money."

Frank looked at Ralph's cart piled high with groceries. Among the items in the cart, Frank noticed two turkeys, sweet potatoes, several bags of fresh fruits and vegetables, two gallons of milk, two cartons of expensive, exotic flavors of ice cream, and on top of the heap, three packages of Oreo cookies. Ralph had many more than ten items.

"Looks like you're getting ready for Thanksgiving," Frank said.

"Yep, the kids are coming home. I buy it, Sue cooks it, and the kids eat it."

"Say, are you going to smoke turkeys again this year?"

"Not this year, Ralph. How about you?"

"No way, Frank. I could never smoke turkeys the way you do. Besides I don't even know which end to light." Ralph laughed at his own lame joke.

The store manager interrupted their conversation and spoke to Ralph. "Sir, please move down to aisle four. We'll be glad to take care of you there."

"My money's no good in this line?" Ralph asked indignantly.

"This is our express line."

Ralph, grumbling under his breath, moved to aisle four, and not a moment too soon. Frank would have been embarrassed for Ralph to witness the exchange that followed. As Frank, gripping his money in his left fist, approached the cash register, the checkout clerk took a break and was replaced by a more familiar face.

"Hey, Mr. Jenkins. Remember me? I'm Annie. I used to work for you at the plant."

"Yes, Annie, I remember you. How are you?"

"I'm fine, Mr. Jenkins, now that I have a job."

"How are your children?"

"They're fine. Growing like weeds. How is Mrs. Jenkins?"

"She has the flu. I'm picking up a few groceries for her."

"Mr. Jenkins, your total is $6.96."

Frank counted out his money. He was three cents short. "I miscalculated," he said to Annie. "I'll have to leave off the candy bar."

"No, sir," Annie said. "I've got three cents. I know that candy bar is for Mrs. Jenkins. She's about the sweetest lady I ever knew. She deserves her Hershey bar."

"Thank you, Annie," Frank said embarrassed and grateful.

"Mr. Jenkins, did you ever get a job?"

"Still looking," said Frank.

"The company didn't do none of us right but especially not you, Mr. Jenkins. As bad as it was for all the rest of us, we couldn't believe the way they treated you. Not after you had worked so hard all of those years for them."

"I know, Annie. It couldn't be helped. None of us ever thought they would just close the doors and walk away. But that's business, I suppose."

"Bad business," said Annie. "I'll be praying for you, Mr. Jenkins. And you tell Mrs. Jenkins I hope she feels better real soon."

"Thank you, Annie. Give your children a hug. Have a good Thanksgiving."

Frank's head was pounding as he carried the groceries to his rusty Chevy pickup. As he opened the creaking truck door, he saw Joe Monroe walking toward him. Joe had been a fellow employee at the plant, too. He had taken early retirement one year before the plant closed. Now he worked part-time as a barber.

"Hello, Frank, how are you doing?" The two men shook hands.

"Doing fine, Joe. Glad to see you." It was nice to see Joe. He was a good friend, and they had enjoyed a pleasant working relationship.

"Frank, I tried to phone you at home. I talked to Beverly. She sounded sick."

"Yeah, she has a touch of the flu. What can I do for you, Joe?"

"Are you still selling firewood?"

"As much as I can. Do you need a load?"

"At least a load, maybe two. How much do you charge?"

"I usually get fifty dollars a load delivered. A load is this truck full."

"Any chance I could get at least one load first thing tomorrow?"

"Sure, I've already got it cut and split. If you buy two loads, I'll make you a special price."

"Great, come to my house early. I need some of the wood to smoke turkeys for Thanksgiving. How early can you get a load to my house?"

"You name the time, and I'll be there."

"How about 6 a.m. sharp?"

"Okay, I'll be there with a load, and if you need more, I'll come back."

"Plan on delivering two. I'll use it all winter."

The men shook hands again.

✳   ✳   ✳

As Frank drove into the cul-de-sac, he could see Ralph's brand new Lincoln Navigator already in the driveway at 527 Camelot Court. Frank turned the 1984 Chevy truck into his own driveway. As he walked to his back door, the scent of wood smoke from the fireplaces of his neighbors filled the cool, damp night air. They were burning the oak logs he had cut, split, and sold to them to try to make ends meet for his family. On the one hand, his labor was going up in smoke; on the other, he had found a way to keep the wolf from his own door and share warmth with his neighbors at the same time. But the wolf was ever lurking.

As he entered the kitchen, Frank could hear Bev coughing. He put the milk into the fridge, placed a pot of cold water on the stove, and entered the dark, chilly den where his wife lay covered in blankets on the sofa. Bev kept the lights off and the heat turned down to save money. Frank turned on a lamp, kissed Bev on the top of her head, and gave her the Hershey candy bar.

"Brought you a surprise," he said. "Chocolate always helps."

"Thank you," said Bev, her head emerging from the pile of blankets.

His head still hurting, Frank went to his backyard and brought in an armload of firewood. In just a few minutes a pleasant fire blazed in his own fireplace. He made two mugs of hot tea with the now boiling water. Frank and Bev sat together on the raised hearth, sipping tea and getting warm.

"What would you like for supper?" Frank asked. "I'll give you two choices. Our surf and turf special rib eye steak, cooked medium rare, with steamed shrimp, or my world famous bologna sandwich?"

Bev laughed, "I think I'll have the bologna sandwich for a change."

"Coming right up," said Frank.

Frank wrapped his denim jacket around Bev's shoulders and made two bologna sandwiches according to his secret recipe: mustard, mayonnaise, and just a dab of Heinz 57 steak sauce. He added a log to the fire and sat down next to Bev. She took his hand, and Bev blessed the food, as she always did. In the Jenkins family Bev was the designated prayer person.

"How are you feeling?" Frank asked.

"I'm better," she said, coughing. "I don't think I've had a fever all day. Sorry I had to miss work this week." Bev worked as a preschool teacher's assistant at a Christian school. She was paid only when she worked and then not enough. The job had no sick days and no benefits.

"Don't worry about it," Frank reassured her. "It couldn't be helped. The children at school probably gave you the flu bug. Besides, I haven't worked either."

"That's not true," said Bev. "You work all the time, cutting firewood, cleaning gutters. You work like a horse."

"I get paid like a horse, too. And I don't mean a race horse, either."

"Frank, I've had a lot of time to pray while I've been sick. I think you'll get a job soon."

"It won't be soon enough," said Frank. "I got the last unemployment check last week. You remember Annie, the single mother with two little children who worked second shift at the plant? She's a checkout clerk at the grocery store. She said she's praying for me, too. She loaned me three cents to buy the groceries."

"Frank, Chip, and Tracy will be home tomorrow. Let's pray that we can have a good Thanksgiving with them."

"Bev, you say the prayers. My prayers don't seem to make it past the ceiling."

✳   ✳   ✳

When Frank's alarm clock went off at 5 a.m. on the Wednesday before Thanksgiving, his headache was gone. He could hear the sound of a steady rain falling on the roof. He was glad that he had loaded the firewood for Joe Monroe after supper the night before. The wood should be dry under the protection of an old tarp held in place by bungee cords. Frank realized that Bev was sleeping more peacefully than she had all week. She did seem to be getting better. He made a pot of coffee and poured a cup to drink while he got dressed. He kissed Bev goodbye and, after several attempts, got the truck started. Harold had promised to find an old starter at the junkyard. Until then, he'd just have to hope for the best. At least the old truck had a good heater, a real help on this cold, rainy morning.

Frank arrived at Joe Monroe's house while it was still dark. He saw the large smoker under the carport. There was a scant supply of firewood piled next to the wall. He backed his Chevy in place, pulled on his work gloves, and started unloading, making a neat stack of fresh firewood next to the old logs.

When the truck was about half empty, Joe appeared at his back door. "You always were a man of your word. You must have gotten up before breakfast."

"Yep," said Frank. "I loaded this last night so it wouldn't get wet. You should be ready to go. The second load will be damp, but I'll keep it separate for you."

"How about a cup of coffee?" Joe asked.

"Sounds good," said Frank.

By the time Joe fixed the coffee, Frank had the truck unloaded. Frank sipped his second cup of the morning while Joe started the fire in the smoker using a few pieces of the old wood and several pieces of the oak, freshly cut by Frank.

"I'm cooking twelve birds today," said Joe. "Family and friends will have them here before eight o'clock. I need to get this smoker going. Are you doing turkeys this year?"

"Not this year," said Frank.

"Are your kids coming home for Thanksgiving?"

"Yes, Chip and Tracy will both get in today," explained Frank. Finishing his coffee, he added, "I'll go get your second load. I'll be back later."

"Frank, could you bring that second load late this afternoon? Maybe it won't be raining by then. Besides, we're going have a good many people in and out of here today. Would late this afternoon suit you just as well?"

Frank was surprised but agreed.

"By the way," said Joe, "let me go ahead and pay you. You said fifty dollars a load, right?"

"Not when you buy two loads. You owe me forty dollars a truck load."

"Here's fifty for one truck load, Frank. You can give me the discount on the second load. See you late this afternoon."

Frank tucked the folded money into his denim jacket pocket and snapped the brass closure securely. The Chevy started on the first try. Frank drove to the grocery store, arriving as it opened. He made his way quickly around the store, picking up a small package of sliced turkey, two cans of cranberry sauce, four large sweet potatoes, a bag of turnip greens, a can of pumpkin pie mix, a pie shell, another gallon of milk, and a package of Oreo cookies. The manager checked him out. When Frank reached into his pocket to extract the folded money, he found a damp index card with a note from Bev written with a permanent marker. He paid for the groceries and asked the manager to return three cents to Annie. The manager grinned and said that he would return the pennies. Back in the truck, with the motor running and the heater blowing, Frank took the damp, crumpled index card from his pocket and read the note from his wife.

> *Frank, I am praying for you.*
> *This scripture verse is for you.*
> *"My God will supply all your needs."*
> *I love you, Bev*

The note was so much like her. Frank was reared as a Presbyterian and a rather nominal Presbyterian at that. Bev, on the other hand, was raised a Southern Baptist. Her family spoke a different language. The first time Frank had Sunday dinner with Bev's family, they had a conversation about a person Frank thought was a distant family member. It took him half an hour to realize they were talking about the Apostle Paul. Prayer was so much a part of Bev's life, that it was often a natural part of her conversation.

Frank's father-in-law and mother-in-law were simple people with a deep faith. Frank remembered how uncomfortable he felt when they said the blessing out loud at a fast food restaurant. To Frank, the strangest of all his in-laws' religious ways was what they called tithing. They said it came from the Bible, but Frank had never heard of it. It was the odd practice of giving to the church one tenth of all of the family income. Bev had tried to convince Frank that tithing was something they should do as a family. "If we are faithful to God, God will be faithful to us," Bev pleaded. Frank just laughed at the idea that giving away money would somehow bring in more income. Their compromise was that Bev could tithe her money, and Frank would decide what to do with his.

Frank read again the note from his wife. Bev really did believe that God would supply all of their needs. Frank believed that God helps those who help themselves.

When Frank returned to his home, Bev was still asleep. He quietly put the groceries away, and he spent the rest of the morning in the garage, watching the rain and sharpening the cutting blades on his chainsaw. In recent months his chainsaw, a rebuilt log splitter, and his old truck had become the means to earning money. Operating and maintaining a chainsaw or, for that matter, keeping a 1984 Chevy pickup truck running, were skills learned, not in his textile engineering degree from North Carolina State University, but growing up on a cattle farm east of Raleigh.

When he graduated with honors in 1973, the job market was wide open. Textile manufacturing was booming throughout the Southeast. But then...*Ross Perot was right*, Frank thought. NAFTA had caused a loud sucking sound of American jobs rapidly moving to other countries, not only to Central America, but to Asia as well. The textile industry in the South had dwindled. Some of the most prosperous companies had vanished. Cotton mills stood empty and crumbling along the rivers of the Piedmont.

The plant that Frank had managed for ten years closed in January. He and others in middle management had an inkling that the company was in trouble, but the sudden decision to close caught them off guard. One day he was making a good living for his family; the next day he was unemployed with no severance pay and two kids in college.

By May he was drawing $287 a week in unemployment, but that ended in early November after the allotted twenty-six weeks. He and Bev had cut expenses in every way they could imagine. He sold his Ford Expedition and bought the old Chevy truck. Bev had an outdated teaching certificate and hoped to get a higher paying position, but she could do no better than the job as a preschool teacher's assistant at the Christian school. Frank had sent rèsumès to every personal contact he had, as well as to numerous employment agencies. The few interviews that he had been granted were dead ends. He was told more than once that he was overqualified.

He had managed to make every monthly mortgage payment on time, but now that his unemployment checks had ended, he had no idea how he would make the December payment. He needed $838 by December 28. The escrow account would take care of property taxes. He wearily made the calculations in his head. Not counting food, gasoline, and other living expenses, plus second semester college tuition for Chip and Tracy, he would have to sell seventeen loads of firewood just to pay the mortgage. He appreciated Bev's note, her faith, and her confidence in God's provision. The idea that God could supply his needs seemed naive at best, if not just stupid, wishful thinking.

Obnoxious Ralph appeared around the corner of the garage and interrupted his thoughts. "Can you believe this rain? I'll be cutting grass on Christmas day."

"Your lawn sure does look green."

"I gave it extra fertilizer and sowed winter rye grass. It is green, but I have to keep cutting it. Why does your lawn look so brown?"

"It's called winter brown, Ralph. I use a secret formula. If it is green and growing, cut it and leave it alone. If not, just leave it alone. Let it live; let it die, just the way Mother Nature intended."

"Beverly doesn't fuss about the way it looks?"

"No, as long as we feed the kids, it's fine with Bev to let the grass starve to death."

"Do you have any idea how much money I've spent on fertilizer and seed just this fall?"

"I have no idea, and please don't tell me. You probably spent more feeding your lawn than I spent on Thanksgiving dinner for my family."

Ralph grumbled to himself as he walked away.

Joe Monroe had been right. It did stop raining by mid-afternoon. Frank loaded the truck with firewood a second time and arrived at Joe's house after five o'clock. He unloaded the wood as he savored the aroma of a dozen smoked turkeys. Monroe friends and family stopped by to pick up their Thanksgiving entrees. When Frank finished unloading the Chevy, Joe handed him several bills. Frank counted fifty dollars. He handed a twenty back to Joe.

"A deal's a deal," said Frank.

Joe took the twenty without an argument. Then he said, "Frank, I cooked one too many birds. Would you do me a big favor and take this turkey home to Bev? I know she isn't feeling well, and if she uses this, she won't have to cook so much tomorrow."

Frank was grateful and accepted the turkey wrapped in aluminum foil. He and Joe shook hands.

"Thanks for the turkey. If you need more wood, let me know," said Frank.

"Will do," said Joe. Then he added, "Frank, stop by the shop some afternoon during the holidays, and bring Chip with you, and I'll give you both haircuts, on the house."

"Thanks, Joe. You're a great friend."

On the way home Frank pulled the rumpled index card from his pocket and read it again. "My God will supply all your needs." He breathed a silent prayer, *Lord, help me.*

✳　✳　✳

Thanksgiving Day was truly a day of thanksgiving for the Jenkins family. Chip and Tracy slept late. Bev served a meal of smoked turkey, cranberry sauce, turnip greens, sweet potatoes, and pumpkin pie. Afterwards they watched the Lions football game on a local television station. Their cable service had been disconnected several months earlier. Then they took a walk around the neighborhood.

That evening as they enjoyed a traditional sandwich of leftover turkey, Frank did something he had never done before. He told his family his concern about the December mortgage payment and tuition for second semester. Though his tone was steady and even as always, he was dying inside. Frank believed that he was failing in his most important responsibility, being a provider for his family. Chip and Tracy had long sensed their dad's unspoken quandary and had made some plans and decisions of their own.

Chip announced that he was a finalist in a bank internship competition. If he got the internship, he would begin work immediately, the bank would pay the tuition for his final semester, and he would be guaranteed a job upon graduation.

Tracy told the family that she had applied for additional need-based grants and a work-study program, funded, oddly enough, by a textile company. Since her college was close by, she could become a commuter student and save the cost of room and board. Frank was stunned by his children's awareness of the family's financial plight and the initiative they had both taken to help with the financial strain. They really were growing up right before his eyes.

Tracy said, "Dad, I want to learn to drive your truck."

"You want to learn to handle a straight drive?" asked Frank. "Why?"

"Who knows when it might come in handy? I might become a trucker babe. By the way, Dad, it's not politically correct to say your truck is a straight drive. Does that make Mom's car a gay drive?"

Frank laughed with his daughter, "I'll be glad to teach you to drive my truck."

On a more serious note Tracy continued, "Dad, when we were walking around the neighborhood today, we had an idea. Chip and I think we know a way to make some money before Christmas, but it will take all of us working together."

Chip and Tracy laid out the plan for a family yard sale. They would both be through with classes by December 16. The yard sale could be held Saturday, December 18. They would each come home a couple of weekends before exams, sort through things, price them, and get them ready for the sale. It would require a lot of work, but Chip added, "Right before Christmas people are in a buying mood."

But do they want to buy our junk? Frank asked himself. Then a second question came to mind, *Is this the reason I sent Chip to college for four years to major in business, so he could put on a yard sale?*

Before the Thanksgiving weekend was over, Chip called the newspaper to learn how to get a free notice in the want ads. Frank started making plywood tables out of scraps of plywood in the garage. Bev quietly started thinking about what she would sell and was pleased to see her family working together. Tracy designed the flyer to be distributed all over the neighborhood.

BIG CHRISTMAS
YARD SALE
DECEMBER 18, 2004

7:30 A.M. UNTIL...
525 CAMELOT COURT

COMPLETE
YOUR CHRISTMAS SHOPPING
AT REASONABLE PRICES

RAIN, SNOW, SLEET, OR HAIL

COME ONE, COME ALL

The next two and a half weeks passed quickly. Bev, completely recovered from the flu and back at school, was looking forward to having her family together for the Christmas holidays. The long-range weather forecast called for an unusually cold, wet winter. Memories of ice storms from winters past made the firewood business boom. Frank was delivering a truckload or two nearly every day except Sundays. Harold had gotten the used starter for the Chevy truck from the junkyard, and Frank's pickup was starting on the first try every time. Chip and Tracy had come home two weekends in a row, selecting, pricing, and preparing for the yard sale.

Everything was going well until Ralph appeared at the Jenkins' door on Saturday night one week before the yard sale. "Frank, I've seen these yard sale flyers all over the neighborhood. You should have checked with us. Your timing is awful. I've registered a complaint with the neighborhood association. You're inviting riffraff from all over town into our cul-de-sac on the day of our family

Christmas party. Sue is very upset. Her mom and dad are planning to arrive before noon, and she will be terribly embarrassed. It's bad enough to have that old pickup truck parked in your driveway and to have a yard as brown as a paper bag. Adding yard sale customers to those disgraces is adding insult to injury."

Frank bit his lip, thought for a moment, and said resolutely, "Ralph, we will make certain no one parks in your driveway or in front of your house. The yard sale should be over by late afternoon. Sorry for the inconvenience, but the yard sale is on."

With that, Ralph, as was his custom, walked away grumbling.

As Frank closed the door, Chip chimed in, "We have a winner in our Most Like the Grinch Contest!"

*   *   *

Tracy had written on the flyer "Rain, Snow, Sleet, or Hail." She left off "gloom of night." When Frank stepped outside his back door on the Saturday morning of the yard sale, most of the above conditions applied. It was a cold, dark, cloudy morning. He hated to awaken his family so early, but they had all asked him to do so. They were really into this yard sale and wanted to do everything in their power to make it successful.

While Bev fixed oatmeal for her family, Frank, Chip, and Tracy set up long plywood tables along both sides of the driveway. They put what Tracy called the money changer's table in the garage with a kerosene heater nearby. Frank propped a large plywood sign next to the garage.

FIREWOOD FOR SALE
PICKUP TRUCK LOAD
YOU HAUL - $40
WE HAUL - $50

Chip, who had researched how to have a successful yard sale, made a sign of his own that he fastened to the back door, over the objections of his mother and sister. The sign read:

NO PUBLIC RESTROOM

"That is so cruel," Tracy said. The sign was their only point of disagreement.

The family unity in this endeavor was pleasing to Bev and encouraging to Frank. He had been especially touched to see the treasures his children had decided to sell. Tracy was selling all of her dolls, including her Snow White Madame Alexander doll. Chip had decided to part with his entire

baseball card collection, including his prized rookie cards. Bev was willing to sell her $33^{1/3}$ rpm record albums, among them Elvis and The Beatles. The family was surprised to see Frank offering most of his fishing gear, including his antique lures, vintage rods and reels, and his johnboat. They were all in this together. Everyone was sacrificing.

Even before they had arranged everything on the makeshift tables, long before the designated time to begin, a white panel truck pulled up in front of the house. A tall man and a short woman, both smoking cigarettes, paced the driveway.

Chip said to them, "We begin at 7:30."

"How much for your baseball cards, buddy?"

Chip had divided the cards into stacks of one hundred, being sure to separate all of the more valuable cards. Those he would sell individually.

"The prices are marked on them," Chip said, "but the sale doesn't begin until 7:30."

"I'll give you twenty-five dollars for your rookie cards," the tall man said, flipping his cigarette butt on the lawn and shoving twenty-five dollars toward Chip.

"No, thanks," said Chip. "They're worth more than that."

"Thirty dollars," said the man, adding a five-dollar bill to his fist.

Frank watched his business major son deal with this predawn persistent jockey lot pro. Chip did not give in. Meanwhile Tracy was talking to the woman.

"I need to use your restroom," the woman said, blowing cigarette smoke in Tracy's face. Tracy pointed to the sign her previously cruel, now brilliant, brother had made.

"How much for your dolls, Honey? I want to give them to my granddaughters for Christmas."

"The prices are marked on each one," said Tracy.

"I'll give you ten dollars for the bunch."

"The Barbie dolls that I played with are five dollars each. Those are the little ones. The larger doll is a Madame Alexander collector doll, my Snow White Wedding Doll. She is priced at seventy-five dollars."

The man offered Chip one hundred dollars for all of his baseball cards. Chip turned him down. The man lit another cigarette and approached Frank. "I'll give you five hundred dollars for everything. I'll load it up, and haul it off. You'll have five hundred dollars, and you can go back inside, get warm, drink coffee, and watch football games."

This guy is running Ralph a close second in the Grinch contest, thought Frank.

"Come back at four o'clock this afternoon," said Frank. "Maybe we can do business then."

"I've made my last offer," said the man.

"Good," said Frank. "Glad that's behind us."

"You're as stubborn as your kids," snarled the man.

"Yeah, I got it from them. They got it from their mother."

The smoking, fuming pair got into the panel truck and drove away.

Bev called from the kitchen, "Hot oatmeal, come and get it."

The family ate a quick breakfast, keeping an eye trained on the driveway. Chip finished first. He grabbed his coat, hat, and gloves and darted out the door. No sooner had he gotten outside than he stuck his head back inside, "Hey, Dad, take a look at this!"

Frank went to the door and into the garage. Ralph was putting a sign in the green grass in his lawn. It read:

YARD SALE
TODAY

Frank walked next door. "Ralph, are you having a yard sale today?"

"Yes, I decided 'If you can't beat 'em, join 'em.' Besides, you've done so much advertising, I thought I'd take advantage of the crowd."

Ralph walked to his garage door and raised it to reveal rented tables and clothes racks full of items for sale. There were no price tags, only one large poster:

EVERYTHING FOR SALE
ONLY $1

"You don't object to a little friendly competition, do you, Frank?"

"Not at all, Ralph, not at all."

By 7 a.m. the Jenkins' yard was filled with yard sale devotees. The cul-de-sac was crowded with cars, trucks, and minivans all morning. People bundled against the cold combed the tables along the driveway, made their selections, and struck deals with Chip and Tracy, who seemed to have a delightful time talking and bargaining. Bev collected the money, carefully recording each item sold, the price asked, and the selling price. Frank noticed that customers who left his house wandered next door to look through Ralph's garage. Few made purchases because Ralph was nowhere to be seen. Ralph was sitting in a chair inside the back door, ready to receive money as selections were made. Whenever a request to use the restroom was made at the Jenkins' home, the family members sent them next door to Ralph.

By lunchtime the sun was peeking from behind the clouds. The ranks of the crowd had thinned considerably. Ralph ventured from his inside perch. "What's going on over here? I haven't sold much at all. You must be giving away diuretics like M & M candy. I have never seen so many people who needed to use the bathroom. Sue has already scrubbed it four times. She says I need to start charging for the facility privilege. Not only that, from now on, I'll have to clean it myself."

"It's all part of customer service, Ralph," explained Frank.

Ralph's face became serious. "I have a proposition for you. Let's consolidate. Let me bring all my stuff over here, and you sell it on consignment."

"I don't know, Ralph. Let me consult my business manager and my partners."

The family agreed. Chip set the terms. "We'll sell your things for a fifty percent consignment fee. Anything that doesn't sell, we return to you or dispose of with our unwanted items."

"That's a deal," said Ralph. "I don't ever want to see the stuff again. Just put the tables and clothes racks back in the garage and close the door. All of Sue's family is coming, and I'll be away most of the afternoon running errands for her."

Frank, Chip, and Tracy moved the tables and clothes racks from Ralph's garage to their brown lawn. When the move was finished, Chip said to Frank, "Dad, Ralph has a couple of business suits and at least one blazer for sale that will fit me. If I get the internship at the bank, I'm going to need some clothes."

Tracy added, "I've seen some women's clothes that will fit me and some that will probably fit Mom. Some of them still have the tags on them."

Frank told his children, "Take what you can use. Put fifty cents an item in Ralph's moneybox. That's fifty percent of one dollar." Then he thought to himself, *Some people have more money than sense.*

After lunch the sun was bright, and business picked up again. Bev continued to keep account of everything.

About two o'clock Frank had the most interesting visitor of the day. He was a distinguished gentleman with gray hair. Frank particularly noticed the tweed jacket and bow tie he was wearing. The man searched the tables and bought a number of nice items at the prices marked; no quibbling, no bargaining. He put his purchases in his car and returned to speak with Frank.

"My name is Jack Woodruff," the man said, introducing himself.

"Frank Jenkins. Welcome to our yard sale."

"May I sit down?" asked Jack Woodruff.

"Please do," said Frank as he offered his own chair and found another for himself at the back of the garage.

For the next forty-five minutes the two men talked. Frank rarely talked with anyone for more than a few brief exchanges, but something about this Mr. Woodruff invited him to open his heart. Mr. Woodruff was a graduate of Georgia Tech but not a member of the famous Woodruff family from Atlanta. He was interested in why Frank and his family were having a yard sale. He listened carefully to Frank's story about the plant closing and his struggle with unemployment. He also learned of the family's sacrifices and the story behind the firewood business.

Near the end of their conversation, Mr. Woodruff identified himself as Sue's father, Ralph's father-in-law. He acknowledged his disappointment that they were selling some of the gifts he and his wife had given Sue's family just last Christmas. He had recognized some of the consignment items; several, he thought, had never even been used. He also confessed that because Sue was their only child, in his attempt to be a good provider, he and his wife had spoiled her.

In a rare unguarded moment Frank said, "Being a good provider is important to me, too. This has been a hard year for me."

"You know, Frank, your children are going to be stronger, better people because they have been through this hardship with you and Bev. You have taught them more in the last year than they could ever learn in college." He concluded the conversation, "You are a dad to be admired. They have a fine heritage."

"It's not me," he said. "They have a very fine mother."

"You and your wife make a good team."

The two men exchanged a handshake and good-byes.

At the end of the day, the entire Jenkins family agreed that the yard sale had been a success. Bev quickly estimated that the family had sold more than seven hundred dollars' worth of their junk and their treasures. Tracy had sold all of her dolls. Bev had sold all of her records, her favorites, to just one buyer, probably a collector, she thought. Chip had sold some of his better baseball cards early in the day. The bulk of the common cards went late in the day to a teenager who bought all that were left for seventy-five dollars. His prized Barry Bonds rookie card, autographed, not by Barry Bonds but by Chip, sold for sixty dollars.

"Did the person know that you had written your name on the back of the card?" Frank asked.

"Yes, I told him I had signed it when I first got it so if I ever lost it, it could be returned."

"And he paid you sixty dollars for just one baseball card?" Tracy asked in disbelief.

"Yep!" answered Chip. "Exactly what I asked for it. Sixty bucks."

Tracy quipped, making reference to the recent baseball scandal, "He must have been on steroids, too."

"Well," said Frank, "I got rid of most of my old fishing stuff, too. Thank you all for helping. We had a pretty good day."

After supper Bev announced the final tally. With sales of $737.28, minus Ralph's commission of $43, the Big Christmas Yard Sale brought in $694.28. The December mortgage payment was due three days after Christmas. He still needed to sell three more loads of firewood just to make the payment. In order to buy groceries or to give a few Christmas presents to his family, he would need to sell even more.

On the Sunday morning before Christmas, the Jenkins family went to church together. The choir was presenting their annual Christmas Cantata. Frank and Bev preferred sitting near the back of the sanctuary. Chip wore one of the blazers he had purchased for fifty cents from Ralph.

Tracy wore a new blouse from the yard sale. Frank was thankful for his family. Bev was just glad they could all be together.

At the time for the offering, Frank looked uneasy. Bev calmly patted his hand. When the offering plate came down their row, it was already full. As it passed, Bev slipped an envelope from her purse into Frank's hand. He glanced at it before placing it face down in the plate. Bev had written a check for seventy dollars, just a little more than one tenth, a tithe, of the yard sale receipts. Chip and Tracy looked on in disbelief. Frank had mixed feelings. On the one hand, he was proud of his wife, and he admired her faith. On the other hand, putting seventy dollars in an already full offering plate was difficult for him to understand. He would have to sell two more loads of firewood.

Frank reached in his jacket pocket and extracted a dirty, crumpled index card. He reread the words written by his wife weeks before. "My God will supply all of your needs …." He really wanted to believe it, but Frank's doubts were stronger than his faith.

When the church service was over, the Jenkins family walked out the side door of the Sanctuary. Before they reached the parking lot, two church members asked if Frank could deliver a load of firewood before Christmas. Frank promised both deliveries on Tuesday. The tithe from the yard sale had been covered by two loads of firewood before he had even left church. Still, he was three loads short of making the mortgage payment. To do anything else for his family for Christmas, even just to buy groceries, he would have to sell several more loads.

He wanted to have the faith that Bev seemed to have, but the plain truth was, Frank was worried. Never in his life had he felt so unsure of his ability to provide for his family. He was tired, so tired, but all he knew to do was to think harder, to work harder, and, oh yeah, to pray harder. The trouble was that whenever he tried to beseech the Almighty, he fell asleep. It happened again Sunday night. Frank tried to pray and fell sound asleep. Maybe God was answering his prayer by giving him what he needed most, some peaceful rest.

Monday morning dawned cold and rainy. Frank awoke with a pounding headache. He had planned to spend all day in the woods on a farm in the northern end of the county where he had permission to cut a few trees for firewood. He and Chip could cut and split enough firewood to meet the demand through the holidays if they worked together until dark. As bad as he felt, Frank knew he had no choice but to work in the rain. He made a pot of coffee, woke Chip, took four aspirin, hitched the rebuilt log splitter to the rusty Chevy pickup truck, and drove to the farm with Chip.

Father and son worked all day long. Frank stayed at the farm cutting and splitting hardwood, mostly oak and sweet gum. Chip drove load after load of firewood back to their home. Tracy, who could not drive a politically incorrect straight shift but wanted to learn, helped unload and stack the wood.

By the end of the day, Frank was coughing, sneezing, and running a fever. It was long after dark when the family sat down to a supper of cornbread and chicken soup. One look at Frank, and Bev knew he had the flu. Nothing could be done except to endure the days of chills and fever until he recuperated. Frank was an impatient patient.

On Tuesday Chip and Tracy delivered the two loads of promised firewood to church members. Frank felt like he was dying.

By Wednesday the weather had turned a little warmer, and Frank had no more orders for firewood. Frank wished he could die.

By Thursday Frank was more worried than sick. He still needed to sell three more loads of firewood, just to make the house payment. Bev was out of school for the holidays. Frank was restless, claiming, "I just had a little bit of flu."

Bev quipped, "Having a little bit of flu is like being a little bit pregnant. You either have flu or you don't."

"I just had flu-like symptoms. I'm better now."

Frank was perhaps better physically, but mentally he was a wreck. His mind was churning. He had to find a way to put together the rest of the money for the house payment. He started rehearsing a speech for his friend Ed Moss at the bank, explaining why his payment was late. Then Frank came to an awful realization. Once the December payment was made, there would be a January payment, then a February payment, and March, and April... Frank's flu-like symptoms became symptoms of depression and anxiety. He would just have to hope and pray that Ed Moss would understand. *Hope and pray; what a novel idea*, he thought. He stretched out on his bed for a quiet moment to pray; and, just like clockwork, he fell asleep.

After an hour or so, Bev came into the room carrying a tray. "How about some hot coffee and two more Tylenol?"

Frank did not answer. He just bolted upright, embarrassed that he had fallen asleep. He hadn't done any work since Monday. He didn't deserve the kind treatment he received from his wife. As he took the two pills and sipped his coffee, he noticed two notes on the tray. On an index card written in indelible ink was the same verse he had carried in his pocket since before Thanksgiving, "My God will supply all your needs." The card was sealed in plastic.

Bev explained, "After I got you tucked in on Monday night, I washed the wet clothes you had worn in the woods all day. When I took your jeans jacket out of the washing machine, I found the shredded note I wrote you before Thanksgiving. I decided if you were going to carry that verse around in your pocket, I'd just make you a new card. I laminated it at school. Maybe it will last a little longer this time."

On the tray was another card, "You had a phone call," Bev said. Frank looked at the note. *Call Jack Woodruff at 727-9185*. "Who is Jack Woodruff?" Bev asked.

"He's Ralph's father-in-law, the man wearing the bow tie at the yard sale. I wonder what he wants?" Frank finished his coffee before returning the phone call. The conversation was a brief, courteous exchange and straight to the point.

"Dad, what did bow tie man want?" Tracy asked later.

"He wants a load of firewood first thing tomorrow morning."

"On Christmas Eve? Did you tell him you had the flu? Can't he wait until next week?" Bev questioned.

"I need to take it to him, Bev."

"Dad, I'll take it for you," added Chip.

"No, Mr. Woodruff wants it delivered to his lake house. It's a long drive. I need to take it to him."

"At least Chip and I can load the truck for you tonight," insisted Tracy. "We'll just see how you feel in the morning."

✳ ✳ ✳

Early Christmas Eve morning, Frank left his home before daylight. He drove his Chevy truck out to the interstate and headed for the mountains. Frank always enjoyed the scenery in this part of the country. The Blue Ridge Mountains are beautiful in every season of the year. The Appalachians dusted with snow are striking. Frank enjoyed getting away by himself. This trip gave him an opportunity to think without going to sleep.

At the exit that led to Jack Woodruff's lake house, Frank stopped at a country grocery store. The small building had wooden rocking chairs on the front porch. A wood-burning stove heated the interior. Frank paid for ten dollars' worth of gasoline, a little less than five gallons. It would be enough to bring the fuel gauge in the truck almost back to half full, enough gasoline to get back home. As he pumped the fuel, he thought about how people complained about paying more than two dollars a gallon for gasoline, yet milk cost more than three dollars a gallon. For that matter, Coca-Cola was nearly four dollars a gallon and bottled water ... the pump stopped at ten dollars.

The road to the Woodruffs' lake house was winding and narrow, lined with rhododendron and mountain laurel. The drive would be spectacular in May.

When he arrived at the house, Frank was surprised. The Woodruff vacation home was a simple A-frame, neat, well kept, and not at all pretentious. The house was anchored on the side of a mountain, overlooking a clear blue lake. The aroma of a wood fire burning in the fireplace mingled with the crisp mountain air. Smoke was rising and drifting from the tall rock chimney at one end of the A-frame. Frank was surprised to see an ample supply of firewood stacked between two poplar trees.

Mr. Woodruff appeared on the porch, wearing the same tweed jacket he wore to the yard sale. He had on a blue shirt, khaki pants, and, of course, a bow tie.

"Hello, Frank," he called from the porch. "Just stack the wood there with the rest. Knock on the door when you're through, and we'll settle up."

Frank stacked the firewood, knowing all the while that Jack Woodruff did not need anymore. There was plenty to be had much closer to this house. Still, he had agreed to pay fifty dollars for the truckload plus mileage. The Chevy's odometer indicated that Frank had driven eighty nine miles one way to get to this place. That was nearly two hundred miles round-trip. Why, he wondered, would this fellow pay him to drive all that way on Christmas Eve for firewood the man didn't even need?

Frank placed the last log on the stack of wood, walked up on the porch, and knocked on the door. The man in the bow tie invited him in and pointed to a ladder-back rocking chair by the huge stone fireplace. Mrs. Woodruff entered the large room with the vaulted ceiling, offering coffee to the two men. Both accepted. As the hostess disappeared into the kitchen, Mr. Woodruff handed Frank an envelope. "Here is one hundred fifty dollars," he said. "Fifty dollars for the firewood. One hundred dollars for the trip. I calculated two hundred miles at fifty cents a mile. That's more than the IRS allows, but it's Christmas Eve."

"Thank you," said Frank, tucking the envelope into his jeans jacket pocket.

Mrs. Woodruff served the coffee in Christmas mugs. "I heard about your yard sale," she smiled. "Jack said it was a family enterprise. You must be very proud of your children."

"Chip and Tracy have a very good mother," Frank said.

The prim lady with white hair responded, "I wish we had done a better job with our Sue. We were so hurt that she and Ralph sold some of the Christmas presents we gave them last year."

Jack Woodruff interrupted, "Frank, don't sell yourself short. Your children have a very good father, too. You know, being an able provider means more than just providing money. There is nothing more important than a solid role model. You and Bev have handled this year of adversity very well."

It was an awkward moment. Frank didn't know what to say. Maybe he had told Jack Woodruff too much about himself.

"Thank you for delivering the firewood, especially on Christmas Eve. Could you make one more delivery for me? My wife and I have a gift for each member of your family. Would you be so kind as to deliver them?"

"Thank you," said Frank. "Of course I will."

Mrs. Woodruff presented to Frank four beautifully wrapped gifts. Frank again expressed his gratitude and said his good-byes. He placed the gifts in the passenger seat of the pickup and drove the winding road from the lake house back to the interstate.

He stopped again at the same country grocery store. This time he filled up the truck with gasoline, added a quart of oil to the engine, and paid with cash from the envelope. A young man with three young children huddled around him waited to buy a gallon of milk and a loaf of bread. A wheel of cheddar cheese was in a case on the counter.

"How much for that cheese?" the young father asked.

"Gim'me fifteen bucks and you can have the milk, cheese, and bread," the man behind the counter said.

"Can't do it," said the younger man. "I got to have gas, too."

With an uncharacteristic impulse, Frank put a twenty-dollar bill on the counter. "I've got kids at home, too," he said. "I'll cover the cheese, milk, and bread, and five dollars' worth of gas."

"Thank you, sir," the young father said. "I lost my job, and we're having a hard time."

"Believe me, I understand," replied Frank as he turned to walk out the door.

As he drove away, his fingers again found the laminated card from Bev in the jacket pocket. This time he didn't even remove the card from his pocket. He knew what it said.

On his way home, Frank made a difficult decision. He still needed one hundred sixty dollars to make the mortgage payment by next Wednesday. He had not quite that amount in the envelope from Jack Woodruff. There was nothing special for Christmas dinner except bologna, round ham, as Chip called it. He had no presents for Bev and his children except for the ones in the truck, though he had thought of something he might do. Frank decided to save the one hundred dollars for the house payment and splurge on his family with the rest. He would buy a few things for their Christmas stockings and cook a special Christmas breakfast. He would just hope and pray Ed Moss at the bank would understand. There were those novel ideas again—hope and pray.

When Frank arrived at 525 Camelot Court late Christmas Eve afternoon, Chip, Tracy, and Bev had just finished decorating a beautiful Fraser fir Christmas tree. Frank was surprised. The family had agreed that they could not afford a Christmas tree this year. Before he could say anything, Chip explained. "Don't worry, Dad, the tree didn't cost anything. I found out that if you wait long enough, you can have as many Christmas trees as you want for free."

Frank placed the four wrapped gifts beneath the tree. "Frank, what have you done?" Bev asked.

"Don't worry, Bev, they didn't cost a thing. I'll explain tomorrow."

"You've had two phone calls, two of Joe Monroe's neighbors. They each want a load of firewood the day after Christmas."

Frank hugged his wife. "That will be enough to at least make the December payment."

"And we'll worry about January when January comes," said Bev. "For now, let's just celebrate Christmas with our family."

✳   ✳   ✳

On Christmas Day, Frank prepared breakfast for his family: scrambled eggs, bacon, grits with butter, toast and jelly, milk, orange juice, and coffee. When the family had gathered around the table, Frank explained that Christmas dinner this year was Christmas breakfast. Their next meal would be Chip's famous round ham, the house special. That suited everyone just fine.

Following the meal, Frank announced, "Santa came last night."

In the living room the Jenkins family found Christmas stockings under the fragrant Fraser fir. Actually, they were mismatched boot socks from Frank's bottom drawer. Each of the three stockings had an apple, an orange, two Bob's Peppermint canes, and some individually wrapped candies. Chip and Tracy each received a package of Oreo cookies. Bev's stocking had a big Hershey Special Dark Chocolate candy bar perched in the top. Bev hugged her husband and said, "Frank, it's Christmas."

Later that morning they sat together around the coffee table where the manger scene was displayed. Bev read the Christmas story from Luke's gospel. As Frank heard the familiar words, his attention was fixed on the tiny figure of Joseph. *Talk about a lousy provider*, he thought. *Joseph couldn't even provide a decent place for his wife to have a baby. And what in the name of heaven did they eat? I guess the poor carpenter did the best he could. I guess it was enough.*

Following a prayer said by Bev, the Jenkins family opened gifts. Frank and Bev were surprised when Chip and Tracy excitedly presented them with large wrapped boxes.

"You have to open them at the same time," said Tracy.

Beverly could hardly believe her eyes. Her children gave her a gorgeous full-length red wool coat. It fit perfectly. Frank was equally astonished with his gift, a nice gray wool overcoat.

"But how?" Bev started to ask.

"Remember that rack of clothes we sold for Ralph the Grinch?" explained Chip. "These coats came off of the rack!"

Tracy announced, "Mom and Dad, you are the proud owners of yard sale outerwear!"

Bev, still wearing the red coat, gave her gifts. The children tore into theirs immediately. Frank hesitated, but Bev insisted he open his gift at the same time. Each one received a handmade cross-stitched bookmark. The wording on each was the same. "My God will supply all your needs." Frank put his arm around Bev, giving her a hug.

Frank handed each of his family members an envelope. Before they could open them, he warned, "There's no money. Just love."

Enclosed in each envelope was a handwritten gift certificate. For Chip, a two-day trout fishing and camping trip at their favorite state park. For Tracy, driving lessons in the Chevy pickup until she learned to drive a straight shift. For Bev, a date night at home once a week with homemade popcorn.

Four more gifts were left under the tree, but before anyone could open them, the doorbell rang. Tracy answered the door, only to find their next-door neighbors, Ralph and Sue. They handed Tracy a paper plate covered in aluminum foil.

"This is leftover ham. We bought two Heavenly Hams by mistake, and don't need these leftovers. Can you use this extra ham?"

Chip stepped forward, "Yes, thank you. We will enjoy it. We were actually thinking of having ham for Christmas dinner." He took the ham to the kitchen, while Bev, still wearing her new red coat, thanked her neighbors.

Sue commented, "What a lovely coat! You look like Mrs. Claus. I got one for Christmas last year almost like yours, a smaller size, of course."

"Of course," replied Bev.

Ralph, fidgeting, revealed the reason for this visit and the gift of leftover ham. "Frank, we're having guests for dinner tonight. Would you mind parking your truck in the back yard out of sight?"

"I'll be glad to, Ralph, anytime."

The Jenkins family returned to their Christmas tree and the four remaining presents. Frank recounted the details of his visit to the Woodruffs' lake home the day before, concluding his story, "Mr. Woodruff did not ask me to go all that way just to deliver firewood. They had plenty of firewood and could have more right from their own property. I believe the mission the Woodruffs had in mind was that I bring these gifts to you."

Tracy opened her gift first. The sight of the Madame Alexander Snow White Wedding Doll brought tears to her eyes. "It's my favorite doll!" she exclaimed. "Look! You can still see the place in the back where I cut her hair when I was a little girl. When bow tie man bought it from me at the yard sale, I told him it was my favorite."

Beverly was next to open her gift, two old record albums "I Wanna Hold your Hand," by the Beatles, and "Love Me Tender," by Elvis. Each album had Bev's initials on the back. "How did he know?"

"I told him, Mom," said Tracy. "I told him they were yours when I sold them to him at the yard sale."

"Wait a minute!" shouted Chip, tearing into his gift. "Yes! My autographed 1987 Fleer Barry Bonds rookie card! Autographed by yours truly. The guy in the bow tie paid me sixty bucks for the card and then gave it back to me?"

"He really must be on steroids," quipped Tracy.

All eyes turned toward Frank. "Open it, Dad," demanded Tracy.

"I bet it is one of your old fishing lures," guessed Chip.

"I don't think so," said Frank. "Those were long gone by the time Mr. Woodruff got to the yard sale."

Frank opened his gift. It was not a fishing lure. It was not anything purchased at the yard sale. It was an appointment book for the new year and a letter. After Frank read the letter silently, he was stunned and fighting to hold back his tears. Bev took the letter from her husband and read it aloud.

December 25th

Dear Frank,

I was very glad to meet you at the yard sale one week ago today. I was quite impressed with your fine family.

I am the president and owner of Southeastern Employment Agency. You will see from my card that we specialize in placing middle and upper-level management personnel. We have many clients who, like you, have lost jobs in textiles. I wish I had a job as a plant manager to offer you. I do not. I do, however, have something I would like for you to consider. I am close to retirement. I have been seeking someone to manage my business for me. My hope was to find a person who had the right management experience and good people skills to do the job. You not only have those abilities, but you have also endured and survived almost a year of unemployment. You might be just the person I am seeking.

The first appointment on your new calendar is a job interview on December 27 at 9 a.m. Please bring a resume with you. Enclosed you will find my card in case you need to get in touch with me.

My wife joins me in wishing you and your family a Merry Christmas.

Warmest regards,
Jack Woodruff

Bev returned the letter to Frank.

"That's great, Dad!" exclaimed Chip.

"Hooray for bow tie man!" shouted Tracy.

With tears in his eyes, Frank put the cross-stitched bookmark from his wife and the letter from Jack Woodruff in his appointment book. Bev wiped his tears, gave him a hug, and said, "Frank, it's Christmas."

she painted forty thumbs on forty gloves,
one for each year the children of Israel
spent wandering in the wilderness.

The Silver Bell

Ginger Lewis sat by her mother's bed in the skilled care unit of the Cypress Point Nursing Home. Trudy Livingston's blood pressure had been slowly dropping since midnight. Her breathing was shallow and slow. Ginger held her mother's wrinkled hand and waited as she had since the nurse called her at 2 a.m.

Twice within the last week Ginger had kept this watch, and both times her mother had rallied. Six days ago, the geriatric physician had told Ginger that her mother only had a few hours to live. Ginger waited through the night until her mother's vital signs improved. Then, two days ago, the nurse had called her at 6 a.m. She went immediately to Cypress Point and again waited at her mother's bedside. Outside her mother's room that afternoon, she spoke on the cell phone to her friend Joyce. In an unguarded moment she uttered something she had thought many times but never before said, "I wish mother could just die."

"How can you say that about your own mother?" Joyce asked.

Ginger had no response.

Joyce pontificated, "We must pray that God's will be done."

Ginger was silent for a moment and then said, "I'm tired. We'll talk later."

Now, napping in a chair, Ginger waited again at her mother's side. After a while, a nurse came in to check Trudy's vital signs. Interrupting Ginger's fretful sleep, the nurse whispered, "I don't think it will be much longer." Ginger closed her weary eyes, still holding her mother's limp hand. Later, Ginger awakened with a sigh, Trudy's breathing stopped, and the long earthly journey of Trudy Livingston ended peacefully.

* * *

"Precious in the sight of the Lord is the death of his saints," intoned the priest, reading from Psalm 116. Ginger listened to the scripture and thought, *If death can ever be called precious, it was my mother's death.* The funeral service for Trudy Livingston followed closely the traditional liturgy prescribed by The Book of Common Prayer. Trudy was a longtime member of St. Jude's Episcopal Church, and Ginger knew that this was just the kind of service her mother would have wanted.

Ginger and Ted Lewis rode with their sons Matt and Mark to the cemetery in the family car provided by the funeral home. Ginger had invited Myrtle, Trudy's sister, to accompany them, but her elderly aunt declined without explanation. That bothered Ginger. She wondered if her aunt was upset with her, but at this point, she simply did not have the energy to pursue it.

The black Cadillac limousine parked near the grave where Trudy's frail body was to be interred. It was next to the plot where Ginger's father had been laid to rest thirty-eight years before. Ginger had visited here several times each year, every year, with her mother: Easter, Father's Day, Memorial Day, Veteran's Day, and Christmas. On those occasions Ginger paid attention to the expression on her mother's face. Today, she felt others looking at the expression on her face. She thought she should be grieving for her mother, but she was not. Instead, she felt that her mother's death was blessed relief, both for Trudy and also for Ginger.

The warm May breeze carried the scent of freshly mown grass and made the afternoon heat more bearable. The service at the cemetery was brief and to the point, interrupted only once by a tiger swallowtail butterfly flitting around the spray of spring flowers on Trudy's polished oak coffin. After a brief pause to admire the winged visitor, the priest concluded the Order for Burial. Taking a handful of the sandy black soil, so typical of the midlands of South Carolina, and sprinkling it on the casket, he recited the words, "Ashes to ashes, dust to dust."

Ginger and Ted had worked for three days packing up Trudy's earthly belongings. They had been trying to sell the home since Trudy's death in early May. A young couple had bought the home on a loan from the Veterans Administration. They expected to take occupancy the first weekend in October, so it was time to clear everything out. The furniture had been easy to dispose of because Trudy had a house full of desirable antiques. Ginger wedged as many of her mother's things into her own home as she could. A few pieces went to Trudy's sister, Myrtle. Ginger donated clothing and household items to the Salvation Army.

The difficulty was that Trudy had saved everything: mayonnaise jars, in case the boys wanted to catch lightning bugs; old toothbrushes, in case something needed scrubbing; paper grocery bags, in case a parcel had to be wrapped in brown paper for mailing. The grandsons were now college students and were far more interested in pursuing girls than fireflies. Everything needed scrubbing, but the house was long past the cleaning power of a used toothbrush. And there were stacks of brown paper bags, enough to wrap everything in the house. Ginger had, in fact, used many of them to wrap her mother's fine china which she would add to the collection in the dining room of her own home.

Ted and the boys had been a big help. But there are some things that only a daughter can do when making decisions about her mother's treasures. The entire process had been a revelation.

She learned things about her deceased mother she had never before known. She found old letters, love letters exchanged between her mom and her dad during their courtship and their all too brief marriage. She found pictures, many of people and places she recognized, and some she did not.

Ginger regretted that she had not spent more time with her mother asking questions before Trudy lost her memory. While she was sorting through desk drawers, early in her mother's dementia, Ginger found a picture of a handsome young man, shirt sleeves rolled up, launching a rowboat into a lake. When she showed the picture to her mother, she asked, "Mother, who is this good-looking man with the boat?"

Trudy gazed blankly at the picture and said, "Child, I don't remember." Then after a reflective pause she added, "There were many boys and many boats."

Her mother's failing memory had become a problem long before Ginger realized it. As she was cleaning out the freezer, she found twelve opened but only partially used cartons of chocolate almond ice cream. She knew that her mother had loved chocolate as much as Ginger did, but her mother was also frugal. The only explanation that Ginger could think of was that every time her mother went to the store, she bought another carton, failing to remember that she already had plenty in her freezer. If Trudy had still had her wits about her, she would have joked about all of the ice cream. "Twelve cartons, one for each of the apostles."

Ginger came to grips with her mother's illness when, late one night, Trudy called her from a phone at the police station in Sumter. Her mother had been to a supper at St. Jude's and had lost her way driving home. The church was only two miles from her home, but Trudy had gone the wrong way, and she just kept on driving, more than fifty miles out of the way. When Ginger and Ted arrived, they found Trudy, confused and crying, sitting with a police officer who was very relieved to see them.

The decision to take Trudy's car away from her created a major crisis. Ted suggested that they ask her physician, Dr. Suggs, to tell her that she could not drive anymore. The doctor agreed, but he wanted Ginger to be present. Ginger took her mother to the doctor's office for a regular visit, and after a routine check-up, Dr. Suggs explained to Trudy that she could no longer drive: "Your short-term memory is not reliable. If you stop at an intersection and you look to the left and see a car coming, by the time you've looked to the right, you are likely to forget that there is a car coming from your left."

The explanation infuriated Trudy, and she threw a royal fit. "You cannot tell me what I can and can't do!" she shouted.

"Mother! Dr. Suggs is trying to help you," said Ginger.

"He is not. He's being mean to me."

"Please don't talk like that," said Ginger, who rarely said anything that created conflict.

"You just shut up, young lady. I'm the adult here!" she screamed at Ginger. Ginger had never before seen that kind of outburst from her normally reserved mother.

Later, when Ginger took her car keys, Trudy uttered a stream of profanity. Before that, Ginger had never heard even one curse word coming from the lips of the dear little church lady who was her mom. Ginger was so astounded and so hurt, she did not say anything. Trudy ended her tirade, saying to her forty-three-year-old daughter, "I ought to wash your mouth out with soap for talking to me like that."

That night, Ginger was terribly upset as she told Ted about the visit with Dr. Suggs. "I have never seen my mother act that way. She was like a stranger." Ginger cried.

"Honey, your mother has lived a secret life that we knew nothing about until today."

"What are you talking about? What secret life?"

"Judging from her language, she spent some time as a sailor."

Ginger laughed even as she cried.

Dr. Suggs was hesitant to give the diagnosis Alzheimer's disease. "That's something we cannot be sure of until an autopsy following death, but your mother has all of the symptoms." The official diagnosis was dementia. Whatever the name, Ginger knew her mother had an ugly, mean disease, and it continued to grow worse over the next four years.

Those years had been extremely difficult for Ginger. As an only child, she had complete responsibility for her mother's care. The decision to move Trudy from her home of fifty-six years into an assisted living facility was heartrending. They had tried keeping Ginger's mother in their own home, but Trudy was unable to be content. After one of her outbursts during a pizza party that Matt and Mark were hosting in their home for high school friends, Ted and Ginger knew other arrangements would have to be made. When they moved Trudy back to her own home with around-the-clock sitters, Trudy pouted, saying they did not love her anymore.

Trudy was a fiercely independent woman, and Ginger admired that. Trudy's husband, Ginger's dad, died in a hunting accident after they had been married only seven years. Trudy had been a single parent and a single woman since Ginger was only five years old. She had to be independent, so when the decision was made to move her to the assisted living facility, her mom protested vehemently. When Ginger told her that she could no longer live alone, Ginger saw a rage in her mother more violent than when she took the car keys. Trudy, as frail as she had become, turned on Ginger, treating her as if she were an enemy, spitting and cursing and hitting. No longer was Ginger the light and joy of her mother's life. Ginger had become the adversary, and she was devastated. The woman she loved and trusted had become a total stranger.

Trudy's anger became suspicion; her suspicion became seething silence. And then Trudy faded into that state that gives Alzheimer's the awful name, the living death. Her body was still alive, but her mind was gone. Ginger watched her once happy, strong mentor become little more than a shell of her former self.

After eleven months at Cypress Pointe, Trudy suffered a stroke. Trudy was paralyzed on her right side and could not speak or swallow. Finally, she slipped into a coma and died ten days later of renal failure. Ginger's Aunt Myrtle, though she was quiet, seemed to blame Ginger for putting Trudy at Cypress Pointe and somehow causing her stroke.

Ginger returned from her painful memories to the task of clearing out her mother's house. She had saved one box to sort through last, a box of her mother's personal items. In it she found a velvet bag in which she expected to find her mother's gold charm bracelet, but the bag was empty. In the bottom of the box, she discovered a Cool Whip container overflowing with a snarled assortment of jewelry. There were strands of cheap costume jewelry, beads, bracelets, and dime-store earrings, the kind her mother wore when she was, in her words, "feeling sassy."

But scrambled among all of the cheap stuff, there was a diamond pendant that Ginger had given her mother for Christmas. As Ginger carefully extracted the diamond necklace from the knotted mess, she also found in the middle of the tangle the gold charm bracelet she was seeking.

There were seven fine gold charms attached to the bracelet; "Seven is the perfect number," she could hear her mother say. Trudy had taken an interest in the numerology of the Bible and often inserted references to numbers from Scripture into her conversations. It was an annoying habit that Ginger had acquired from mimicking her mother.

Ginger noticed that besides the seven gold charms there was one silver bell. *Why would mother have a silver bell on a gold charm bracelet?* It was a question that begged for an answer, and Ginger could think of no one left who would know. She tucked the gold bracelet with the silver bell into the soft velvet bag where it belonged and tightened the drawstring. She placed it neatly into the jewelry box with the diamond pendant and crammed the cheap stuff back into the Cool Whip container. The jewelry box itself was a treasure, handmade by Ginger's grandfather for his older daughter as a wedding gift. Carefully crafted from cherry wood, fitted with tiny brass hinges and a brass hasp, the box was a keepsake. The lid of the jewelry box was inlaid with the wood of holly and walnut, light and dark. Her mother's initials were clear: GML for Gertrude Moore Livingston. Ginger ran her finger over the initials, admiring the box for only a moment, wrapped it in one of the numerous brown grocery bags, and placed it in the top of the United Van Lines box. She wiped the perspiration, the result of the warm September evening, from her brow, sealed the last box with packing tape, and wrote across the top with a black magic marker,

MOTHER'S PERSONAL THINGS.

A voice from another room called out, "Hey, Mom, have you got one of Grandma's mayonnaise jars? We want to catch lightning bugs one more time."

"Take ten mayonnaise jars," Ginger responded, "one for each plague on Egypt."

* * *

The next three months were a time of transition for Ginger. Because she had been the primary caregiver for her mother, she now had more time alone at home. There were no more trips to the nursing home, no more difficult doctor visits, and no more anxiety about medications. Matt and Mark were away at Furman University, and Ted was as busy as ever with his work as an engineer. Integrating her mother's furniture into her home took some doing. Finally she decided that she had to sell a few antiques and did so through one of Ted's business acquaintances who also ran a monthly auction.

The more difficult transition was the emotional adjustment. She still had not really grieved for her mother. Trudy's death had been such a relief that for several weeks, Ginger avoided talking about her mother's death for fear that she would be misunderstood. Though her tears flowed easily before Trudy's death, after her mother died, Ginger became zombie-like and unable to cry. Should she feel sad, as others seemed to think? Or was it okay to feel glad, which seemed unacceptable and certainly unspeakable, especially around people like Joyce? Ginger was in a double bind, and she slipped into a depression.

As the weeks became months, her despair deepened. She slept too late, struggling to get out of bed, she stayed up too late watching TV, and she ate too much chocolate almond ice cream. As a result, she had gained five pounds and become a David Letterman fan, staying up almost every night until the Top Ten List was given.

When Ted was out of town on business, Ginger's days and nights ran together. At one point she spent four days in her pajamas, rarely getting out of bed. When Ginger allowed herself to think about her mother's death, she felt guilty because she could not feel sad that her mother was gone, and she felt mad, believing that others would disapprove of her sense of relief. Trudy's death was a blessing for Trudy, but for Ginger, her mother's death had become the source of deep inner conflict. She was at war with herself, and there was no victory and no peace in sight.

"Maybe you're angry," Ted said the Sunday after Thanksgiving.

"Angry about what? Angry at you for bringing it up?"

"I don't know, just think about it."

Ginger did think about it, and she *was* angry. She was angry that her mother's mind had departed long before she died. As the disease progressed, when Ginger looked into Trudy's vacant eyes, her mother was absent. Her mother had always been her best friend. They had gone through so many things together: proms, graduation, the wedding, and the births of Matt and Mark. Trudy was so vibrant, full of life and energy, until the illness invaded her mind like an alien monster from a science fiction movie.

"You haven't been yourself since your mother died," Ted commented.

"My mom died a long time before her funeral," said Ginger abruptly.

"Maybe you need to talk to somebody, you know, a professional."

But talking to somebody was not Ginger's natural inclination. She usually kept things to herself, unspoken.

As Christmas approached, Ginger was still mad, sad, and worried. The associate pastor at St. Jude's, an older woman, was offering an Advent Bible study on the life of Mary, the mother of Jesus. Ginger had been attending each week hoping to find something that would help, but she found little consolation. The study was more academic than devotional. Still, one line from the Gospel of St. Luke had lodged in Ginger's mind. "And Mary kept all of these things and pondered them in her heart." She certainly understood the concept of a pondering heart; it was the constant activity of her heart and mind. Whatever the name—introspection, soul-searching, meditation, reflection, or pondering—Ginger was preoccupied with a tumble of thoughts much of the time.

Among the things going through her mind were two in particular. Ginger had done extensive reading on Alzheimer's disease. Though she opted not to have an autopsy performed on Trudy, she was sure that her mother was a victim of the disease. She also knew that there is a strong genetic link in Alzheimer's. In fact, Trudy had often spoken of the aging problems of her own grandmother, referring to them the old-fashioned way as hardening of the arteries. Ginger was afraid that she might have the dreaded disease and thereby put the same burden on her children that she had experienced as Trudy's primary caregiver. She could not imagine Matt and Mark, as much as they loved her, expending the time and the energy required to care for an Alzheimer's patient. She certainly did not want them to go through the agony. She would just rather die before she lost her mind.

The other thing that often occupied Ginger's thoughts was related, not to her mother's illness, but to Trudy's death. Ginger realized that with Trudy's death, she and Ted were now the first generation in her family. Ted's parents were both deceased, so it was as if they had moved to the front line. They were the only thing separating Matt and Mark from death. In the normal course of events, Ginger and Ted would be the next to die. For most of her life, Ginger's mother had been her strength, a wall defending her against the onslaught of death. Now, Ginger was the wall.

Ginger fumbled for her keys that always seemed to make their way to the very bottom of her oversized purse. Her fingers were numb from the cold December wind. Balancing herself on the top step, her arms loaded with groceries, she found the key. Inside, the warmth of the kitchen gave her a moment of comfort as she looked for a place to put her burden down. The weight of the groceries now shifted to the kitchen counter, bringing relief to her aching joints. She draped her coat and scarf over a kitchen chair and kicked off her shoes. Her toes wriggled with gratitude.

As she put the perishable groceries in the refrigerator, the chocolate almond ice cream in the freezer, and folded the brown paper bags for safekeeping, Ginger glanced at the sink filled with dirty dishes. She checked the crock-pot where chili was simmering for the evening meal. She grabbed the half-full mug of coffee left over from breakfast and put it in the microwave oven, setting the timer. As she waited for the coffee, she filled the sink with hot, soapy water. When the microwave signaled that the coffee was hot, she dug into the last brown grocery bag for half-and-half and the new bag of Pepperidge Farm Chocolate Chip Cookies. She sat down, propping her feet up on the chair that already held her coat, with her back to the soaking dishes. Having lightened her coffee with cream, she placed two cookies on a fancy Christmas napkin. Two was the right number, one for the Old Testament, and one for the New Testament. Besides, one serving, according to the labeling on the side of the package, was two cookies. How could you ever expect to keep track of fat grams and calories if you deviated from the correct serving size? This was her time to relax. Christmas was only a week away. She had taken only a few sips of coffee and eaten just one cookie when the telephone rang.

Joyce wanted to go over some last minute details for the Christmas drop-in for the Green Thumb Garden Club. Joyce hosted the drop-in every year and was careful never to have it too early. It had to be the week before Christmas in order for Joyce to have all of her decorating completed. Then there was the food preparation. She always had enough food for fifty, even though there were only fifteen women in the garden club. In another unguarded moment Ginger had made a silly mistake. "Is there anything I can do to help?" she had asked Joyce. Ginger knew it was the wrong question even as the words came out of her mouth. Joyce said that everything was under control except for one little detail. The party favors were not ready.

Ginger offered to take care of the favors. She should have realized that the favors would have to be done Joyce's way or no way at all. Joyce was the master of overcontrol, especially for the Christmas drop-in for the Green Thumb Garden Club. For her, it was the social event of the season, and it had to be done right, meaning *her* way.

Joyce had decided that the party favors this year would be a pair of garden gloves for each member of the garden club. But, as if she had received a vision from Martha Stewart herself, Joyce wanted the thumb on each glove to be painted green. Ginger had spent the last week painting green thumbs on twenty pairs of OshKosh B'Gosh gloves. The five extra pairs were for unexpected guests. First, she did one pair just to be sure she understood Joyce's plan. Of course the shade of green was wrong.

"Not Hunter Green," Joyce protested. "Meadow Green, that bright green that is so trendy this year."

Ginger had searched the supplies of acrylic paints at the local craft store for Meadow Green. She found Palm Green, Turtle Green, Money Green, and Green with Envy. With chagrin, she remembered the words of Kermit the Frog, "It's not easy being green." She finally settled on St. Patrick Green. She stuffed tissue paper into each glove thumb. Then, she put brown paper bags on the kitchen table. She covered the bags with a layer of waxed paper before painting forty thumbs on forty gloves, one for each year the children of Israel spent wandering in the wilderness.

Now Joyce was calling, the day before the drop-in, to ask one more favor. She just didn't have time to fix a platter of fresh vegetables with her special Benedictine Dip.

"You know, I always like to have a vegetable platter because at least two of the girls in the club are vegetarians. Could you please fix the vegetables? I'll be glad to give you the recipe for the Benedictine Dip. I'll send it to you by e-mail right now."

Of course, Ginger agreed without a word of complaint. As she hung up the phone, she realized that even though she had just come in from the grocery store, she would have to go back, buy the vegetables, and make the dip. In a moment of revelation, she asked herself, *Why am I trying so hard to get Joyce's approval?*

Of course, she would never get it, because with Joyce, enough was never enough. Alone in the safety of her home, Ginger erupted like a seething volcano, profanity spewing like magma from deep inside. She uttered many of the same words she had heard from her demented mother when the car keys were taken from her. With gritted teeth and clinched fist, she screamed and then screamed again. When the explosion was over, Ginger thought, *I wish I had said that to Joyce, and I wish my mother had heard it!* And then, on second thought, she was glad she had been alone.

Ginger shoved her coffee cup back in the microwave and punched the timer. She looked at the one cookie on the Christmas napkin and took two more from the bag to put beside it. Okay, three cookies, one for each member of the trinity. Or if you count the one she had already eaten, four cookies, one for each Gospel. If Joyce didn't leave her alone, she might just go for Ten Commandments. She sat down with her feet up, with the hot coffee and cookies, to try to make sense out of the nonsense of her life.

✳   ✳   ✳

It had been more than seven months since her mother's death, but the pain Ginger felt in cold December was more intense than the pain she felt on that warm day in May when her mother was buried. Ginger wanted to weep, and for a few minutes, she thought she might. But no tears came. Christmas was only a week away, but for Ginger it might just as well be a year away.

The lingering fatigue of being the primary caregiver for her mother had merged with the exhaustion of strange, tearless grief. It was important to her to be strong and positive for her family. It wasn't so much a matter of keeping up appearances as it was fulfilling her typical role of being the calm, steady person when the foundations were shaken. But she knew that if she could cry, she would feel better. She tried to make herself cry in the shower after Ted had gone to work, but to no avail. Now, the boys were home from Furman for the holidays, she had bought all of the groceries she needed, and she had done all of the decorating she intended to do. If she could just get beyond Joyce's drop-in, then maybe she could look forward to Christmas.

Ginger checked her e-mail. Sure enough, there was the recipe for Benedictine Dip from Joyce. After reading through it, Ginger hit the delete button. *This is much too involved*, she thought. *I'll just chop up a cucumber in some ranch dressing. No one will know the difference.* Angrily, she wrote down a short grocery list on a note pad, put on her shoes, donned her coat and scarf, and grabbed her purse for a return trip to the store. The afternoon sky was gray and overcast. It fit her mood exactly.

 At the grocery store, the vegetables Ginger needed for the vegetable platter were picked over. The cauliflower was mushy; the broccoli heads were splotched with brown; the yellow squash and the zucchini were small and pitted with scars. There were none of the peeled baby carrots, so she selected a bunch of carrots that she would have to peel and slice herself, a task she hated. Then she thought about it and slammed the carrots down on top of the display of celery. *There won't be any carrots on the veggie platter for Joyce.*

 If only Joyce had told me about this earlier, she thought. *All the veggies looked so much better when I was here earlier in the day.* And then, she thought, *it serves Joyce right! I'll fix a cruddy veggie platter.* She was glad she didn't need bananas. They were all very, very ripe or very, very green. Her personal theory was that there are only about fifteen minutes in the life of a banana when it is fit to eat. She thought about all of the green thumbs she had painted on the garden gloves. Acrylic paint should be available in Banana Green, Zucchini Green, Broccoli Green, and Fried Green Tomato. Why in the name of heaven should there be acrylic paint named for a saint, Saint Patrick Green? Why, for that matter, should a vegetable dip be named for Saint Benedict? Why, in the name of all things holy, should trivial things be connected to holy people? And then, out of nowhere, popped another question, a question dormant in her mind for nearly four months. *Why did my fashion-conscious mother have a silver bell on a gold charm bracelet?*

Ginger wheeled by the salad aisle and picked up a large bottle of ranch dressing and pushed her cart to the express line. The weather forecast now included a chance of frozen precipitation. Threatening winter weather always made the grocery store lines grow longer. As she waited in line, Ginger glanced at the tabloids. GRANDMOTHER RETURNS FROM TRIP ABOARD UFO YOUNGER THAN HER GRANDCHILDREN. Ginger could see it now. Interviews with Regis Philbin and Oprah Winfrey. Thousands of women lining up to be the next UFO passenger. 450 POUND WOMAN DIES AFTER ONE TOO MANY CHOCOLATE CHIP COOKIES. Perish the thought. The man in line ahead of her placed three gallons of milk and three loaves of bread on the checkout counter.

"Milk and bread, milk and bread. Every time it snows, hundreds of people sit at home eating milk and bread," the checkout lady chattered. "Why milk and bread?"

"I really don't know," answered the man. "I just get what my wife tells me to get." The man paid for his milk and bread. Ginger put her groceries on the counter.

"Paper or plastic?" the clerk asked.

"Paper," said Ginger.

"No milk and bread for you?"

"Not this time," said Ginger. "I got my milk and bread earlier today."

"Why?" asked the clerk.

Ginger explained, "If the power goes out, my family can eat cold cereal with milk and peanut butter sandwiches with the bread. When the forecast is for winter weather, I buy milk and bread, cereal and peanut butter."

"Express Line Only. Ten items or less," the sign above her read.

She had exactly ten items. *One for each beatitude*, she thought. She knew that Matthew only listed nine but Luke recorded her personal favorite, "Blessed are you who weep now, for then you shall laugh."

As she headed to her car, Ginger passed the Salvation Army volunteer. She put her change into the kettle, and the ringing of the bell made her think again of the silver bell on her mother's bracelet.

As she drove home, she listened to a cassette tape of Christmas music Ted had given to her. "Maybe this will help get you in the Christmas spirit," he had said. The music was beautiful. The choir sang "O, Holy Night."

Ginger hummed along until one line caught her attention. "The weary world rejoices."

How can that be? How can anyone or any world rejoice if they were as weary as Ginger felt? The cassette choir sang, "I Heard the Bells on Christmas Day." Ginger could not get that silly silver bell out of her mind. Then it occurred to her that there was one person who might know why her mother would put a silver bell on a gold charm bracelet, Trudy's only sister, Ginger's Aunt Myrtle.

As she came through the back door with her second load of groceries for the day, Ginger kicked off her shoes. She was surprised to see that someone had washed and put away all of the dishes. The sink was almost clear except for two bowls and two glasses. There was a note on the kitchen counter. "Mom, we've been invited to a progressive dinner with the college group from church. We'll be home about 10:00. We got started with a bowl of your chili and a glass of milk. You're the best, Mom. Love, M&M."

Ginger was disappointed the boys would not be at home for supper but not at all surprised. They were constantly on the go and always needed refueling. In fact, Ted would sometimes say that Ginger functioned as an air traffic controller, monitoring takeoffs and landings, preventing collisions, and resupplying her family. As she waited for Ted to come home, Ginger started preparing the vegetable platter for Joyce's drop-in.

She thought about how her own mother had managed their home when Ginger was growing up.

Trudy rarely got upset; she was the calm when anyone else was the storm. After Ginger's dad died, Trudy had worked as a secretary in the local school system. Though they had never been wealthy, her mother had been a good provider. Trudy was a strong, resolute woman with a simple, yet deep faith. One of Ginger's pleasant memories was that, as a child, whenever she was hurt or afraid, she would run to Trudy and put her head in her mother's lap. Her mother would gently stroke her hair to comfort her. As silly as it seemed, that was something Ginger missed.

It was from her mother that Ginger had learned so much about the Bible. It was at her mother's knee that she had learned to pray. Since Trudy's death, Ginger had found it difficult to pray. She felt that her words never got beyond the ceiling. But as difficult as praying had been, crying had been impossible.

When Ted came home, Ginger was nearly finished preparing the crummy veggie platter. The hard part was done. She could easily finish after supper. Ted gave her a kiss and washed his hands at the kitchen sink, ignoring the two chili bowls and the two milk glasses. Ginger asked him to fill the sink with hot soapy water, which he did. She asked him to get four pieces of Tupperware, with tops, out of the cabinet. Ted was an engineer, but he claimed to be Tupperware challenged. He seemed completely unable to puzzle through the task of matching Tupperware lids with Tupperware containers. What's more, he had to think twice to remember which cabinet the Tupperware lived in. He thought it moved around in the middle of the night to deliberately confound him. He thought the same about coat hangers. Ted imagined they moved around in the closet at night, intentionally entangling themselves. Perhaps it was some sort of mating ritual to make little coat hangers. Ginger excused Ted from the kitchen and got the Tupperware herself.

Ted and Ginger lit candles and enjoyed their chili supper together. Near the end of the meal, Ginger asked, "Do you remember the box of mother's things marked PERSONAL? Do you think you could find it?"

"I know right where it is," Ted said. "What do you need?"

"There is a jewelry box with her initials on it. I would like to have it." After supper Ginger cleared the table, loaded the dishwasher, and returned to the preparation of the veggies for the garden club drop-in. Ted found the jewelry box and put it on the table. The more Ginger thought about it, the more she knew she needed to talk to Aunt Myrtle. She should visit her before Christmas anyway. When the second-rate vegetable platter was prepared, Ginger covered it in plastic wrap and made a sign in bold letters, DO NOT EAT. The boys thought anything in the refrigerator was fair game unless otherwise marked. Then, Ginger realized that she had forgotten to buy the cucumber to make the Benedictine Dip. There was no way she was going back to the grocery store. The plain ranch dressing would have to do.

With the vegetable platter safely stowed in the refrigerator, Ginger sat down with the cherrywood box. She opened the velvet bag and took out the charm bracelet. She looked at each of the seven gold charms—a terrier dog, a mailbox, a fish, a birdhouse, a Valentine heart, a church, and a train. She was sure there was a story behind each one. She looked carefully at the silver bell. It was a little larger than the gold charms and quite tarnished. Ginger polished the bell and noticed for the first time that it would actually ring. The tone was a small but clear sound. Ginger tried on the bracelet, shaking it on her wrist. She decided to wear it. The coming-out party for her mother's gold charm bracelet with the silver bell would be the Green Thumb Garden Club Drop-in at Joyce's house.

Only nine of the members of the garden club showed up. The others, including both vegetarians, were unable to come. They thought that the OshKosh B'Gosh garden gloves with the green thumbs were "just darling."

They all agreed that Joyce's home was "just lovely."

The consensus of opinion was that the dip was "just the best ever." Joyce offered to share her recipe with any who wanted it.

Ginger thought, *I'm just going to throw up!* But she said nothing about the dip or the gloves. When the drop-in was over, Joyce gave her five extra pairs of the green-thumbed garden gloves. Several members asked about Ginger's new charm bracelet. She gave no explanation other than to say, "It was my mother's."

"Oh, part of your inheritance," said an older woman.

"You know, gold charm bracelets are very much in style," said a younger woman.

A woman, now sporting a pair of the garden gloves added, "After my mother died, my husband gave me diamond earrings to help me stop crying. I called it the ministry of jewelry."

As Ginger left with an almost untouched platter of second-rate veggies, she was intrigued by the concept of a ministry of jewelry and wondered if her mother's bracelet could become that for her.

*   *   *

The next four days were easier, but still the Christmas spirit escaped Ginger. If anything, she felt more morose because, in the season to be jolly, she just couldn't find any joy. With an attitude of resignation, she decided that this year Christmas would just simply have to be endured. The weary world may rejoice in Christmas carols, but it was not part of Ginger's Christmas. The entire season was like the Green Thumb Garden Club Christmas Drop-in. Ginger would be grateful when it was all over.

On Christmas Eve Ginger went to see Aunt Myrtle. She paid her a surprise visit early in the afternoon. She took a Christmas gift with her, and she wore the charm bracelet. Giving Aunt Myrtle a gift was not just an obligation, though that was part of it. Aunt Myrtle was now her closest relative apart from Ted and her two sons. Ginger also wanted her mother's sister to tell her all she knew about the bracelet. Ginger rang the doorbell and waited. Surely Aunt Myrtle was at home. Where on earth could she be? She rang the doorbell a second time. Still no answer. Ted had cautioned her, "Remember your aunt is so deaf she can't hear it thunder without her hearing aids." Finally, Ginger opened the storm door and knocked loudly. Her persistence paid off.

When Aunt Myrtle answered, she was putting in the second hearing aid. Her response to the sight of her niece was immediate. "Oh, my child," she said as she embraced Ginger. "I am so glad to see you."

Ginger was taken aback by Aunt Myrtle's sudden warmth. She had believed that for the last eleven months her aunt had blamed her for her mother's stroke and eventual death. That did not seem to be the case at all. Myrtle fixed each of them a cup of hot tea with lemon. They sat together in her small cozy parlor. Ginger took off her shoes, and the two women talked together for more than an hour. As they remembered Trudy—sister to one, mother to the other—they shared stories together. Myrtle did much of the talking, which was fine with Ginger.

"Gertrude and I were more than sisters; we were best friends. We were together all of the time. Our friends called us Mert and Gert or sometimes, Myrtle and Girdle. After your father died we were closer than ever."

"I'm sure mother's death has been difficult for you."

Though cataracts dimmed her eyes, Myrtle noticed the gold charm bracelet. "I see you have Trudy's charm bracelet."

"Yes," Ginger said, shaking her wrist. She moved from her chair and sat on the oriental carpet at Myrtle's feet. "Tell me about the bracelet." Ginger held it close so Myrtle could see it better.

Myrtle fingered the charms as she explained. "Your father gave Trudy the bracelet the Christmas they were engaged to be married. Each Christmas he gave her a charm as a way of remembering something special that had happened to them. The little dog was for the year they got MacTavish, a Scottish terrier. The birdhouse was the year they were expecting you. I don't remember what they all mean but there should be seven of them for the seven years they were married."

"You know, seven is the perfect number," Ginger said.

Myrtle paused and said, "I owe you an apology."

"For what?" asked Ginger.

"You remember you invited me to ride in the family car at Trudy's funeral?"

"Yes, but you need not apologize."

"At least let me explain. I didn't want to ride in the family car because I didn't think I could be appropriately mournful. I was so relieved when Trudy died that I was almost giddy."

Ginger felt tears welling up in her eyes. "You felt that way?"

"Yes, I had often thought what a blessing it would be for you and for your mother if she could die before she lost her faculties. Then after she had the stroke, I was ready for her to go to heaven."

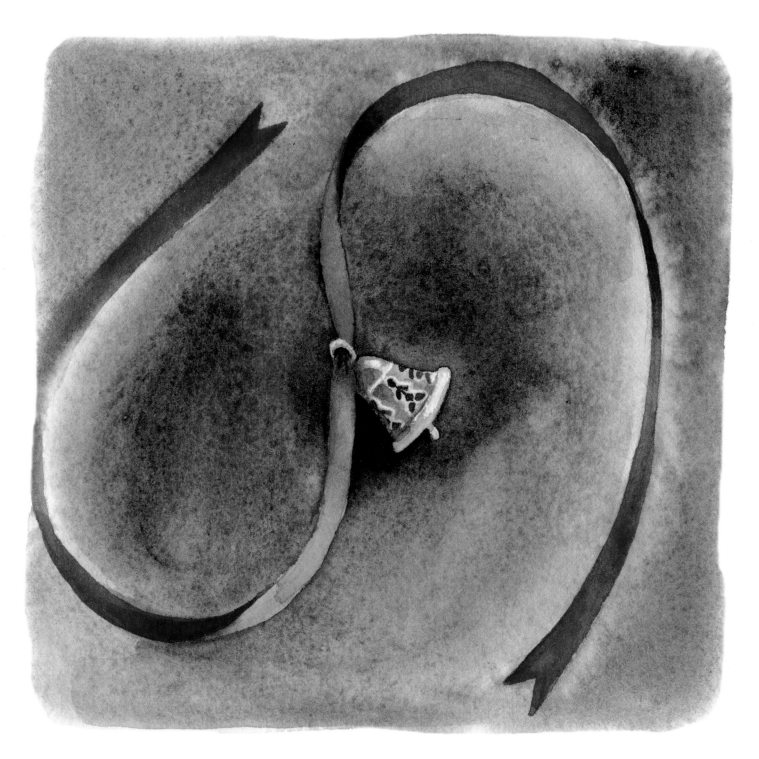

"Aunt Myrtle, I thought you were upset with me because I put mother in a nursing home."

"Mercy, no! I was proud of you. There was no way you could take care of her in your home."

Tears trickled down Ginger's cheeks. "Thank you for understanding."

"I have often thought about how fortunate your mother was to have a daughter like you. You cared for her so lovingly, even after she became so difficult."

Those words of affirmation absolved the guilt Ginger had felt for almost a year. Like an artesian well when it is first tapped, her tears gushed from deep within. Then, like a child seeking comfort, she leaned toward her aunt, putting her head into Myrtle's lap. It was just what Ginger had done as a little girl when she needed reassurance from her mother. Myrtle stroked the graying hair of her niece, as Ginger wept. The grief became contagious and Myrtle's tears mingled with Ginger's.

After several tissues and some time, the women gathered themselves.

They sat together in silence for a few minutes looking at the charm bracelet. Ginger said, "Aunt Myrtle, tell me about the silver bell." She held the bracelet closer so Myrtle could see.

Aunt Myrtle touched the bell, breathed deeply, and continued. "Your father was killed in a hunting accident in late October. You were only five years old at the time. I was not married, so your mother and I had a lot of time together. There were many people in our church that were kind and helpful to your mother, but she was inconsolable. Your mother was a private person and kept her feelings to herself. In her bereavement, she said very little to anyone about her loss.

"But there was a sister, a nun, from Saint Francis Catholic Church down the street from St. Jude's who was especially kind. She was an older woman who, years before she became a nun, had been engaged to be married. The love of her life died before their wedding. She was heartbroken and eventually entered a convent with the Sisters of Clare. She believed that God had called her to minister to grieving women. Right before Christmas she came to visit your home. She told Trudy that every time a child of God dies, the bells of heaven ring. She told the Christmas story the way you've always heard it, but she added one thing. Legend has it that when the shepherds visited the Holy Family in the stable in Bethlehem, they gave the Christ child a little lamb. But they gave to Mary a small silver bell, a bell worn by newborn lambs.

"The nun gave your mother a silver bell for Christmas. She called it Mary's bell. She said any woman who had the heart of Mary could wear the silver bell. Though Mary was afraid when the angel Gabriel visited her, she submitted to the Lord as His handmaiden. She had a servant's heart. When Mary went to visit her cousin, she was called blessed by Elizabeth. After Jesus was born, Simeon told Mary that her heart would be pierced by sorrow as if by a sword. A woman who has the heart of Mary has a heart filled with blessing and a heart filled with sorrow, the heart of a servant. The nun who told the story showed us the tiny bell she wore around her own neck, and said that it reminded her of the scripture, 'Mary kept all these things and pondered them in her heart.'

"That's interesting. That's a verse I recently read at an Advent Bible study at St. Jude's."

"Your mother put the bell given to her on the charm bracelet because it reminded her of the most important thing that happened in her life that year, your father's death. But every year at Christmas for the next several years, she would take the bell off the charm bracelet and wear it on a red ribbon next to her heart."

"I didn't realize it was the same one on the charm bracelet," said Ginger.

"Trudy said the silver bell put her in the Christmas spirit," said Myrtle. "It was a reminder that Christmas is always a mixture of joy and sorrow."

Ginger blotted her eyes as she heard the story. "Now I remember," she said. "I remember that she wore the bell every Christmas when I was little. She called it her Christmas jewelry. I always thought my father had given it to her."

Myrtle and Ginger spent nearly two hours together on Christmas Eve, laughing and crying with each other. It was a time of healing for both of them.

Ginger gave Myrtle the gift that she had brought, a piece of her mom's cut glass. But the gifts Aunt Myrtle had given her were priceless, the gift of tears and the story of the silver bell. The two women embraced, "I hope you have a Merry Christmas, Aunt Myrtle."

"And I hope you will have a blessed Christmas," replied Myrtle.

✳   ✳   ✳

Back at home, Ginger found a pair of needle-nose pliers and carefully removed the silver bell from the charm bracelet. She threaded the silver bell on a narrow piece of red satin ribbon and wore it next to her heart. Ginger spent some time by herself wrapping gifts for her family. When all the gifts were wrapped, she added three more. Into three gift bags, one each for Ted and the boys, she placed a pair of OshKosh B'Gosh garden gloves with Saint Patrick Green thumbs. Christmas would come after all. A weary world, a weary Ginger, really could rejoice.

Ginger invited Ted and the boys to go with her to the Christmas Eve service at St. Jude's. The family had never gone to a Christmas Eve service before, and the guys did not understand, but they went along anyway. As they sat together in church and heard the scripture lessons and the Christmas carols, Ginger felt at peace for the first time in a long time. She touched the tiny bell over her heart. Through the silver bell, she was somehow connected to Mary, to a nun she had never met, and to her mother. She felt a bond with all women who had the heart of Mary, who knew the strange mixture of the joy of blessing mingled with the sorrow of grief. And Ginger kept all these things and pondered them in her heart.

The Return of Alan Shepherd

Christmas Eve was cold and damp. A light mist had been falling since early morning, and the temperature hovered just above freezing. Now the mist had turned to light rain. Alan Shepherd adjusted the windshield wipers of his Helms rollback wrecker to compensate for the increased precipitation.

He had made service calls all day—four fender benders, three dead batteries, two flat tires, and a kitten in a Bradford pear tree. It might just as well have been a partridge. By the time Alan got to Widow Oakley's house, the feline, as usual, had managed to get out of the tree on its own. Mrs. Oakley was one of his dad's old girlfriends. She had always called Alan's dad to fix her problems, not only car trouble, but also any kind of home emergency. Now she called Alan. The kitty call was the third from Alma Oakley in December. Each time, little Muffin, the kitten, had made her escape from the same pear tree before Alan arrived.

On the radio Barbara Mandrell sang "Christmas at Our House." Alan didn't want to hear Christmas music, especially not a song about a cozy family Christmas by a woman named Barbara. He had two stations programmed on the wrecker radio that played what he liked, all country music all the time. Of course, both stations would spin an occasional Christmas song, but it was easy enough to change to the other station. The deejay on WSSL 100 was making stupid Christmas jokes.

"Did you hear about the dyslexic angel? Spent all Christmas night singing about a guy named Leon to the tune of 'The First Noel.' You know, 'Leon, Leon, Leon, Leon'...." With a quick push of a button, Alan changed the radio back to WESC 92.5, the other country station.

The weather lady on television had warned that there was a slight chance the rain might turn to freezing precipitation before ending Christmas night. No white Christmas but a very wet, maybe even icy, Christmas was ahead. The rain and the cold had kept Alan busy, just the way he wanted to be at Christmas. Some days his AAA Motor Club connection could be annoying, but today it was good for business and good for him. He wanted no free time to think, no time to reflect. He had dreaded Christmas coming, and he was glad to see Christmas Eve fading into night. There was nothing for him to celebrate and no one he cared to celebrate with. In one more day, Christmas would be over for another year, and Alan was glad.

The wrecker, with Shepherd's Towing and Auto Repair painted on both cab doors, pulled into the parking lot of the Waffle House. Alan pulled up the hood of his bright yellow rain slicker as he slammed the wrecker door. There were only a few customers on Christmas Eve. Most people, Alan thought, must be at home with their families. He peeled off the wet slicker as he walked in, tossing it dripping into an empty booth in the smoking section, and went to the men's room to wash the day's accumulation of grease and grime from his chapped, cracked hands. When he returned to the booth, Julie, the waitress, had already poured a mug of steaming hot coffee for him.

"What'll it be for Christmas Eve?" Julie asked.

"I'll have the high cholesterol special," said Alan, shaking two packs of sugar into his mug.

"One double cheeseburger, add bacon, with French fries and onion rings coming up," Julie shouted.

Alan sat down to wait for his evening meal, picked up a copy of the morning paper left by a previous customer, and lit up a Marlboro. The sports page was missing, so he read only the headlines and the captions under the pictures. His cigarette smoke filled the smoking section of the restaurant.

Julie brought the food piled high on the plate. Refilling his coffee, she asked, "What's Santa Claus gonna bring you?"

"I don't know. Maybe some Christmas lites."

"Christmas lites?"

"Yep, I've got a couple of six-packs in my refrigerator."

"That's it? That's your Christmas?"

"I'd be glad to have a pair of well-filled stockings if you want to help me with the Christmas lites."

"No way, big guy! I'm playing Santa Claus for my kids. I don't like stockings anyway. They don't wear well with jeans."

"Okay, then," said Alan, "I'll have Christmas lites alone."

"What you need is a pair of work gloves. Look how chapped your hands are."

Julie turned her attention to another customer. Alan ate his cheeseburger in silence. Thanks to the cold rain and the slick roads, he had spent his day working both I-26 and I-85. He had to skip lunch, so the cheeseburger and trimmings were lunch and supper. Julie came back and put a small bottle of hand lotion on the table. "Use this," she said. "It might help some." As she refilled his coffee mug, she added, "I hope this weather doesn't turn bad. I'm supposed to drive to Columbia to be with my sister for Christmas Day. Driving a carload of kids on a busy highway in bad weather is not my idea of fun."

"I'll be working all day. If you need me, call me, and I'll come get you," he said, rubbing the lotion into his hands.

Julie became serious. "You know you're killing yourself, Alan. The cigarettes, the beer, the cholesterol, not to mention your killer work hours."

"We all have to die sometime from something."

"But you could put it off for awhile."

"Maybe so," he said, standing up and putting his slicker on. "But there's really no reason to. Life is just one wreck after another, and the last one takes you out." He paid his bill and gave Julie a ten-dollar tip. "It's Christmas. Do a little something extra for your kids."

"Keep the lotion," she said. "Merry Christmas."

"Thanks," Alan said as he put the lotion in his pocket.

Back in the truck, Alan lit a cigarette and headed down Highway 29 toward home. The rain was steady; the air had turned colder. A call from the AAA dispatcher came over his cell phone. A late model BMW had hydroplaned into a ditch up on Highway 11 near Gowansville. Alan stoically accepted the interruption and made a detour on his way home, taking I-26 west toward Campobello. He turned up the volume on WESC. George Strait wailed his hit song, "All My Exes Live in Texas." Alan changed to WSSL. Both of his ex-wives lived in Texas.

The first marriage, a mistake from the beginning, had not even lasted a year. He met Susie at a Houston bar. Her long red hair, big green eyes, and tight blue jeans caught his eye, and she caught Alan. They had a torrid romance that became a quick marriage when Susie took an in-home pregnancy test. After a honeymoon in Cancun, they returned to Houston to begin married life. Susie had a miscarriage a few days later and promptly went back to the bar scene. It was as if they had never even been married. Alan tried to have the marriage annulled, but Texas law required a divorce. He had to pay a large chunk of change to a lawyer and also to Susie.

His second marriage had been more promising. He really did love Barbara, but after nine years and no children, she decided she just didn't love him anymore. Barbara, a physical therapist, had left between Thanksgiving and Christmas four years ago with a doctor she met at the hospital Christmas party. After that, Christmas just wasn't the same. Nothing was the same. He hated to admit it, but he still loved her even though she had married the doctor and already had a baby.

Somewhere beyond Inman, Alan passed a nativity scene on a frontage road paralleling the interstate. The life-sized, two-dimensional figures had apparently been cut from plywood and recently painted. The scene was illuminated with floodlights. All the figures but one were huddled together under a crude shed made from rough slats. The lone shepherd was standing outside in the elements. Mary, Joseph, and the wise men were gathered around the manger under the shelter out of the rain. The cold rain caused the paint to run on the figure of the poor shepherd.

The wrecker took the Highway 11 exit and traveled through Campobello toward Gowansville. Beyond a sawmill and lumberyard, Alan passed a peach orchard on the left side of the road. The BMW was right where the dispatcher said it would be. Alan turned on his red flashing emergency

lights as a well-dressed, distinguished-looking man with a large Augusta National golf umbrella got out of the car. He felt the need to give Alan all of the details. He and his wife had been to a Christmas party at the Cliffs of Glassy, a gated community on top of Glassy Mountain. On the way home his wife was fussing at him for drinking too much. He became angry, stomped on the accelerator, and the car skidded on the wet pavement into the ditch. Friends had stopped and offered to take his wife home. She gladly accepted. He had stayed with the car as the AAA dispatcher had said he must.

After the rambling soliloquy, he snapped as if Alan were an underling, "What took you so long?"

As he examined the car, Alan explained, "I was outside of Duncan when I got the call. I came as fast as I could."

"Just get it out of the ditch and I'll drive it home," said the impatient man.

"I'm not sure you can drive it at all," Alan said. "The undercarriage is low on this car and this is a steep ditch. You may have quite a bit of damage under there."

"Just get it out and let me try to drive it."

Alan slogged into the ditch filled with rainwater, hitched a cable to the tow point, and eased the car out of the ditch as carefully as he could. Once the BMW was back on the pavement, the man was ready to go. Alan asked for the man's AAA card to fill out the necessary paperwork. "My wife has the card," the exasperated man said. "Just let me pay you."

"Are you sure you don't want me to take you and your car to your home? You can get your card from your wife, and I can do the paperwork there."

The man reluctantly agreed. Alan pulled the BMW up on the rollback, secured it in place, and invited the man to get into the cab. The two men rode together back to I-26, past the manger scene with the shepherd standing in the rain, down to the Highway 29 exit, and on to another gated community between Spartanburg and Lyman. Lulled by the rhythm of the windshield wipers, his head thrown back on the headrest, the distinguished-looking man slept and snored as if he were a Skid Row drunk. Alan smoked and listened to country music as he drove.

When the man and his BMW were safely at home and all of the paperwork was completed, Alan headed to his own home. It would be Christmas Day in a couple of hours, and Alan would be glad when it was over.

The rain fell harder now. Weather Woman might be right. Alan was almost home, back to the same house he had lived in as a kid, a place where Christmas had once been a happy time. His mom had always made Christmas cookies with those little sprinkles on top. His dad had even enjoyed putting up the Christmas tree. He backed the wrecker into the driveway and went inside the dark house. He was like Macaulay Culkin—home alone—with no wreath, no tree, no nativity scene. Christmas was still in the attic, but Christmas lites were in the fridge. Alan took a long, hot shower and put on dry clothes. He settled into the La-Z-Boy recliner that had been his dad's. He turned on the TV with the remote and opened the first of his Christmas lites. He watched the weather channel, paying special attention to the weather babe. She announced a winter storm watch. No snow was expected. Just continuing cold rain, changing to sleet and freezing rain by Christmas night. After admiring the cute meteorologist, Alan switched to a movie channel, drank all six of his Christmas lites, and slept in the recliner until early Christmas morning.

❋   ❋   ❋

When Alan woke up before daylight on Christmas Day, he could hear sleet falling against the windows of his house. The television set was still on, so he switched back to the weather channel. The temperature had dropped lower than predicted, and the winter storm watch had changed to a winter storm warning. Significant accumulations of ice were expected, especially on bridges and overpasses. He climbed out of the recliner, threw away his beer bottles, and washed his face. He made a pot of fresh coffee and toasted a Pop-Tart. The uniform of the day was long underwear, wool socks, a heavy wool shirt, jeans, and boots. After his first Marlboro and second cup of coffee, he pulled on his yellow rain slicker, locked the door, and climbed into the wrecker.

After the cab warmed up and the windshield was cleared of ice, he pulled the big truck out into the street. The radio played "Christmas in Dixie." Trees and power lines were showing accumulation, but so far, the roads were okay. Alan drove to the nearest Hardee's. He had seen a sign indicating they would be open on Christmas Day until 2 p.m. With a double order of bacon, egg, and cheese biscuits and another cup of coffee from the drive-through, he headed to his shop. After the biscuits and coffee, he smoked another cigarette.

Shepherd's Towing and Auto Repair had been in business since shortly after his dad returned from World War II. The shop only had two bays, one with a hydraulic lift. By some standards, the business was no great shakes, but it had provided well for the Shepherd family. Alan opened one bay and backed the wrecker into it before closing the door. His Christmas plans included tidying the shop. After cleaning and arranging his tools, he straightened the tires and oilcans on the back wall. He cleared the floor so he could remove as many grease and oil stains as possible. Just as he finished, the telephone rang.

"Shepherd's Towing and Auto Repair. Alan Shepherd."

"Are you working today?" the voice asked.

"All day long. What can I do for you?"

"This is the dispatcher for AAA Motor Club. We're trying to get a tow truck up to the Saluda Grade. We've got a big mess up there. There are three vehicles we're trying to move to the Tryon exit. You're going to pick up a gold Jeep Grand Cherokee with Ohio tags. The North Carolina Department of Transportation has the interstate blocked. You'll have to stop at their checkpoint."

"I'll get there as soon as I can. What are the roads like?"

"Very hazardous and getting worse. Be careful."

Alan drove to I-26 and headed for the mountains. The Saluda Grade seemed to always ice over before any other roadways. He lit another Marlboro and asked himself, *How in the world did my life come to this?*

In February three years ago, a year after Barbara left, Alan's mother had suffered a stroke. His dad begged him to move back home to Spartanburg. Alan held a good job in Houston, chief mechanic for a Ford dealership, the largest in the Southwest, but he hated Houston. It was home of both ex-wives and NASA's Johnson Space Center, a town where the name Alan Shepherd always brought a double take, if not a snide comment. Still, he put off the move back to South Carolina for another two years.

His name had always caused him grief. Though the first American astronaut spelled his name Shepard and Alan's name was spelled Shepherd, the two names sounded exactly the same. It was the way his dad had intended it to be. Alan Shepherd was born May 5, 1961, the very day Commander Shepard rode his Freedom 7 Mercury Space Capsule on a fifteen minute, 302-mile flight into history. Walter Cronkite and Alan's mother had both breathed a deep sign of relief at about the same time. Alan's dad had been more interested in the space flight than in the birth of his son. Because he and Commander Shepard had served on the same naval destroyer at the end of World War II, he had named his son—his only child—for the astronaut. It had been a problem for Alan all of his life.

Commander Shepard, Mission Commander of Apollo 14, was the fifth man to walk on the moon. The name Alan Shepard had appeared on every news broadcast for several days in early 1971. Young Alan was nine years old at the time, in the fourth grade. His friends called him "man in the moon" or "space cadet." By the time he was in junior high school, they all wanted to see him do Michael Jackson's moonwalk. Alan's biggest problem was his dad, who wanted him to get an appointment to the U.S. Naval Academy. Alan couldn't even get an appointment with his high school principal. He did make it to The Citadel, but only after being on the waiting list until after he graduated from high school. He applied to please his dad, but the Fourth Class System was just not for him. He was a knob for one semester, and then he dropped out. The next fall, he did what he really wanted to do and enrolled at Spartanburg Tech in auto mechanics. It was what he did best. Being up to his elbows in grease was his delight.

Just past Inman, Alan saw the nativity scene to the left of the interstate. The holy family and the wise men looked fine, even with icicles hanging from the shed roof. The poor shepherd who had been out in the rain on Christmas Eve was covered in ice on Christmas Day. Alan let that sink in for a few minutes. An ice-cold shepherd on Christmas? He dismissed the thought from his mind and lit another cigarette.

By the time Alan crossed the North Carolina state line, the interstate was much worse. Two cars were stranded in the median and several more on the shoulders of the highway. The rest area near Tryon was crowded as were the service stations and fast-food restaurants at the Columbus exit. The tops of the mountains were white with ice and snow. The interstate going up the Saluda Grade looked like a demolition derby track. Alan stopped at a checkpoint. He pulled up the hood of his slicker, lit a cigarette, and got out of the truck. Leaning against the truck, Alan struck up a conversation with a trooper whose hard-brim hat was trimmed with icicles.

"Cold enough for you?" asked Alan.

"Wish I was home with my wife and kids," said the trooper.

"When is your shift over?"

"Six tonight. Still got a long day."

For a few minutes neither man said anything more. Alan's cigarette smoke combined with the foggy vapor of their breath in the cold air to create a cloud. Alan looked up at the Blue Ridge Mountains. White Oak, Hogback, and Round Mountain with their frosty glaze looked like a Christmas card. He loved these mountains. Long before the interstate was built, he had spent summers at the Boy Scout camp near Saluda. The old twisted highway would be even more hazardous in weather like this.

"I remember the old Saluda Grade," said Alan, breaking the frozen silence.

"Yep. My uncle painted on the old road," said the trooper.

"Painted?"

"Yep. He was a hellfire and brimstone preacher. He painted all of those Jesus signs that are nailed to trees and posts at nearly every switchback. Some were painted right on the rocks. You know, 'Jesus Saves,' 'Jesus Died for Your Sins,' those signs."

Alan remembered the signs. "You could use one of those signs at the top of the mountain today. 'Jesus Died for You on the Saluda Grade.'"

"You got that right," said the trooper.

Finishing his smoke, Alan said, "I see the mess. I'm here to get a Jeep Cherokee."

"Good. It's about halfway up. We're just trying to get the ones stuck in the middle of the highway off to the side. We've got this stretch closed up past the Green River. North Carolina guys are working the upper end. We need you to help on this end."

"Let me see if I can get up there."

"Take your time with that rollback on this ice. Take the Jeep down to the Tryon exit. Park it on the side of the road on that wide shoulder just before Tryon. Then come back and get another one."

"Will do," said Alan. It was just what he needed, a busy, busy Christmas. He saw the gold Cherokee with Ohio tags. It was a four-wheel-drive vehicle that had skidded on the icy interstate and slammed into the center guardrail. It spun back into the middle of the highway, blocking both uphill lanes. Alan thought, *People think four-wheel-drive will exempt them from the danger of ice, and Yankee drivers are the worst.*

Even wreckers are not exempt. As Alan tried to back up to the Jeep, the tires on the truck started spinning. Alan drove down to the bottom of the grade, got up enough speed to take him above the Jeep. He pulled to the shoulder and turned around. Pumping his brake, he managed to move into position to load the Jeep. The bed of the rollback whined as it dropped to the ground, becoming a ramp. Alan took the long cables with tow hooks to the battered Jeep. Kneeling on the icy pavement, he attached the first cable to the left side of the axle.

He stretched his body under the twisted bumper to find the right side of the axle. Holding the bumper with his left hand, he reached under the Cherokee with his right hand. Just as he attached the cable, his left hand slipped across the jagged edge of the torn bumper. Alan felt a sharp pain in his left palm followed by the warm rivulet of his own blood. He struggled to his feet, his boots slipping on the now blood-splattered ice. Examining his left hand, he knew the ripped palm would require stitches. With his right hand he took a first aid kit from under the seat of the wrecker and found a roll of sterile gauze. He wrapped the entire roll around his left hand as tightly as he could, but he had no adhesive tape. Baffled only for a moment, he searched his toolbox and uncovered a roll of electrical tape. Using his right hand to wrap the black tape over the gauze on his left hand, he tore the tape with his teeth. *Yep. Julie was right*, he thought. *I do need work gloves.*

Since the Jeep was already hooked, Alan worked the mechanical winch to pull it up on the rollback. He secured the Jeep with his good hand. He found a discarded plastic bag in the truck floorboard and packed it with ice that had accumulated in the tall grass along the shoulder of the highway. He pressed the bag of ice into his throbbing left palm and slowly eased the truck, steering with one hand, down the Saluda Grade to the Tryon exit. He clumsily unloaded the Jeep. A representative from AAA said he would take care of the owner of the Jeep and the paperwork.

Though he could have gone to St. Luke's Hospital in Tryon, he didn't think about that until after he had crossed the South Carolina line. Instead, Alan made his way to the Emergency Room of Spartanburg Regional Medical Center. As he passed the roadside nativity scene, he thought again about the ice-covered shepherd.

There was no shortage of patients in the Emergency Room on Christmas afternoon. Alan judged that about a third of them had coughs, colds, and flu. He had not had a flu shot so he tried to keep his distance. There were several who had injuries that were weather related, including an elderly woman with a broken hip. She reminded Alan of his mother. When an ambulance brought in an older man with an apparent fatal heart attack, Alan stepped outside in the sleet for a cigarette.

One hour passed, then another. Alan understood why the people who wait are called patients. Finally an ER doctor examined his injured hand. A pretty blonde nurse with a sharp needle gave him a tetanus booster shot, and a young, attractive brunette surgical resident used twelve stitches to sew Alan's left palm back together. "Go home and get some rest," she ordered. "We'll give you a couple of pills for pain. Keep your hand iced and elevated as much as possible. You need to make an appointment with your surgeon day after tomorrow."

✳   ✳   ✳

It was late Christmas afternoon when Alan got home. He scrounged in his refrigerator for something to eat. The pickings were slim: a half jar of pickles, half a block of moldy cheese, peanut butter, grape jelly, and a six-pack of Christmas lites. He opted for a peanut butter and jelly sandwich for his Christmas dinner, so he made two sandwiches, using only his right hand. He would save the beer for later. He noticed that the red light on the answering machine was blinking. Alan put a pot of coffee on to brew as he listened to the message.

"Hi, Alan. This is Spencer. Please give me a call as soon you come in. It's an emergency! I'm in Hartsville. Thanks, Buddy."

Spencer didn't bother to leave a number, but Alan saw it on the caller ID Spencer, his roommate for the one semester he attended The Citadel, was nicknamed "Spencer the Jerk" by their fellow knobs. Though he was now a state representative from the Pee Dee area, as far as Alan knew, he was still a jerk. *I wonder what he wants*, Alan thought to himself. He took off his yellow rain slicker, hung it near the back door, and poured a cup of black coffee. Then he used the now empty bread bag filled with ice on his sore left hand. After he ate his sandwiches, he returned the call to Spencer.

"Merry Christmas," the voice boomed.

"Hello, Spencer, this is Alan Shepherd returning your call."

"Hey, Buddy. Long time no see. Hope you've had a good Christmas. How's Barbara?" It *had* been a long time.

"Barbara and I divorced nearly four years ago, Spencer. How's Jean?"

"She's great. We just had all three kids here for Christmas. Sorry, I didn't know about Barbara. How are your mom and dad?"

"Mom died in the spring a year ago. She had another stroke. I had only been back home three months."

"Well, at least you had a little time with her. How about your dad?"

"Dad died earlier this year of a heart attack, Spencer."

"Too bad. When I looked up the number for Shepherd's Towing and Auto Repair, I thought I would get your dad. I was surprised when I heard your voice. I guess you're running your dad's business."

"Right."

"Listen, friend, I need a favor. My daughter—her name is Lisa Daniels—and our son-in-law were visiting here for Christmas, like I said. They left Hartsville this afternoon to drive back to their home in Knoxville. We got a call from them a few minutes ago. They called on a cell phone from a parking area on I-26 just north of Cross Anchor. The phone was not working well, maybe a bad connection or a weak battery. They are driving a Ford van but are having mechanical trouble. Could you go help them out? I have an AAA Plus card."

"The weather is turning bad here, Spencer, but I'll go now. I'll get the card number later."

"Thanks, Alan. Oh, one more thing. My daughter Lisa—she's pregnant."

"What's your son-in-law's name, Spencer?"

"Don't laugh, Alan. His name is Jack, Jack Daniels. He's from Tennessee."

Alan didn't laugh, but he did consider. Being Alan Shepherd living in Houston was probably not as bad as being Jack Daniels from Tennessee. Alan could only imagine the jokes that unfortunate fellow had tolerated.

Alan slid into the wet yellow rain slicker again. He set his coffee cup in the kitchen sink and pulled the back door closed, locking it behind him. His hand was throbbing again, but he could not take one of the pain pills if he was going to drive. It would just have to hurt.

The air seemed even colder than before. Ice covered the bed of the rollback, but the cab was still warm. He drove out Highway 295, being careful of the slick road. Power company trucks were trying to restore electricity to hundreds of customers. This was much worse than Weather Woman had predicted.

The deejay on WSSL spoke up. "There's a chance of some icy weather tonight," he warned. "Be careful out there." *No one should be allowed to give a weather forecast*, Alan thought, *without first being required to look out of a window.*

"I'll have a blue Christmas without you," Elvis started singing. Alan changed back to WESC.

Last year at Christmas, he and his dad had gone to Atlanta to visit cousins. On the drive back from Atlanta, they had talked together about Christmas without Mom. In the weeks after that, he had felt closer to his dad than ever before. Then his dad had died suddenly the week before Father's Day. All through December, every time someone had asked him, "Are you ready for Christmas?" Alan had just answered, "Yep."

Alan turned the wrecker toward 221. Sleet was mixed with freezing rain now—a wintry mix, Weather Babe would call it. As he made his way south toward the interstate, he saw, in his rearview mirror sand trucks working on the bridge where 221 crosses 295. "I'll be home for Christmas," the radio chimed. He remembered his mom and Christmas. She had always fixed a big Christmas dinner with homemade pecan and apple pies. Each year, she put the nativity scene in the center of the table and read the Christmas story from the Bible: "And there were in the same country shepherds abiding in the fields."

His dad would always interrupt with the same wisecrack, "At least these Shepherds have a roof over our heads."

"We'll have snow and ..." Alan changed stations.

Another corny Christmas joke from the deejay, "If athletes have athlete's foot, what do astronauts have? Missile toe, of course, get it? Mistletoe?"

Though the ramp onto I-26 had been sanded, driving was still treacherous. The road was almost deserted as Alan drove eastbound toward Clinton. The parking area was on the opposite side of the highway just before the interstate crossed the Enoree River bridge. He probably could not cross the median there. There had been too much rain, and the ground would be too soft. He would have to drive past the parking area to turn around at the first emergency vehicle turnout. Sleet was heavier, and ice was accumulating on the interstate. Soon this stretch would be as treacherous as the Saluda Grade had been this morning.

Just as he thought about the hazards of the morning, the rollback started skidding sideways. Alan did not use the brake, but tried to steer against the skid with his one good hand. No use, the big truck did a 360, spinning a full circle in the middle of I-26.

Fortunately, there was no traffic. Alan pulled over to the shoulder and lit a Marlboro. The sand trucks would never be able to keep up with this mess. He eased the wrecker back onto the highway. Once he got the van loaded, the rollback would drive better. The extra weight would give it more traction.

As Alan passed the parking area on the opposite side of the interstate, he spotted the Ford van. It looked to be about ten years old. He had seen plenty of them before. He could tell it was a conversion van. Somebody had spent a lot of money to make it real pretty. The trouble with conversion vans was that all the converting was cosmetic. All the converting in the world didn't change a thing under the hood. Alan remembered something his dad had told him once. Conversion vans are like some converted people—all surface, no real change where it really counts—inside.

After making the flip-flop and heading back toward Spartanburg, Alan drove up the ramp into the parking area. The van was completely dark, but a young man with a frightened look on his face jumped out into the wrecker's headlight beams. He was waving frantically as Alan pulled up beside the van and lowered his window.

"Your name Daniels?"

"Yes, Jack Daniels. My wife is going to have a baby. She went into labor right after I called my father-in-law. Please help us."

Alan made only one attempt to jump-start the van. He was almost certain the timing chain was bad. A Ford van this old was bound to have major problems.

"Please, mister, hurry."

Alan backed the wrecker up to the van, lowered the ramp, and started hooking the cables and the chains. Everything was covered with ice. His left hand was aching, but the cold weather numbed some of the pain. "Get your wife into the cab of the truck," he directed. The young woman slowly made her way to the wrecker but stopped midway as she doubled over with a contraction. As Alan pulled the van onto the truck bed and made it secure, he muttered, "They closed down the Woodruff hospital. We'll have to go straight to Spartanburg Regional Hospital. The van can just go along for the ride." He did not want to deliver a baby. Even AAA Plus would not cover that.

The three crowded into the cab, and the wrecker slowly pulled out onto the interstate. The extra weight did give better traction.

"We've had Lamaze childbirth classes," the husband said, as if to reassure himself. "They told us to get to the hospital when her contractions were ten minutes apart."

The young woman grabbed her husband's hand as another contraction took her breath away. "It's only been five minutes since the last one. Lisa, try to hold on."

"I don't have any control over this, Jack. Are you an idiot? Do you think I want to give birth to this baby on the interstate?"

Alan certainly did not want her to have her baby on the interstate. "We're headed straight to the hospital."

"Thanks. Please hurry," Lisa groaned as she pressed both hands on the truck dashboard, bracing against yet another contraction. "Please ... hurry."

"Silent night, holy night," the radio offered as a lullaby. "All is calm, all is bright." *Nothing could be further from the truth*, Alan thought. It wasn't calm. It wasn't bright. It was hectic. It was frantic. It was sleeting. It was slippery. He was hurrying with care. He noticed disabled cars spaced like so many mile markers all along the highway. One 18-wheeler had spun off the road. Highway 221 would be too icy, and there were just too many hills. He would have to go all the way to Reidville Road. Lisa's next contraction seemed harder. She groaned more emphatically. Alan dialed 911 on his cell phone.

"This is 911. What kind of emergency are you having?"

"A baby is about to be born in my truck!" Alan shouted. "Give me EMS! Quick!"

"Right away, sir."

The brief pause seemed to last for an eternity. "This is EMS. May I help you?"

"Yes, this is Alan Shepherd—Shepherd's Towing and Auto Repair. I've got a woman in my truck who is about to have a baby."

"Has she had a baby before?"

"Not in my truck! I don't think we can make it to the hospital. Can you meet us?"

"Where?"

"How about my garage?"

"That's near The Beacon, right?"

"Right."

"We'll meet you there."

SHEPHERD'S
TOWING AND AUTO REPAIR

Alan had done nothing to prepare for Christmas, but Christmas had come to him anyway.

Having a garage near The Beacon was a good thing. Every police officer, sheriff's deputy, fireman, and paramedic knew where The Beacon was.

"It came upon a midnight clear," the radio foretold. It was coming all right, and certainly before midnight. But clear it was not. If anything, the sleet was heavier.

Lisa was in hard labor, groaning more loudly with each contraction, as the wrecker, loaded with the van, lumbered down Reidville Road. Her husband, Jack Daniels from Tennessee, had almost nothing to say. The Lamaze classes hadn't covered labor in a wrecker. Jack had run out of ideas. No wonder that in the cowboy movies they always sent the husband to boil water. Husbands just need something to do. The wrecker turned off the road to the repair shop. Alan quickly raised the heavy bay doors with his good hand and drove inside with the van just clearing the top of the door. Moments later, the ambulance pulled into the other bay; the blaring siren was silenced, but the blue lights still flashed. Two paramedics jumped out.

"Where's the little mama?"

"In the cab," Alan replied. The word on the front of the ambulance was written backwards, Alan noticed. ECNALUBMA. Framed in a rearview mirror, it would read AMBULANCE. Alan could only think of Leon and dyslexic angels. Angels in uniform—blue angels, at that.

"She's already crowning," the female blue angel exclaimed. "Get the stretcher and the OB kit. This baby is on the way. Gentlemen, give us a little privacy here."

Thank goodness somebody knew what to do. Alan stood by the tire rack at the back of the garage.

"Hold on, sweetie," the paramedic coached. "I've been through this three times myself."

"In this garage?" Lisa shouted.

"No, honey. I've got three kids myself." Then to the male paramedic, "Hand me those sterile drapes."

Alan chuckled. He had cleaned the garage, at least by garage standards, earlier in the day just to keep busy. At the time he had no idea that he was preparing for this. Grease and oil stains still spotted the floor.

"Now, Lisa, push hard!" the blue angel commanded. Lisa gave an extended growl from deep within as she pushed as hard as she could. "You're doing great, sweetie. Here comes your baby!"

The flashing light from the ambulance reflected off the silver oilcans stacked against the wall. Alan heard it all—the excitement of a young father, the agony and the ecstasy of a young mother, and then the cry of a baby.

"A little girl!" the paramedic proclaimed.

"Let me see her!" Lisa demanded.

"Just a minute. Let me clean her up a little." The blue angel clamped and cut the cord, wrapped the baby in a blanket, and handed her to her shivering mother.

Alan Shepherd took a step or two closer. He could hardly believe it.

For a moment, nobody said anything. The flashing blue light of the ambulance illuminated the faces of a little baby, a young mother, a befuddled father, two blue angels, and a stunned Shepherd whose heart was beginning to thaw.

"This is what makes it all worthwhile," said the male blue angel. "We see so many hurt people, so many injured, so much tragedy, so much dying. But this is a miracle. A birth always is." Then after a pause, he added, "Say, what happened to your hand?"

"I cut it up on the Saluda Grade this morning. Spent all afternoon in the ER waiting for twelve stitches."

"Looks like it's been bleeding again. Let me get my wound kit and wrap it again."

While the male blue angel took care of Alan's hand, the female took care of Lisa and the baby. Finally the woman angel said, "We're ready to go here. We've got to get Mama and this little girl to the hospital." The other angel added, "Come on, Daddy, you can ride up front with me."

"Thanks, Mister," Jack said, almost as an afterthought. "I bet you never thought something like this would happen in your garage."

The ambulance backed into the road and headed for the hospital. Alan sat down for a moment. He would fix the van later after his hand was better. He was sure it was the timing chain; they always go bad after 100,000 miles.

He glanced at the sign on the wall.

MAKE CHECKS PAYABLE TO
SHEPHERD'S TOWING AND AUTO REPAIR

Alan picked up a felt-tipped marker and scrawled another line.

MAKE CHECKS PAYABLE TO
SHEPHERD'S TOWING AND AUTO REPAIR
AND DELIVERY ROOM

Alan sat awhile in silence pondering what had happened.

Once the van was unloaded, he stepped outside his garage. The sleet had stopped, and a few stars now sprinkled the sky. He checked his watch and lit a cigarette. Christmas was almost over. Alan had done nothing to prepare for Christmas, but Christmas had come to him anyway. A baby had been born in his shop on Christmas Day. It was like a living nativity with a young mother, her frightened husband, two welcoming angels, and one surprised Shepherd. There were no strangers from the East bearing gifts, but Alan had even figured that one out. He picked up the phone and ordered takeout from one of the only restaurants open on Christmas, one of his favorites, New China. That was certain to give him an encounter with at least one stranger from the East bearing gifts. Moo Goo Gai Pan, egg rolls, and a Christmas lite sounded mighty good.

Alan remembered as a boy going to church with his mother to see the Christmas pageant. He had dropped out of church when he dropped out of The Citadel and had only been back in church four times since—for two weddings and two funerals. Maybe he would go to church again, or maybe not. He would see. But this Christmas the pageant was not in a church, it was in his shop. A baby was born.

Alan picked up his Chinese food and drove the rollback to his home in Duncan. When he reached his street, all of the homes in his neighborhood, including his, were without power. He took the flashlight from the truck and his takeout food and walked to the house. He paused for a moment in his front yard and turned the flashlight off. Without electric lights to interfere, the stars in the sky were unusually bright. Inside, Alan hung up the yellow rain slicker. A red blinking light caught his attention—four messages were on the answering machine, now operating on battery power.

The first message was from Alma Oakley. "Alan, I hate to bother you on Christmas since I'm sure you have the day off, but my kitty has gone up the pear tree again. That's where the bird feeder is hanging. I think she might be trying to catch a little bird. Could you please come get her down? I'm afraid she'll freeze to death in this weather."

The second message was also from Mrs. Oakley. "Alan, never mind. Muffin came down from the tree by herself. Thank you anyway."

The third message was a voice he did not expect to hear. "Hi, Alan. This is Julie. Thought you'd like to know that the kids and I are staying in Columbia tonight with my sister. We decided the roads were just too bad. We'll be back tomorrow after some of the ice melts. I am sure you are busy. Take care of yourself. And Alan, Merry Christmas!" Alan was not only surprised to hear Julie's voice, but he was also taken aback at how glad he felt to hear from her. He would go by the Waffle House and tell her about his Christmas adventure.

The fourth message was not a surprise. It was Spencer the Jerk. True to form, there was not one word of thanks. "Hi, Alan. I'm a new grandfather. Lucky you, Buddy, getting to see my granddaughter on Christmas. By the way, Jack and Lisa are fine and so is Jennifer. They named her Jennifer Noel because she was born on Christmas."

"The first Noel the angels did say, Was to certain poor shepherds..." Noel to Shepherds. It had happened again, just as it had so many years before.

Alan pulled down the disappearing stairway into the attic, using his right hand. After a brief search with the flashlight, he found the box with his mother's nativity set. He made his way to the kitchen table and took a candle from the drawer. He placed it in a glass holder and lit the wick. He placed the figures of Mary, Joseph, and the baby Jesus on his kitchen table along with one lonely shepherd. By candlelight, he silently read the Christmas story from St. Luke, Chapter 2, in his mother's Bible. When he got to verse 20, he was stopped short. "And the shepherds returned, glorifying and praising God for all they had seen and heard."

It had been Christmas after all, and in the flickering light of Christmas night, Alan Shepherd returned.

The Healing Wreath

Frances McLean poured a fresh cup of coffee and tinted it just the right color with half-and-half cream. She plopped down in her favorite chair, kicked off her shoes, and propped up her tired feet on the ottoman. Her day had not gone exactly as she had expected. She did have the car serviced, and she managed to change the filter on the heating and air conditioning unit. She had paid most of the bills. The things she had not done were the things she had most wanted to do. She had to cancel her hair appointment because it took so long to get the car serviced.

Frances also wanted to have lunch with the Widows Might, a support group of caring women who had lost their husbands. Frances had been to their meetings only a few times, but she had known friends in the group for several years. The group name was a play on words. The story of the widow's mite in the Bible demonstrated what one widow could do for God. The Widows Might encouraged women, bereaved following the deaths of their husbands, to join together to strengthen each other and to reach out to others. Frances' husband, Charles, had always made fun of the group's name. Whenever someone mentioned the Widows Might, Charles would ask, "The widows might what?"

Now, with Charles gone, Frances needed the group. She hated to miss the Christmas luncheon but was fearful that she might burst into tears at the slightest provocation. Rather than risk losing her composure in uncontrollable weeping, she used a ready excuse. She had bought the wrong size furnace filter and had to return to the hardware store to exchange it for the right size.

Frances wanted to watch "As the World Turns," but she had missed it because the bills had to be in the mailbox before the mailman came. She did not mind missing her soap opera occasionally, but Friday's programs were usually a wrap-up of the crisis of the week and a tantalizing cliffhanger for the week ahead. In these last days before Christmas, postal pickup and delivery had become predictably unpredictable.

As Frances savored her coffee, she thought with surprise, *This is good!* Charles had often tried to teach her to make coffee the way he made it, but she had steadfastly refused his attempts. "Making coffee is the husband's role," she would counter. Charles would tease her, explaining to others why he was the designated coffee person: "Frances has found proof in the Bible that the husband's job is to make the coffee. In fact, she found it in the title of her favorite book in the Bible, Hebrews. Get it? He brews."

Enjoying a cup of coffee was only one reminder of how much she missed Charles. Her husband had been her rock. He was the one who got the car serviced, who changed the furnace filter, and who paid the bills. She never had to worry about those chores before Charles' death in March. Her husband just did them. Of course, she had to nag him frequently about taking out the garbage, putting away his clothes, and changing light bulbs. But the car, the furnace, and the bills he did automatically.

But what Frances missed most about Charles was not what he did. Most of all, she just missed being with him. Charles was her best friend. They walked together, prayed together, laughed together, cried together, and slept together for forty-one years. She couldn't believe it, but she missed his snoring. She missed hearing him whistle, and she missed hearing him sing in the shower; most of all, she missed his touch. She felt her deepest grief when she woke up in the middle of the night, alone.

Remembering all of their good times together, Frances again felt overwhelmed with a terrible mixture of sadness and anger. *How could Charles just die and leave her so alone? I could just kill him!* she thought to herself. Then she smiled at the irony of wanting to kill a dead man, especially the man she loved so much. *It just isn't fair,* she thought as her eyes flooded with tears. *And if I cry in my coffee, it will be his fault for making my coffee taste salty.* She cried anyway. Maybe it was irrational, but Frances was still mad at Charles for leaving her, even though dying was not his decision.

As Frances wiped her tears away with the gingham napkin, the telephone rang. She checked the caller ID. It was her sister-in-law, Eva. Frances let it ring twice more. *I have to answer,* she thought, *or Eva will be here in a skinny minute to see what's wrong with me.* She reluctantly answered the phone.

"Hello, Frances McLean speaking."

"Frances, where have you been? I've been trying to call you all day."

"Hello, Eva, how are you?"

"I'm fine except I've been worried sick about you."

"I've had a busy day, Eva, but, really, I'm fine."

"Frances, Lucille said you canceled your hair appointment, and Marjorie said you were not at the Christmas luncheon for the Widows Might. Where have you been all day?"

"I've been taking care of some personal business."

"What kind of personal business?"

"Oh, just having the car serviced, paying bills, a few things like that."

"Frances, are you just now getting around to having the car serviced? That should have been done before Thanksgiving. And your bills should have been paid at the first of December. Frances, you are not doing well!"

It never ceased to amaze Frances how much Eva knew about her routine and how intent she was on trying to manage her life. She could be so overbearing!

Eva continued her lecture, "You're spending too much time moping around and feeling sorry for yourself. I have a big surprise for you. I'll be by to pick you up at eight o'clock tomorrow morning. Eat breakfast early, dress in casual clothes, wear that Christmas sweater Charles gave you last year, and be ready."

"Eva, I really don't ..."

"Frances, I won't take no for an answer. Be ready at eight."

"Good-bye, Eva."

"Good-bye to you, Frances. Be ready at eight. And, Frances, it's time to change your furnace filter."

Frances hung up the telephone. She could think of only one word to describe her sister-in-law, one her mother had taught her not to say. *I should not have taken that call*, she scolded herself.

Frances refilled her coffee cup and stood staring out of her kitchen window. The leaves still clung to the oak trees at the back of the yard. This past fall had been without a real cold snap, and the leaves had not put on their usual display of brilliant autumn colors. They just died and turned brown. It was as if the trees were grieving right along with her.

She glanced down at the windowsill and saw a Ziploc bag containing two black licorice twists. Frances had always given Charles licorice for Christmas. It was his favorite candy, and he especially liked the long licorice twists. He rationed himself, enjoying only one or two a week, making them last as long as possible. The twists in the Ziploc were the last two left over from last Christmas. She kept them where Charles had left them on the windowsill. Frances couldn't stand the thought of throwing them away, and she certainly was not going to eat them. In fact, she and Charles had an agreement that after he ate licorice, she would not kiss him until he brushed his teeth.

It had been a difficult year. Charles had died suddenly in March though he had always been the picture of health. In January he had passed a complete physical exam with flying colors. He and Frances had planned a week at the beach with all three of the children in June. But on a cold night in March, Charles went to bed with a headache. He took two aspirin and died in his sleep. The required autopsy revealed a cerebral hemorrhage.

Frances was in shock, so numb that she could hardly remember anything the pastor had said at Charles' funeral. Her biggest concern had been for her children. Charlie had been just like his dad, the Rock of Gibraltar for the rest of the family. JoAnne, their youngest, tried to keep her composure, but it was too much for her. Their oldest, Alison, a third-year resident in neurology, tried to find comfort in her medical knowledge. Her children missed their daddy, and Frances, try as she might, could not fill the void.

The children had been as much help as they could be. Frances understood that they all had their own busy lives. JoAnne and her husband had a new baby. Charlie and his wife had two children and a new business. Alison was trying to finish her residency and move into a neurology practice. All three children called home at least once a week to check on their mother. They visited occasionally, but the truth was that the children expected Frances to go right on being their mother in spite of her grief.

The family had vacationed together in June just as Charles had planned, but being together at the beach had been difficult for everybody. In order to help Frances enjoy their summer vacation, Charles had always done some of the cooking. The children especially looked forward to his made-to-order omelets, his cold boiled shrimp, and his sautèd scallops. In his absence none of that was on the menu for the week. Charles led family beachcombing expeditions to the inlet at low tide and star hikes on the beach after dark. The children went through the motions, but it was just not the same without their dad. Frances missed their times alone, sipping fresh coffee as they watched the sunrise from the beach house porch, and their walks together on the beach after supper. She was glad when the week was over.

At Thanksgiving the children and grandchildren all came home for the dinner Frances had prepared, just as she had always done. But being in that house without Charles was again difficult for everyone. When JoAnne and Alison set the table for Thanksgiving dinner, they inadvertently set a place for their dad. When they gathered around the table for the blessing, traditionally offered by Charles, the entire family felt the stabbing pain inflicted by his empty place at the table. Frances bravely said the prayer, but it was just not the same. Even little Charles III toddled around the house all Thanksgiving Day looking for his grandpapa. He did not find Charles, but he found a piece of licorice from a secret stash. When Frances found her grandson, he was covered in black candy. He greeted her with that same black-toothed grin she had seen so often when her husband had been eating licorice. Frances sank down beside her sticky grandson and hugged him, laughing and crying at the same time.

Cynthia, Charlie's wife, decided to invite the family to their home in Charlotte for Christmas. It would be easier for everyone, she thought. Alison would be able to come from Durham for the day. JoAnne and her family would come down from Greensboro, and Frances could drive up on Christmas morning.

For Frances, it would make Christmas a little easier. She would not have to do much cooking, though she would probably make a special Apple-Cranberry Bake they all enjoyed. It was a dish that traveled well. She would not have to decorate the house this year. Charles usually did most of the Christmas decorating anyway. Frances had no idea how to put up a Christmas tree or to string the lights on the tree. She had absolutely nothing remotely resembling Christmas spirit. She was just trying to survive the holidays.

A bright red cardinal perched on her windowsill and chirped in anticipation, startling Frances from her reverie. She had not filled the birdfeeder in several days. That was another one of Charles' routine tasks. The cardinal flew across the yard and found comfort in the dark green leaves of a holly tree Charles had planted when they first moved to this house. The red berries perfectly matched the cardinal's feathers, but it was the crushed brown oak leaves at the back of the yard that fit Frances' mood exactly.

Frances checked her watch, the one her husband had given her for their fortieth Christmas together. She set the clock by her bed to correspond to the time on her watch. She resented having to set her bedside alarm so early. She enjoyed sleeping late, especially on Saturday morning. Now, she had to set the alarm so she could get up and be dressed and ready when Eva came to pick her up. Frances did look forward to an early bedtime, but she knew she would need to be well rested to endure Eva.

The early bedtime was not to be. No sooner had Frances placed her head on the pillow than JoAnne called, asking about home remedies for colic. Frances tried to be as loving and comforting as she could be. She resisted the strong temptation to say that it was only sweet justice that JoAnne should have to put up with a colicky baby since JoAnne had been one herself.

After suggesting all of the remedies she knew, none of which had met with much success years earlier, she spoke motherly words of reassurance and love, "This too shall pass." It was both a limp clichè and an enduring truth.

When the good-byes were said, Frances thought, *Being a mother never ends.* Even though she had lost her husband, her children still depended on her as if nothing had changed. Then she reflected on her words to JoAnne, "This too shall pass."

Does that hold true for all of life's difficulties? Would the pain of her grief and the brokenness of her heart ever end? Would she just have to outgrow the sorrow of her husband's death like a bad case of colic? Again her tears flowed. Sobbing, she whispered into her pillow, "Charles, how could you?" Then she slept.

* * *

On Saturday morning Eva arrived ten minutes early. Frances was dressed but hardly ready. Getting ready for Eva was impossible. Eva came into the house, brushing past Frances.

"I thought you were going to wear the Christmas sweater Charles gave you last Christmas."

"No, Eva, it was just too warm."

"Well, you don't look very much like Christmas."

Frances did not respond. She didn't feel very much like Christmas and much preferred to be left alone.

"Did you change the furnace filter?"

"Yes, Eva, I did that yesterday, before you called."

"Where are all your Christmas decorations?"

"I've decided not to decorate this year. I won't be here for Christmas. I'll be in Charlotte with the children."

"You mean they're not coming home for Christmas?"

"No, they were just here for Thanksgiving, you know. Cynthia invited me to have Christmas at their house. It will be easier for all of us."

"Easy! Why should Christmas be easy? Besides, you have to decorate. You'll never get in the Christmas spirit if you don't decorate."

Frances did not expect to get into the Christmas spirit. Christmas without Charles just didn't seem like Christmas.

"Well, at least you have your nativity scene out," said Eva. "That's a start. Where is the beautiful snow globe collection Charles gave you?"

"The snow globes are still in the attic, Eva."

"In the attic! You can't enjoy them there!"

"They are just fine right where they are. I'm not planning to get them down this year."

"You've got to at least put up a tree."

"Eva, Charles always put up the tree. I'm not planning to decorate a tree this year either."

Eva noticed the Ziploc bag containing the two black licorice twists. She picked it up and started for the garbage can. "These things need to be thrown away."

"Don't you dare!" Frances shouted. "Don't even think about throwing that licorice away!"

Eva was stunned. "What do you intend to do with it?"

"I'm not sure, but that's for me to decide, not you, Eva!" It was unusual for Frances to be so adamant with Eva.

"Frances, Charles is dead and gone. I miss him as much as you do. He was, after all, my brother. I knew Charles much longer than you did! I changed his diapers and taught him how to walk. You've got to get over Charles and do things for yourself. You have moped around long enough. Now, let's go. I have a surprise for you that is going to help."

Frances felt like screaming, but she did not. She remembered Charles' nickname for his older sister. He affectionately called her Caterpillar, because, as he put it, "She's the closest thing to a bulldozer I've ever run into."

The two women walked together to Eva's car, a silver Pontiac Vibe.

"How do you like your new car?" Frances asked, getting into the passenger seat.

"I love it! I bought it for one hundred dollars above invoice."

"How does it drive?" It was the wrong question. Eva drove just like her nickname, just like a bulldozer.

Frances hated to ride with her sister-in-law. She could feel every muscle in her body tensing. In fact, she hated doing anything with Eva. Why, on a Saturday morning, should she allow herself to go through this misery?

"Eva, where are we going?"

"You'll see," the bulldozer snapped, as she changed lanes and made a sudden left turn. "Just relax."

Frances could not relax. She did not look forward to whatever the surprise was. Just getting there safely would be enough of a surprise.

Eva whipped the silver Vibe into the parking lot of the Good Earth Garden Shop, stopping right on top of a painted line on the pavement, thereby occupying two parking places instead of just one. The shop was already a flurry of activity even at 8:15 on a Saturday morning in December. Red, pink, and white poinsettias were on display, as were paper white narcissus and bright red amaryllis, all in full bloom. The chain link fence served as a showplace for Christmas wreaths of every kind. Fraser fir trees lined the upper parking lot, waiting to find a home for the holidays.

Frances had a terrible thought. "Surely Eva is not going to make me buy a Christmas tree."

But Eva had a different plan. "I want to give you your Christmas present early this year," she said.

"What is the present?" Frances asked reluctantly.

"I know you have seen Martha Stewart on television."

"Not since the interview with Barbara Walters before she went to prison."

"Yes, it's all so unfair. But never mind that. Today you're going to meet the Martha Stewart of the South. Her name is Martha Jane Stuart. She's from Atlanta, and she's teaching a class here today. Enrollment was limited to fifteen people so I registered both of us. Merry Christmas, Frances."

"Why, thank you, Eva. How thoughtful. What kind of class?"

"Well, Martha Jane does all the things Martha Stewart does but with a Southern twist. She makes flower arrangements with goldenrod and Queen Anne's lace. She makes baskets out of Kudzu vines. And she has the best recipes. She makes pies that are out of this world. Kentucky Derby Pie and Mississippi Mud Pie are her specialties. Her black-eyed pea and okra relish dip and her grits casserole are the best you ever tasted."

"What kind of class, Eva?"

"Wreath making. Martha Jane makes the most beautiful Christmas wreaths out of plain old muscadine and scuppernong vines. You'll love it, Frances. You need to do something to get your mind off yourself. It's just two Saturdays and besides, I've already paid for it. You have to do it!"

Frances was especially glad to see that several of her friends from the widows' group were also registered for the class. Their company put her at ease. Martha Jane Stuart from Atlanta was an ample woman. Frances' first impression was that Martha Jane had enjoyed Kentucky Derby and Mississippi Mud pie maybe a bit too often. Grits were probably a staple in her diet, too. She was a pleasant woman whose soft Southern accent made it easy to listen to her.

The class was really about wreath making. Martha Jane suggested that the best, fullest wreaths could only be made by gathering wild vines and weaving them to the desired size. The entire hour and a half was spent watching Martha Jane Stuart from Atlanta demonstrate the weaving technique for a grapevine wreath. Each participant had a turn weaving one length of vine into the wreath. Eva hovered over Frances, making sure that her strand was properly woven. Frances finally just handed it over to Eva to complete, realizing that her sister-in-law would never be pleased with her half-hearted attempt.

Near the end of class, Martha Jane acknowledged that many of her former wreath-making participants preferred to purchase grapevine wreaths pre-woven from pruned runners from domestic vineyards.

After trying their hand at the craft, most women in this class also agreed that they would rather purchase ready-made wreaths. The owner of the Good Earth Garden Shop was delighted to oblige.

As the class ended for the morning, Martha Jane explained that each wreath would be unique. Each should have a theme. She displayed two wreaths. One, created for a family with a new baby, was decorated with pacifiers, baby rattles, and baby socks. The second, intended as a teacher gift, featured pencils, rulers, and the plastic letters, A, B, C.

As class ended, Martha Jane gave final instructions. "Either make or purchase your grapevine wreath, select a theme, and have fun. Next Saturday bring your wreath, and be prepared to share your creation with the class."

Following the class, several other women gathered around Frances and asked how she was doing with the holidays. She told them she was still having a difficult time being alone.

"Be gentle with yourself," one said.

"Call me if you need to talk," offered another.

"The holidays are difficult, especially the first year," counseled a third.

Martha Jane had been listening to the conversation. "My husband died seven years ago. I wish I could promise that you'll get over it. I have gotten better, but I still miss him. I teach these workshops because it keeps me busy and allows me to earn a little extra money."

Frances thanked the group and said her good-byes. Martha Jane said, "Thank you for coming. I know it wasn't easy. I look forward to seeing you next Saturday. If you don't feel like making a wreath, don't worry. Please, just come and be with us." With that, Martha Jane gave Frances a hug.

Frances purchased a ready-made wreath. Whatever the price, she thought it a real bargain not to have to go into the woods to gather her own grapevines and weave them herself. For Eva, nothing would do but to go through the entire process from beginning to end. "If I am taking the class from Martha Jane, I am going to do it the right way! I refuse to cheapen the experience by using a store-bought wreath." With Eva, it was all or nothing.

For Frances, the experience could not be cheapened. It was not about making a wreath. It was about making it through the holidays without Charles. The class had been a better gift than Eva could have imagined. Wreath or no wreath, Frances had found something she needed—a gentle gift of grace from women who shared her pain and understood her grief.

The wreath-making class had been good for Frances, not only in the support she found, but also in the distraction it was providing for Eva. Charles had often said of his older sister, "Eva needs a project, or else she'll make you her project."

Frances had definitely been Eva's project for several months. It was one of the reasons the children wanted their mother to leave town for Christmas. They had had their fill of turkey and Eva at Thanksgiving. Frances tried to be understanding of her sister-in-law. Of course, Eva really did have good intentions, but those good intentions were the kind that paved the road to hell. At least that's the way it often felt to Frances. It is a road designed for bad vibes and their bulldozer drivers.

Frances tried to remember that Eva's life had been difficult. She had cared for both of her aging parents in their home. Her father died nine years before her mother, and her mother never quit grieving. Frances realized that her sister-in-law had used up most of her patience with grieving widows on her own mother. It was, perhaps, the reason Eva wanted Frances to get over Charles' death so quickly.

Though Eva never married, she had two relationships that held promise. The first, when Eva was a young woman, ended abruptly when Eva's fiancè left town with an older woman. Eva learned later that they were married. It was a heartbreaking loss for the young Eva. Frances always thought that what seemed to be a hard heart in her sister-in-law was really a defense against another broken heart. The defense did not, however, prevent another broken relationship.

Eva met Bill on one of her trips with the travel agency where she was employed for thirty years. She was in her late thirties when they met. After a time, it seemed that Eva and Bill would marry. Their courtship lasted for well over a year, and they were together for nearly every social occasion. Eva had told Charles and Frances that she expected to receive an engagement ring for her birthday. When that didn't happen, she said she was sure Bill was waiting until Christmas. Bill did give Eva a diamond, but it was a pendant, not a ring.

Unfortunately, Bill became one of Eva's projects. She became obsessed with doing a complete makeover of Bill. A country boy at heart, he would rather eat pinto beans and turnip greens at the kitchen table set with a plastic plate and only one fork. Eva tried to train Bill to feast on portabella mushrooms and artichoke hearts in the dining room with a place setting of fine china and three forks. Bill would have enjoyed Martha Jane Stuart's cheese grits casserole and her black-eyed pea and okra relish dip. Charles had given a succinct commentary on the relationship between Eva and Bill. "You just can't make a racehorse out of a plow mule."

Even without an official engagement, Eva started planning the wedding of the century. When she did, Bill disappeared. Like everything else Eva did, the planning was perfect down to the last detail. But, as Charles put it, "She had the whole thing under control, everything except the groom." Eva seemed unable to learn from her mistakes. It was easier and less painful to blame somebody else. In the case of the wedding flop, Bill got the blame.

Eva's newest obsession was making her own wild grapevine wreath. Frances was grateful Eva had found a new project. Maybe she would have a short break at least until the wreath was done. The wreath-making class had been a good Christmas gift after all. The class members had been caring and supportive, and Eva had something else to occupy her time and attention for a week. In fact, Frances did not hear from Eva until Wednesday. The telephone call came right in the tension-filled middle of "As The World Turns."

"Frances, what are you doing? Have you made your wreath yet?"

"Hello, Eva, how are you?"

"Frustrated! It's been raining all week, and I haven't been able to gather the wild grapevines to make my wreath. It's supposed to clear up tonight and turn colder. I'm leaving right after lunch tomorrow to go to the Pickens' farm. Are you sure you don't want to go with me so you can make a real wreath?"

"No, Eva, I haven't changed my mind. I won't go this time."

"Have you finished decorating that store-bought wreath?"

"No, I haven't even started. I've just been thinking about it."

"Well, it's high time! You know, the last class with Martha Jane Stuart is Saturday. You certainly don't want to show up empty-handed."

"No, Eva, I won't go empty-handed. This time, I'll drive. Be ready with your beautiful homemade wreath at eight o'clock sharp!"

"I'll be ready. I have it all planned. I'll gather the grapevines tomorrow afternoon, weave the wreath tomorrow night, and decorate it Friday. It will be beautiful! I'm going to make it large enough to fit on the big double doors on the front of the house. It will be just the right decoration for the entry."

"It sounds spectacular. I'll pick you up Saturday morning."

"Why don't you let me drive, Frances? You know how slow you are."

"No, I'll pick you up this time. It's my turn to drive."

"Don't be late. I want to have my wreath there early."

"Good-bye, Eva."

Frances took a deep breath. Wouldn't Eva's plan for a double-wide Christmas wreath make it impossible to use the entrance?

Friday, the day before the final class with Martha Jane Stuart, Frances decided to venture into the attic to look for a few items to use as decorations on her wreath. She hated going into the attic. Just opening the disappearing stairway was difficult for her. Charles had always accepted that task. As far as Frances could remember, the last time the attic had been opened was when Charles put the Christmas decorations away last New Year's Day.

Frances set out on an adventure armed with the proper equipment: a flashlight in case the one attic light bulb should burn out, the portable telephone so she could call 911 just in case something happened to her, a broom to fend off the critters she always expected to find in the gloom overhead, and a plastic trash bag to haul away the treasures that had turned to trash with the passage of time. To her equipment she added a strawberry bucket, left over from summer's bounty. It was just the right size to gather and carry down whatever treasures she gleaned for decorating her wreath.

Standing on tiptoe, a well-equipped Frances tugged at the rope that opened the stairway. Dust, bits of insulation, and other debris, including a few acorns, sifted down from the gaping hole in the ceiling. Frances did not want to know how the acorns got into the attic. Frances unfolded the cumbersome stairs and cautiously climbed within reach of the light cord. The stairs beneath her creaked as the light above her clicked on. With the phone and trash bag tucked into the pockets of her oldest housecleaning attire, she pushed the broom in ahead of her, guided by the flashlight beam. She paused to listen for scurrying sounds. There were none, so she ventured further into the attic.

Charles had built shelves in the attic several years ago after considerable nagging on her part. Thank goodness for the shelves that brought some order out of the attic chaos. Scanning the labels on the plastic storage boxes along the shelves, she intended to open only the one marked

FRAGILE ORNAMENTS

Frances pulled herself into the attic and opened the special box, which held the ornaments she and Charles had purchased for their first Christmas together forty-one years earlier. Charles was in the Army at the time. They had feared that he would be sent to Korea. Instead, he was given a desk job in Germany. They got married, and she went with him. Though they were far away from both families that first Christmas, they were together, and that was all that mattered. These fragile ornaments had been on their tree every Christmas since.

Charles had carefully wrapped these special ornaments in fresh paper towels straight off of a new roll. No smudgy discarded newspaper would do for these keepsakes. Frances unwrapped the tiny treasures, examining each one. She selected only three: a glass angel; a Christmas tree, hand carved in German quillwork; and a hand-painted porcelain shepherd holding a lamb. She loosely rewrapped the three ornaments and tucked them safely into her strawberry bucket. Then she closed the box and placed it back on the shelf.

As Frances prepared to make her descent, her eyes swept past another label:

FRAGILE SNOW GLOBES

Even her cursory glance told her immediately that something awful had happened. Black, sticky goo covered the sides of the box. As she lifted the lid, the strong odor of mildew overwhelmed her. She had packed her snow globe collection in the box, each piece carefully padded with Christmas hand towels. Apparently, over the sweltering summer, the tightly closed plastic box simmered in the attic, holding so much heat that the water seals on the globes had melted. The water had drained from every globe, causing the wet towels to mildew inside the box. The glass globes had disintegrated, and all of the contents were black with mildew. Everything was ruined. Frances, shocked in disbelief, cried out into the attic, "Oh, Charles."

With considerable distress, Frances threw towels and broken glass into the trash bag, searching for anything she might be able to salvage from the wreckage. She thought about all of those Christmases past when Charles had surprised her with a new snow globe. He did not give her one every year, but each was a reminder of her husband. As the magnitude of her loss sank in, she slumped to the floor of the attic and wept.

After a while, Frances composed herself. Most of the contents of the box were now only trash. In the moldy debris she found one small familiar wooden carving of the Holy Family. She recognized it as the centerpiece of the very first snow globe Charles had given her that Christmas in Germany. She took a tissue from her pocket, moist with her tears, and wiped the mildew from the faces of Mary, Joseph, and the baby Jesus. The cleanup would require more than a damp tissue. She folded the Holy Family figurines into the tissue and placed them in the strawberry bucket with the other ornaments. She put the garbage bag into the plastic box and closed the lid. It was a little like closing a coffin. *This is all just trash*, she thought as she climbed carefully down from the attic. She took the box filled with snow globe ruins all the way outside to the garbage can.

Once the mildewed garbage was out of the house, Frances spent the rest of the day making her wreath. The Holy Family got a good, gentle scrubbing with an old toothbrush and a dusting of baking soda. She took several twist ties from the box of trash bags and stripped away the paper from each one. Using the exposed thin wires, Frances attached the Holy Family salvaged from the broken snow globe and the three keepsake ornaments from Germany to the woven grapevine circle. Each piece she added was from her first Christmas with Charles. The theme of her wreath, the first Christmas of her marriage, was clear.

The one thing worth holding on to is love.
Love is right at the center of Christmas.

Frances laid the wreath aside and walked out into her backyard. Much to the delight of the waiting cardinal, she filled the birdfeeder with fresh seed. Then with hand-pruning shears, she snipped short sprigs of dark green leaves adorned with bright red berries from the holly tree Charles had planted years before. Back inside the kitchen, she secured the holly cuttings among the twisted grapevines. The finishing touch was a bright red velvet bow attached with wires long enough to make a suitable door hanger for the wreath. After Frances hung the wreath on her front door, she took several steps back to admire her creation. It was not a double-wide, but it was a beautiful little wreath.

Thinking about the double-wide wreath reminded her to check with Eva just to be sure they were clear about the Saturday morning plan. When Eva answered the phone, Frances knew something was bothering her.

"Frances, I'm glad you called. I won't be able to go to the class tomorrow."

"Why not, Eva, what's wrong?"

"I'm not sure. I'm not feeling well at all. I've made an appointment to see Dr. Marshall early in the morning."

"Is there anything I can do?"

"Please just give my regrets and apologies to Martha Jane Stuart and the others. I so wanted them to see my wreath."

"Would you like for me to take your wreath?"

"Oh, no. Just ride by in the morning and look at it. It's on the front door. By the way, you won't be able to use the front door of my house until after Christmas. The wreath is so large, it blocks both doors. I am so disappointed I can't make it to the class. I worked so hard on my wreath."

"I'll drive by in the morning. Please let me know if I can help."

"Thank you, Frances. I just need to try to get some sleep."

"Good-bye, Eva."

✳   ✳   ✳

As Frances left her house Saturday morning, she removed the wreath from her front door. The clear, cold air made the weather finally feel like December. The warmth of the Christmas sweater Charles had given her the year before was comforting in the morning chill. Christmas was just six days away, and Frances was beginning to sense the Christmas spirit. She put the wreath on the passenger seat of her car. She was sorry Eva didn't feel well, but this morning she would enjoy going to the class alone.

Frances drove slowly past Eva's house, the house her parents left to her, the one she had lived in all of her life. On the double front door was an enormous wreath that covered the top half of both doors. A massive burgundy velvet bow, streamers trailing all the way to the floor, matched the size of the wreath.

Eva certainly has a sense of proportion, thought Frances. Her double-wide wreath, decorated with an assortment of glittering attachments that gleamed with the reflection of hundreds of flashing multicolored lights, was a sight to behold. *What was her theme?* Frances wondered. *Maybe it was Mardi Gras at Christmas.* Charles would have described the wreath in one of the colorful ways he usually described tacky Christmas decorations. "Looks like Santa's revenge." Frances was relieved Eva had not accepted her offer to take the wreath to the class.

The class at the Good Earth Garden Shop was not so much a class as it was a time of sharing. Martha Jane asked the participants to show their wreaths and explain why they had chosen those particular decorations. One young mother told about her family's summer vacation at the Outer Banks of North Carolina. Her husband and children had enjoyed beachcombing every day. She had decorated her wreath with seashells and other interesting items found in the sand. Another woman had created a wreath with a garden theme by using colorful seed packets and lightweight garden tools. The only man in the group chose a fishing motif for his wreath, including several antique lures and even a miniature rod and reel like the kind intended for ice fishing.

After the others had taken their turns, Frances was asked to show her wreath to the group. She explained, "As some of you know, my husband, Charles, died suddenly in March. We were married forty-one years, and this is my first Christmas without him." Tears welled up in her eyes.

Martha Jane spoke to give Frances a moment to gather herself, "You've done a marvelous job. Tell us about the four ornaments."

"The first Christmas we were married, we lived in Germany. Charles was in the Army, and we were away from our families at Christmas for the first time. But we were together, and that's what mattered most." Frances paused and blotted her eyes with a tissue. "Charles brought a small Christmas tree to our apartment just before Christmas. We shopped together for the only three ornaments on our little tree that first Christmas. These are the three: a glass angel, a carved wooden Christmas tree, and a porcelain shepherd." She explained the sad discovery of her ruined snow globe collection in the attic the day before. "The Holy Family was the centerpiece of the first snow globe that Charles gave me."

Then Frances added, "You know, this Holy Family was the only thing I could salvage from a mess of mildew, broken glass, and disappointment. It has taught me an important lesson: sometimes life is just one big jumble of brokenness, loss, and sadness. But the one thing worth holding on to is love. Love is right at the center of Christmas."

By the time Frances had finished explaining her wreath, several of the women in the class were wiping tears from their eyes. Martha Jane passed around a plate of homemade Christmas cookies, and the man who made the fishing wreath was pouring cups of coffee. "Calories and caffeine always help," he said, apparently trying to ease his own discomfort.

Back at her home, Frances hung the wreath on the front door. As she walked into the house, the phone was ringing. It was Eva. She was beside herself, but Eva was often beside herself. She explained that Dr. Marshall had said he had never seen anything like it. He even considered putting Eva in the hospital. His diagnosis was that she was afflicted with a severe allergic reaction that must be treated with steroids. In other words, the gorgeous Christmas wreath on her front door was not a grapevine wreath at all. It was a poison ivy wreath.

"Frances, this is December. Have you ever heard of anybody breaking out with poison ivy for Christmas? How was I to know? There were no leaves on the vines. They looked just like grapevines to me. I won't be able to go to a single Christmas party. I can't even go to the choir cantata."

"Eva, I'm so sorry. Is there anything I can do to help?'

"No, not one thing. By all means, stay away from my front door. I have the most beautiful poison ivy wreath in town."

"Eva, what will you do about the wreath?"

"I've already called the police department. They have a special squad that specializes in disposing of bombs, toxic waste, and hazardous material. My wreath qualifies, and they will come to get it. Good riddance!"

✳ ✳ ✳

On Christmas morning Frances woke up early for her trip to Charlotte to be with her children. As she stood by the kitchen window and finished her morning coffee, she watched the bright red cardinal. He was chirping a Christmas greeting in gratitude for the freshly filled feeder. Though today was her first Christmas without Charles in forty-one years, Frances was determined to make the best of it. She breathed a prayer for strength and prepared for her drive to Charlotte.

She had several items to put into her car: three pies, one Apple-Cranberry Bake, four gift bags, and two Christmas wreaths, the one on her front door and a second wreath she had made for Eva. Frances secured the pies and the Apple-Cranberry Bake in the back floorboard of her car. Then she arranged the gift bags in the passenger seat and placed the wreath for Eva on the back seat. Finally, she took the wreath from her front door, which now looked empty without her only Christmas decoration.

Bundled in her Christmas sweater, Frances locked her home and drove to Eva's house. It was a pleasant time to drive. Almost no cars were traveling on Christmas morning. Parking her car in front of Eva's house, Frances took one pie, one gift bag, and one wreath up the steps to the front door. The massive double-wide wreath was gone. No decoration hung on Eva's door.

After Frances placed the pie and the gift bag in front of the door, she hung the wreath on the

nail where the huge wreath had been. It was too early to ring the doorbell, so she left a card in the gift bag that read:

Dear Eva,

I hope you are better. I'm on my way to Charlotte to be with the children, but I wanted to leave you three gifts. I made the Mississippi Mud Pie according to the recipe from Martha Jane Stuart, and I made a wreath for your front door, just a simple store-bought grapevine wreath decorated with a few sprigs of holly from my yard. It is the largest wreath I could find. The gift bag holds a practical gift, a bottle of Calamine lotion. I am sure you can use it.
Eva, thank you for your gift to me. The wreath-making class has helped me get through the holidays. I am sorry your wreath made you so ill. For me, the experience of making the wreath and the support of our classmates were sources of healing. I still have a long way to go, but the healing wreath has helped.
I love you, Eva.

Merry Christmas!
Frances

Frances rearranged the two remaining pies and the Apple-Cranberry Bake for the trip to Charlotte. She had one more stop to make at the Green Pastures Cemetery. On the driveway near the grave for her husband, Frances stopped the car. She carefully removed each of the fragile ornaments from the Christmas wreath, the healing wreath. The glass angel went into a gift bag for Alison. The porcelain shepherd would be a gift for JoAnne. The carved Christmas tree was for Charlie. Each of the children would receive one of the ornaments she and Charles had enjoyed for so many years.

Frances walked to the grave through the winter rye grass, still wet with dew. She stood quietly at the bronze marker of her husband, Charles L. McLean. Though she knew Charles was not in this place, it was here that she felt she could talk with him. *Charles, I miss you.*

Frances gently removed the Holy Family from the wreath and put the figurine in her coat pocket. She wanted to be sure to show it to her children and grandchildren when they read together the Christmas story from the Bible at dinner. She took the simple grapevine wreath with sprigs of holly and a red bow and placed it on the bronze marker on the grave. From the other coat pocket, she took the Ziploc bag containing two black pieces of candy that had been on her kitchen windowsill since last March. She removed the two licorice twists left over from last Christmas and tucked them into the grapevine wreath.

"I love you, Charles. Merry Christmas."

The Christmas Quilt

Mary Alice McCall was tired, bone tired. She was also elated. She was exhausted, and she was exhilarated. She lifted the last of the boxes onto the tailgate of the dark green Ford Explorer and mopped the perspiration from her brow. This last box was the most important. The carton with the Uncle Ben's Long Grain Converted Rice logo on the side contained the treasure she had been seeking. For all of her fifty-two years, she had heard family stories about the Christmas quilt.

Her grandmother had shown the heirloom to her several times, explaining to her that one day it would belong to her, Mary Alice. It was often the subject of conversation at McCall family reunions. It had become a source of strife within the family. But Mary Alice, who was the rightful owner, according to her mother's will, had been unable to locate it since her mother's death.

The keepsake was nowhere to be found in the renovated mill house in Spartanburg where her mother had lived. Mary Alice did not think it had ever been in Spartanburg. She thought it had always been right here, at the family home in Bamberg, in the Lowcountry of South Carolina.

The trip back to Bamberg from Spartanburg had been well worth the effort. Though her three cousins had searched the old home place diligently, they had been unable to find the missing heirloom. The cousins had been through the house over and over again, taking everything except the trash. But the quilt, along with a few other things, was right where Mary Alice thought she might find it.

Finally, this treasured part of her inheritance was firmly in her possession. With a red marker she wrote FRAGILE across the top of the box. Then in larger letters she wrote THE CHRISTMAS QUILT.

Mary Alice slammed shut the tailgate of the sport utility vehicle, wiped her glistening face again, and drank the last swallow of her bottled water. Pulling herself into the driver's seat, she started the engine and turned on the air conditioner. She hit the button that raised the rear window, fastened the seat belt, adjusted the rearview mirror, and drove down the long twin tracks of the driveway to the main road. In the rearview mirror she could see the house, now nearly 185 years old. At the road she parked the SUV. Leaving the engine running, she got out to snap one last picture with her camera. As she stood looking back down the long driveway, a sandy avenue lined with massive pecan trees, the old homeplace looked like a movie set straight out of *Gone with the Wind*.

Mary Alice framed the picture in the viewfinder of the digital camera, careful to include the green and golden leaves of the pecan trees, just beginning to turn to brilliant fall colors, and a patch of blue October sky. She was also careful to position a tree limb in the picture to block out the bent, crooked television antenna mounted on the rusted red tin roof. She put the camera on the passenger seat and stood looking down the lane toward the house, thinking back on her family's history.

This was the home where both her father and her grandfather had been born, upstairs in the master bedroom. It was here that she spent so many happy summer days with her grandfather and grandmother. Her grandfather taught her to fish in the Edisto River. He took her for rides in the pony cart along the curved sandy drive beneath the pecan trees.

Under these pecan trees, along the boulevard, as her grandpa called it, she had learned to ride a bicycle. Even after she moved to Spartanburg with her mother, they always returned to this home for Christmas. This spacious old home absorbed Christmas decorations the way her grandmother's fruitcake soaked up her grandfather's fine bourbon whiskey. At Christmas there was always an enormous red cedar tree in the foyer at the foot of the stairs. It took every available McCall to wrestle it into place. According to Mary Alice's grandmother, the tree had to be a little over fourteen feet tall in order to touch the ceiling. The whole house was filled with the fragrance of cedar. The tree was decorated with lights, garlands, and ornaments made in school by children and grandchildren. Some decorations were so old nobody could even remember who had made them.

There was always so much good food. And there were so many pecans. These trees had been the most productive in Bamberg County. From Thanksgiving until New Year's Day, anyone who sat down to rest, even for a moment, was handed a wooden bowl filled with pecans to crack, shell, and pick. As her grandfather presented the bowl of pecans, he would say, "While you're resting, make yourself useful." The apple salad and the sweet potato soufflé were filled with chopped pecans. Every cake and every dish of ice cream had pecans added. There were pecan rolls for breakfast and pecan bread for lunch. Guests and family alike delighted in delicious pecan pancakes and pecan pies. While Mary Alice enjoyed a piece of pecan pie every now and then, she thought that when it came to pecans, the McCall family had taken a good thing a bit too far.

In an attempt to create a substitute for his Kentucky bourbon, her grandfather had tried to find a way to ferment pecans to make Christmas spirits for Grandma's fruitcake. When the attempt failed, he tried to persuade Grandma to use cheaper corn liquor, made by local bootleggers. Grandma would not hear of it. Of course, she loaded the fruitcake with pecans, but her recipe called for Kentucky bourbon and she would accept no homemade substitute. Grandpa considered this use of fine Kentucky bourbon a tragic waste. To his mind, sipping was the only suitable use for good Kentucky bourbon. Whenever he was offered a piece of Grandma's fruitcake, he joked about taking it to the old wringer washing machine to try to squeeze a glass of liquid out before he ate the cake. The juice, he thought, would be better than the cake.

One of Mary Alice's cousins made a dessert she called Better than Sex. Mary Alice wouldn't know about that. She did know that her cousin's dessert was a creamy, chocolate concoction, filled, of course, with pecans.

For Mary Alice, Christmas had changed dramatically. The house that had been in the McCall family since it was built in 1818 now stood empty. The last of the heirlooms were packed into the four boxes in the back of the dark green Explorer. The house, a desperate bequest from Aunt Evelyn, now belonged to the citizens of Bamberg County. It was to become the County Historical Museum. As she drove along the blacktop road, past the Bamburg Airport and through an industrial development area that occupied what had once been the cotton fields of the McCall plantation, two questions entered her mind. *Now, who will shell all of those pecans?* And, making her way onto the Charleston Road, *What in the world will I do with the Christmas quilt?*

The drive toward town past the white cotton fields of October brought back memories of her grandfather. Every time they rode to town together, he would tell her the same stories, rich in local history. All of this land used to be part of Barnwell County. Bamberg was originally known as Lowery's Turnout. It was a way station on the Old Stage Coach Road between Augusta and Charleston, the road that went through the middle of the McCall plantation, now U.S. Highway 78. When Mr. Bamberg bought the station, he changed the name. The county and the town adopted his name in 1897. Grandpa remembered it well. He was seven years old at the time.

Grandpa's favorite stories were about the War Between the States, or the War of Northern Aggression, as he preferred to call it. He told how George Jay Washington McCall converted the plantation to the manufacture of boots and saddles for the Confederate Army. At that time the McCall plantation had five hundred slaves, a fact Mary Alice found difficult to reconcile with her deep belief in human dignity. In her Advanced Placement U.S. history class, she always made it a point to confess this family flaw to her students. The institution of slavery, she thought, was an apt example of the Old Testament teaching that the sins of the fathers will be visited on the children to the third and fourth generation. The ongoing racial conflicts in this country, especially during the late sixties, her teenage years, were simply a matter of cause and effect.

Just outside of Bamberg Mary Alice turned left into Memorial Gardens. She parked her vehicle near the front of the cemetery where her grandpa and grandma, her father, and her mother were buried. She stood looking at the four graves. The marker above her grandparents' grave read Robert E.L. and Alice McCall. The headstone for her parents read R.E. Lee and Louisa McCall. She found comfort in knowing that after so many years her parents were side-by-side. She bowed for a moment of silent gratitude for the people who had loved her so much. She knew it would be a long time before she would be back to visit this place. She probably would not return until Aunt Evelyn's funeral.

In the town of Bamberg Mary Alice drove past the Methodist Church where her grandparents and her parents had been members. It was the church where Mary Alice had been baptized as an infant, wearing the same handmade gown her father had worn at his christening. She took a left at the traffic light past the old courthouse and the Confederate Memorial, turning the SUV onto the 301/601 highway heading toward Orangeburg.

As Mary Alice continued her drive across the Edisto River Bridge, she thought to herself, *This is the most beautiful place on earth*. The tall trees were gracefully draped in Spanish moss. The black water flowed calmly past a lone black man fishing from the bank. She recalled the many hours she and Grandpa spent fishing along the river. He would always say, "The bream might not bite but the 'skeeters will."

A red-tailed hawk flew up from the grassy shoulder of the road, clutching a small animal in its talons. The shoulder on both sides of the road sloped into ditches filled with dark swamp water. Above the pine trees and scrub palmettos a pair of Carolina buzzards soared, searching for road kill.

As Mary Alice continued her drive north, she recalled her grandpa's most passionate Civil War story. When he recounted, yet again, the well-rehearsed details of the scorched-earth tactics of General William Tecumseh Sherman's army, he told the story as if it had happened only yesterday. Once Sherman had marched to the sea destroying much of Georgia, he turned the Yankee army back north and brought them through South Carolina. On the way from Savannah to Columbia, the Union Army devastated the town of Barnwell. One of the Yankee officers reported to General Sherman that, following their raid, the town should change its name from Barnwell to Burnwell. Sherman laughed. By the time a detachment of Union troops arrived in this part of the county, the faithful Confederates had burned all three bridges over the Edisto River, both wagon bridges and the railroad bridge to keep the Yankee army from moving north toward Columbia. That was just what Sherman wanted. He wanted everything in his path burned. As offended as Mary Alice was by the institution of slavery, she was equally repulsed by the horrors of war.

Though he was born twenty-five years after Sherman's march, Grandpa remembered stories of the Yankee soldiers who set fire to the McCall home on three different occasions. The first time, federal troops ignited the roof of the house, and the very same Union soldiers put out the fire when they realized women and children were still inside the house. A Yankee sergeant gave the order to burn the house, and a chivalrous blue-coated lieutenant from Kentucky ordered that the flames be doused. Less than a week later, Sherman's soldiers set fire to the house again, this time at the kitchen on the back of the home. A slave woman, Queen Esther, rang the big alarm bell. All the slaves came running and put out the blaze with a bucket line hauling water from the well. Several days later the house was torched again on the front porch. This time Grandpa's Aunt Margaret, a courageous lady, put out the fire using the wet quilt that she grabbed from soaking in a washtub. That is why, he explained, her mother's quilt, which would one day belong to Mary Alice, had one corner singed by the fire.

When Mary Alice finally found the quilt earlier that morning, one of the marks of identification she looked for was that burned corner.

As she neared the town of Cope, Mary Alice admired the flat terrain, so different from the Upstate. Every house and doublewide seemed to have a boat in the front yard, and hanging from a clothesline in the side yard, rows of freshly washed laundry flapping in the stiff breeze. Her Explorer fell behind one of the ever-present logging trucks. Whenever she saw those massive trucks loaded with logs, she breathed a prayer for one of her fellow teachers. Her friend's husband had been tragically killed just before Christmas two years earlier when, blinded by the early morning sun, he drove his car into the back of a logging truck that had stopped to make a left turn. The trauma was never far from her thoughts when she was driving into the sun this time of year. Mary Alice gave the truck a wide berth. It was also the way she usually related to her Aunt Evelyn, giving her a wide berth, staying as far away from her as possible. But today she had to see her. Evelyn would expect her to stop by, and Mary Alice had questions to ask her annoying aunt.

Evelyn McCall Bauknight was Mary Alice's only aunt, her father's younger sister. In fact, Aunt Evelyn was sixteen years younger than Mary Alice's father. She was just five years old when Mary Alice came into the McCall family. So, Evelyn was ten years closer in age to her niece than to her beloved older brother, Mary Alice's father.

The relationship between Evelyn and Mary Alice had always been strained. In some ways Evelyn was like an older sister who never failed to give Mary Alice advice, usually unwelcome. In other ways Evelyn was like a spoiled stepsister, an only child who had felt displaced by her adopted niece. She took it upon herself to remind her niece that Mary Alice was really not a McCall, at least not by blood.

During her happy childhood days Mary Alice lived at the old homeplace in Bamberg. Evelyn usually spent all of her time in the house with her mother. Mary Alice loved her grandma, but she enjoyed most of all her time with her grandpa. When he talked with her about her adoption, he always said, "It's not the blood that matters. McCall blood has been mixed and mingled so many times that there's nothing special about the blood. The most important thing is the name and the way you live up to it."

Mary Alice's father, Lee McCall, had served in the Army in World War II. He married a young lady he met while he was at Camp Croft in Spartanburg in 1945, just after the war. Louisa had lived and worked at Beaumont cotton mill, but after their marriage she moved with her husband to his home in Bamberg. For five years they had no children, though they wanted a baby very much. In 1950 a family doctor told them about a little girl who had been born in Barnwell County. The infant needed a good home. The doctor and Grandpa's lawyer arranged the adoption so everything would be legal, and the little girl became a McCall, Mary Alice McCall. Less than a year later her father was called back into the Army and sent to Korea. It was there that he was killed.

Lee McCall's death was difficult for everyone in the family. Grandpa and Grandma lost their only son. His death meant the McCall name would not continue because Lee and Louisa did not have a son. For Evelyn, the death of her big brother seemed to intensify her resentment toward Louisa and Mary Alice McCall. It was as if Evelyn blamed them for her brother's death. From then on, Mary Alice could do nothing to please her Aunt Evelyn. Evelyn was critical of everything. She resented the fact that Louisa had named her daughter Mary Alice. "Alice should have been *my* name saved for one of *my* girls," Evelyn complained, as if her grandma's name could be bestowed on only one granddaughter.

Evelyn resented the way her father, Mary Alice's grandpa, took his adopted granddaughter under his wing after Lee died in Korea. Even though Mary Alice lost her father, a man she really never knew, the constant ongoing bitterness of Aunt Evelyn was far more difficult to bear. Mary Alice would always believe that the reason her mother moved back to Spartanburg was to get away from the incessant harangues of Evelyn. Most of the time Mary Alice avoided her aunt, but today she wanted to ask her about the quilt, the quilt her mother had left behind.

Mary Alice drove the Ford Explorer into Columbia right at the peak of rush hour traffic. *Columbia is hotter than half of Georgia*, she thought as she turned the air conditioner to maximum cool. Aunt Evelyn lived in a subdivision on Lake Murray. She seemed never to be at home, so Mary Alice used her cell phone to call ahead. For a change, Evelyn was not only at home, but she was expecting Mary Alice to come by to give her a full report on the search for the Christmas quilt.

Mary Alice had asked Aunt Evelyn's permission to go back to the old house in Bamberg one last time. Her aunt told her that the girls, Mary Alice's three cousins, had already gone over the house with a fine-tooth comb and that there was absolutely nothing left. The sisters had divided all of the furniture and other items among themselves. They did leave a few of Grandpa's old tools in the barn for Mary Alice, if she wanted them, but there was no sign of the quilt.

Mary Alice had asked nicely if she could conduct one last search, and Aunt Evelyn gave grudging permission. Just as she had expected, Mary Alice found the old home stripped of all the items she had remembered so fondly. The way her cousins had ransacked the place, taking everything of value but leaving behind piles of trash, reminded her of Grandpa's stories about General Sherman.

Mary Alice had gone straight to the closet in the master bedroom, a closet that was lined with cedar. Behind a row of shelves, just where her grandpa had showed her years before, she found the secret hiding place. It was where the family had stashed the silver when Sherman came through on his march to Columbia. It was a closet within a closet. It was where Grandpa had kept all of George Jay Washington McCall's Confederate money just in case the South ever did rise again.

When Mary Alice removed the shelves and opened the creaking secret door, she was greeted with a musty odor and evidence of mice. But she found the treasures she was seeking. There was a small metal box filled with the remaining Confederate bills, two boxes of old letters saved by the family over the years, and the Christmas quilt stuffed inside the Uncle Ben's Long Grain Converted Rice carton. It was a moment of joyful relief. Mary Alice had found her inheritance! She expected that Aunt Evelyn would ask only about the quilt, and Mary Alice would show her only the quilt.

Evelyn McCall Bauknight's home was a condominium with a view across Lake Murray, very different from the old homeplace in Bamberg where she had lived with her husband until five years ago. Uncle Luke was a good and long-suffering man. His life was marked by one failed business venture after another. Grandpa had paid Uncle Luke and Aunt Evelyn out of debt more than once. When Uncle Luke died, Aunt Evelyn moved away quickly, hoping to sell the family home immediately. She expected to receive a small fortune for the old plantation, but Uncle Luke had sold most of the land through the years just to make ends meet.

Finally, after the house had been vacant for five years, Aunt Evelyn decided to give the house to Bamberg County to cover the delinquent taxes. She received credit for a charitable contribution and a guarantee that the house would be listed on the National Register of Historic Places. Evelyn wanted to mark the McCall plantation with one of those nice metal signs put up by the Highway Department. The old homeplace became the future site of the County Museum.

When Mary Alice arrived at Aunt Evelyn's condominium on Lake Murray, that old feeling of apprehension flooded over her. She paused a moment to gather herself before ringing the doorbell, dreading this encounter with her disagreeable aunt.

The first question out of Aunt Evelyn's mouth was, "Did you find the quilt?"

Mary Alice asked if she might come in.

"Of course," Evelyn said. "Would you like a piece of pecan pie with some butter pecan ice cream on top?" Mary Alice would have just a small piece of pie and a glass of water.

Though Aunt Evelyn was eager to see the quilt, Mary Alice wanted to hear the story first. Aunt Evelyn told the tale with passion and attention to detail that reminded Mary Alice of her grandfather's way of spinning a yarn.

"A family slave named Queen Esther made the quilt in about 1850. She was the plantation seamstress, a kind and intelligent woman. She could card cotton to make thread on a spinning wheel, and then, using the thread, weave cotton fabric on a large loom inside a shed located next to her own cabin. The resulting homespun muslin fabric was dyed with tea or indigo and made into clothing for the slaves. She also used muslin as the backing for the quilts that she made.

Queen Esther made all of the clothes for the McCall family by hand from store-bought fabric.

For her efforts, she was allowed to keep the scraps. It was from these scraps that she cut carefully sized pieces. From the squares, rectangles, and triangles she made beautiful quilts. Her quilts usually had just a single, simple design in each panel. The patterns had descriptive names—Bear Paw, Flying Geese, Drunkard's Path, and Log Cabin.

The Christmas quilt was made of red stars on a white background. Queen Esther called the pattern The North Star. Nobody in the McCall family wanted anything with the name north in it. To the family, the pattern was the Star of Bethlehem."

Mary Alice asked, "So that's why it's called the Christmas quilt? The stars are Christmas colors."

"Not just that," Aunt Evelyn explained. "There's more. The McCall family had a standing joke that Queen Esther made so many quilts that she didn't have enough room in her cabin for all of them. She always had at least one quilt hanging on an old split rail fence beside the road. Other people said she was just showing off her work. They all thought that she used the star quilt more often than any of the others because most of the time it was the one draped on the fence airing out. On chilly days Queen Esther would sit on the porch of her cabin bundled up in the red and white quilt. It was often admired by friends and neighbors, but especially by the McCalls.

"McKendree McCall fought with Robert E. Lee and Stonewall Jackson early in the war. Like other Confederate soldiers he had to provide his own bedroll. He asked Queen Esther for a quilt and she gave him the star quilt to take with him. He took the quilt with him to war. He only fought in three battles before he was wounded. The quilt took a bullet right through one of the stars, and McKendree took a bullet in the knee. Since he could no longer march, he was given a horse and sent home to search for Confederate deserters and runaway slaves. He gave the quilt back to Queen Esther and apologized for the bullet hole. She never mended the hole.

"Soon after his return McKendree McCall got married. McKendree was my great-grandfather, your great-great-grandfather. Of course, you're not really a McCall," Evelyn asserted as an afterthought. "The family had so admired the quilt and McKendree had taken it to war, so Queen Esther gave it to his bride as a gift. Queen Esther wanted the quilt to always stay in the McCall family. So when the oldest son stepped over the broom, which was the way slaves described marriage, his mother was to give the quilt to his bride on the first Christmas after their marriage. That's another reason why it's known as the Christmas quilt.

"The Christmas quilt stayed in the McCall family. Queen Esther was often asked to make more quilts with the same pattern, but she never got around to it. After McKendree returned from the war and got married, Queen Esther's favorite quilt pattern seems to have been Drunkard's Path. That's the one that hung on the fence most often. After Abraham Lincoln emancipated the slaves in 1863, all of Queen Esther's quilts disappeared. The McCalls thought they had all been given to freed slaves. Only the Christmas quilt, given to McKendree McCall and his bride, stayed in the family. When Sherman's army came through, Aunt Margaret used the quilt to put out the fire set by

Log cabin

Flying geese

Wagon wheel

Crossroads

Bears Paw

The patterns were simple,
the messages were clear.

his soldiers. That's why the quilt is singed on one side.

"McKendree and his wife had two sons, Robert E. Lee McCall and Stonewall Jackson McCall. When Robert got married, the quilt went to his wife. My father, your grandpa, was Robert E. Lee McCall, Jr. Your adopted father was Robert E. Lee McCall III. He was my brother, Lee."

"So, my mother was given the quilt by Grandma the Christmas after my father and mother were married?"

"Yes," answered Evelyn, "but after Lee was killed in Korea, the quilt should have come back to me. You're not even real family. One of my daughters should have the quilt since your mother couldn't have a son. You're not even married."

"No, I'm not married, but I am the last person with the McCall name. Grandpa always taught me that my name matters more than blood."

Evelyn gave an audible gasp and had a stunned look as if Mary Alice had thrown a bucket of ice cold water on her. Even though she was fifty-two years old, it was the first time Mary Alice had ever talked back to her aunt. With some satisfaction she asked, "Now, would you like to see the quilt?"

"Yes, I would. Where did you find it?"

"I found it in a secret hiding place Grandpa showed me years ago. It was where the family hid the silver when Sherman came through."

"My girls got that silver after Luke died. Do you know they sold it all? Said they didn't have time to keep it polished."

Mary Alice went to the Explorer to get the quilt while Evelyn gathered herself. As she walked back into the condominium, Mary Alice had an uneasy feeling. She had only opened the box once, just to peek at the quilt, the star design, and the burned corner. She had not even taken the quilt all the way out of the box. Evelyn would want to see the whole quilt, burned corner, bullet hole, and all.

Evelyn was aghast that the quilt had been kept in a common rice box. But then, Aunt Evelyn had spent a good bit of her life being aghast. As the two women unpacked the antique, they were saddened to see its poor condition. The quilt had deteriorated badly. There was evidence that mice had made a home in the box. The muslin backing of the quilt was shredded. The cotton batting was falling away.

Evelyn shrieked, "Get it out! It's nothing but junk. Your mother ruined my heirloom!"

Mary Alice took the damaged quilt outside and spread it out carefully on Evelyn's patio. Dry rot had destroyed nearly half of the muslin backing. Mice, attracted by the cottonseeds remaining in the old batting, had done their damage. Still, there was much to be admired. A sudden gust of wind from the lake blew away some of the loose batting. Mary Alice threw a handful of the shredded backing into a garbage can.

"Throw it all away," Evelyn demanded.

But Mary Alice examined the top piece of quilt. She saw the bullet hole and looked again at the singed corner. The fine needlework was amazing. Tiny stitches connected the small red triangles of cloth. Delicate quilting held the top cover to the homespun muslin backing, securing the hand-carded batting between them. The batting, still containing cottonseeds that had escaped Queen Esther's vigorous carding, was the trademark of antique Southern quilts. *Surely this fragment of history could be salvaged,* thought Mary Alice.

"Hang it on a fence somewhere. That's what they say Queen Esther did with it most of the time. She just hung it on an old rail fence outside her cabin next to the road."

Feeling deflated, Mary Alice slowly packed what was left of the Christmas quilt back into the Uncle Ben's Long Grain Converted Rice box. She wasn't sure what converted rice was, but she certainly had a quilt that needed converting. She returned the box to the SUV and went back to the condominium to say goodbye. Evelyn was standing in the doorway.

"Aunt Evelyn, I am sorry the quilt is damaged. I have a friend who will know whether it can be salvaged."

"Don't bother! Louisa should have returned the quilt to me after Lee died. I would have taken care of it. Now it is ruined. I don't care what you do with it. Just take it away from here. I never want to see it again."

"Goodbye, Aunt Evelyn."

Without so much as a kind word, Evelyn shut the door.

✳   ✳   ✳

For Mary Alice, the day had begun with such anticipation. Though her trip to Bamberg and the old house had been difficult, she was excited to find the quilt. She was exhausted, and it was time to go home. As she drove away, she started to cry. And then she screamed aloud until her throat ached. As much as she tried to prepare herself, her aunt's words always hurt. She could understand why her beleaguered mother left Bamberg and moved back to Beaumont. Leaving the former cotton plantation to return to the cotton mill must have been difficult but not nearly as difficult as living with Evelyn. Leaving the old homeplace and returning to a mill house was a major transition, but it was a change from strife to peace. Mary Alice appreciated her mother more than ever.

Evelyn's words, "You're not even married," cut to the quick. That was true. Mary Alice was never married. She was once engaged. She met Bill in Bamberg the summer before her junior year in high school. He was visiting his grandparents for the summer, just as she was. Their grandmothers introduced them. Bill was from Hartsville and had two years left in college at The Citadel.

By the end of the summer, they were deeply in love, the first love for each of them. Mary Alice returned to Spartanburg for her junior year in high school. Bill went back to Charleston. They saw each other rarely, but they wrote letters several times a week. They met in Bamberg at Christmas and again spent all of their second summer together. Both families, and especially both grandmothers, encouraged their relationship. Bill gave Mary Alice an engagement ring, a diamond that had belonged to his grandmother, on Christmas Eve on the porch of the old McCall house. The wedding was planned for the following summer in Bamberg after Bill graduated from The Citadel and Mary Alice graduated from high school.

In April, right after Easter, Mary Alice got the letter. Bill had attended The Citadel on a Navy ROTC scholarship. He was ordered to report to Parris Island one week after graduation. He would be commissioned as an officer in the Marine Corps. In 1968 being in the Marine Corps meant one only thing—Viet Nam. Their wedding would have to be postponed indefinitely.

After he was sent to Southeast Asia, they continued to write, but his letters were few and far between. Mary Alice wrote love letters as if she were making diary entries, always expressing her affection for Bill. On the other hand, Bill wrote as if he were a war correspondent sending terse reports from the front lines. Even that was all right with Mary Alice as long as he ended with the line "I love you." After a time, that disappeared and then Mary Alice just didn't hear from him anymore. Was he dead? Was he a prisoner of war? Was he missing in action? For two years Mary Alice heard nothing. Even Bill's family did not hear from him. Bill never returned, at least not to South Carolina. Mary Alice finally heard from Bill's family that he was married and living in California with his wife and their child. Her heart was broken.

"You're not really a McCall," Evelyn had said. Mary Alice had not only accepted her adoption, she was grateful that Lee and Mary McCall had chosen her. Her mother had often reminded her that she was a special person. Mary Alice had learned as a child in Sunday school that all of God's children are adopted. Her mother taught her the intriguing verse from the Old Testament book of Esther: "Who knows but what you have come to the kingdom for just such a time as this?" Mary Alice knew that she had a place and her life had a purpose. She wasn't sure that Evelyn had ever learned that about herself. She wondered if Queen Esther had found her place and her purpose. Maybe it was quilt making.

By the time Mary Alice unloaded the Explorer, she was exhausted. She fixed a steaming mug of Lemon Lift tea, and then she took a long, slow shower.

"Thank Heaven for leftovers," her grandpa had taught her. "They're like money in the bank." Over a bowl of yesterday's chicken noodle soup, freshly reheated in the microwave, she continued to reflect on her day.

Her curiosity about the quilt remained. She was only a beginner at quilt lore, but she knew someone who was an expert. She dialed up her best friend from college. Jo answered in that same perky voice that always gave Mary Alice a boost. "Come to Charleston," Jo invited. "Come next weekend. Matt and the boys will be away on a camping trip. We'll have all weekend to catch up and talk quilts. By the way, don't wash the Christmas quilt. I'll help you with that next weekend. Just hang it up, air it out, and pack it in something besides the rice carton, like maybe a Rubbermaid box, something befitting a treasured antique. And Mary Alice, bring some Efferdent tablets with you."

By late Sunday afternoon Mary Alice had decided to alter her lesson plans for the week. As a well-seasoned teacher, she felt that it was her prerogative to change the syllabus. When she majored in history at Wofford College, Dr. Lewis Jones had reminded her that there was often a teachable moment for learning certain segments of history. A good teacher had a knack for timing the discussion of certain subjects to the interest of the students or, as in this situation, to the whim of the teacher.

Mary Alice's trip to Bamberg on Friday to look for the quilt had become a day of class preparation as well. She was interested in the antebellum South and especially the institution of slavery.

On Monday she announced to her AP U.S. History class their focus of the week. Mary Alice would lecture each day. Then on Friday the students would submit a two-page report on a relevant topic of their own choosing. Subjects had to be approved ahead of time, no later than Wednesday. After all, she reminded them, this was a college-level class.

On Tuesday Mary Alice told her class about the Underground Railroad. It was neither a railroad, nor was it underground. It was a route of escape, a way from slavery to freedom. It was a cooperative effort by those who opposed slavery to help fugitive slaves reach freedom in the North. The story of the Underground Railroad began in 1833, when slavery was abolished in the British Empire, including Canada. From that time until Abraham Lincoln issued the Emancipation Proclamation in 1863, thousands of slaves escaped from plantations in the South and fled to the promised land of the North or on to Canada.

Bounty hunters patrolled the roads leading to the North trying to capture runaway slaves. This period of American history produced heroes like Frederick Douglass and heroines like Harriet Tubman. An escaped slave from Maryland, Harriet Tubman became a conductor on the Underground Railroad, leading more than three hundred slaves to freedom.

By Wednesday the AP U.S. history students had received approval for the themes of their Friday reports. Mary Alice had been teaching long enough so that for her there were few surprises. The topics followed a predictable pattern: biographies of Frederick Douglass, Abraham Lincoln, and Harriet Tubman; reports on the music of slavery; discussions on the politics of slavery; and papers on issues leading up to the Civil War.

Friday morning before school, Mary Alice packed the dark green Ford Explorer for her trip to Charleston. The Christmas quilt was carefully folded into a Rubbermaid container in a manner befitting an antique. Though the quilt had been hanging on a makeshift clothesline in the spare bedroom, Mary Alice had not washed it. After school, she would be off to visit Jo for the weekend,

Efferdent tablets in hand, though she had not the foggiest idea what they were for.

The students in her class had done a good job with their written essays. Mary Alice asked Brad to give his as an oral presentation on the music of slavery. With guitar in hand, he sang for the class. He included several songs in his presentation. He concluded with "Follow the Drinking Gourd." He explained that the drinking gourd to the slaves was the constellation we know as the Big Dipper. The two stars in the cup of the constellation are called pointer stars that align with the North Star. To follow the drinking gourd is to follow the North Star, to travel north to freedom.

✳   ✳   ✳

Mary Alice always enjoyed being with Jo. They had both been educated at Wofford College. They were a part of the first graduating class to include women. Jo had entered college right out of high school. Mary Alice had worked in the cotton mill and waited. At first she waited for Bill. Then she waited to find herself. Her grandpa finally told her that it was time for her to get on with her life. He offered to pay for her education.

Mary Alice and Jo were enrolled in Wofford as day students. In spite of their seven-year age difference, they became friends immediately. They were both from single-parent families. Both lived with their mothers. When they graduated, Mary Alice became a teacher. Jo followed her father's wishes and his footsteps and entered law school. There she met Matt, now her husband.

Matt and Jo lived on Rutledge Street, just south of Calhoun Street, in downtown Charleston. Their home was one of the old single houses with a side door facing the street, opening onto a long porch. It was just the kind of home in just the kind of neighborhood that Jo had dreamed about as a college student. Two incomes as Charleston attorneys made their lifestyle possible.

When Mary Alice arrived at Jo's house, the two women greeted and hugged each other. Then in the next breath, Jo exclaimed, "Get the quilt! I can't wait to see it!"

Mary Alice got the quilt while Jo fixed two glasses of sweet iced tea. They spread the quilt on a wicker divan on the porch, sipped tea, and admired Queen Esther's handiwork. Mary Alice told the family story about the Christmas quilt. In the course of their conversation, Jo said, "Your quilt reminds me of something I have been reading. Ozella McDaniels Williams was a quilt maker here in Charleston and was a regular vendor at the Old Market on Meeting Street. She not only made beautiful quilts, but she also revealed a story hidden in the quilts of the antebellum South. The book, *Hidden In Plain View: A Secret Story of Quilts*, was written by Jacquelin Tobin, an historian, and Raymond Dobard, a professor of art history. They tell the story of Ozella and her quilts, and, I think, the story of your quilt, too."

"Really? What is it?" asked Mary Alice.

"For years scholars have speculated that runaway slaves, fleeing to the safety of the North along the Underground Railroad, had some means of communication. How would they know which route to take? How would they know where to locate safe stations of refuge? How could they find food and water? The secret communication of the Underground Railroad was perhaps contained in the various patterns of quilts. According to the oral tradition revealed by Ozella, slaves seeking freedom received directions and encouragement from quilts."

"But how?" asked Mary Alice.

"On every plantation a slave woman was designated as the seamstress. She not only made and repaired clothing for the plantation owner and his family, but she also saved scraps of material and made quilts for herself, her family, and her fellow slaves. It was quite common to see quilts hanging to air outside the seamstress's cabin."

"Just like Queen Esther!" said Mary Alice.

"Exactly!" Jo continued. "According to Ozella, the quilts displayed gave messages to escaping slaves. The patterns were simple; the messages were clear. A Wagon Wheel motif indicated that transportation to freedom was available. A Bear Paw quilt signified that food and water were close. The Flying Geese design advised slaves not to stop but to keep moving north. The Crossroads arrangement was a signal to change directions. The Log Cabin pattern indicated that a station where weary slaves could find refuge and rest was nearby. The Drunkard's Path quilt gave warning that bounty hunters were in the area and escaping slaves needed to take an indirect route."

"So," said Mary Alice, "when McKendree McCall came back from the war to look for runaway slaves, Queen Esther used the Drunkard's Path quilt to give warning."

"That's right!" Jo concluded. "The North Star design on your quilt was just like the song 'Follow the Drinking Gourd.' It meant follow the North Star. The North Star was a symbol of hope and encouragement. The North Star quilt meant, 'Don't give up. Continue the journey to freedom.'"

So Queen Esther had found her purpose in life, and it was far more significant than making quilts. In her own way Queen Esther was a freedom fighter living on the McCall plantation. That realization made Mary Alice proud.

Jo and Mary Alice had a busy weekend together. They walked to the Battery, looking out on Charleston Harbor where the Cooper River and the Ashley River join to form the Atlantic Ocean. They walked to Rainbow Row and shopped on King Street. They had shrimp and Southern grits for brunch at the Hominy Grill. Across the Cooper River at a restaurant on Shem Creek called Slightly Up The Creek, they enjoyed a Lowcountry dinner featuring gourmet collard greens. They went to church on Sunday morning in the Holy City at the First Scots Presbyterian Church.

Much of their weekend was occupied with quilts and talk of quilts. The Charleston County Museum featured a special quilt display and symposium. In her study Jo had a library's worth of books on quilts. Together they washed the Christmas quilt using Efferdent denture tablets.

"Are you sure it is safe to wash this one-hundred-and-fifty-year-old quilt with Efferdent?" Mary

Alice asked.

"Yes, I am," said Jo. "I learned it from my grandmother. It is guaranteed to remove all of the stains."

"How did your grandmother learn to use it?" asked Mary Alice.

"It was one of those Eureka moments," answered Jo, "like Firestone spilling rubber on a hot stove or what's-his-name discovering penicillin. My grandmother accidentally turned over the glass that was holding her dentures as they soaked. It splashed into the sink where she was washing her white blouse!" Just as Jo said, the Efferdent cleaned Mary Alice's antique quilt beautifully.

Together Mary Alice and Jo went to the old market. Jo explained, "Tourists often believe that this was where slaves were sold. Actually, there were several places where that happened, but not in the old market area." Mary Alice learned that Ozella McDaniel Williams had died several years before, but other quilt makers verified her story. As Mary Alice watched African-American women making sweetgrass baskets, selling flowers, and selling quilts at the Old Market, she could not help thinking of Queen Esther, a woman who had lived more than a hundred years before her, a woman whom she had known about for only one week, but a woman she respected deeply.

As the weekend came to a close, Mary Alice prepared to drive back to the Upstate. She still was not sure what to do with the Christmas quilt. Jo had a suggestion.

"Mary Alice, the quilt is a beautiful example of a mid-nineteenth century antebellum folk art. It is especially valuable to you and the McCall family. In its present condition, it is unusable, and you can't enjoy it. I have an idea, but you'll have to trust me with your heirloom. About half the quilt can be preserved in close to its original state, but the rest of the quilt needs to become a cutter."

"What's a cutter?" asked Mary Alice.

Jo explained that old quilts in poor condition could be cut up and made into a variety of keep-sakes as a way to continue to enjoy the heirloom, even when it has been damaged by time, and to salvage the sections still in good condition. "I know someone who does that kind of work. If you want to leave the quilt with me, I'll see what I can do."

Mary Alice agreed reluctantly, but she had confidence in her friend. "Thank you, Jo. Give Matt and the boys my love."

"Be careful driving home," said Jo. "I'll drop this in the mail to you before Christmas."

＊ ＊ ＊

Every year since Luke Bauknight's death, Mary Alice visited her Aunt Evelyn, her three cousins, and their families on Christmas Eve. Luke had always insisted that the family should include Mary Alice in the Christmas Day festivities at the old homeplace. Evelyn did not want anyone who was not really family to be present on Christmas Day. Now, with Uncle Luke dead and gone, Mary Alice was welcome only on Christmas Eve.

The truth was that Mary Alice was never really welcome. The decision to visit Evelyn was always difficult, especially when her cousins were included. For this Christmas Eve visit, the three cousins did not even think of bringing their own children. They simply didn't want their children to know Mary Alice, though she was the only remaining person with the McCall name. The cousins consciously excluded their children because they did not consider this annual visit with Mary Alice a family event. To their minds, Mary Alice was not family. Mary Alice had long since given up the hope of knowing those children. This was the only family she had, and these four women were really the only enemies she had.

As she drove to Lake Murray to visit her aunt and her cousins, Mary Alice pushed herself beyond the anger that so often came over her when she thought of her only remaining family. She knew that her anger was prompted by her hurt. She had debated whether or not to make the trip this year, especially after her unpleasant visit with Evelyn in October. She went because she had unique gifts to give. Maybe next year she would not make the effort, but this Christmas she was going.

Mary Alice always took four gifts, and she always received four gifts. This year she was excited about the surprise gifts she had for Aunt Evelyn and the cousins. Mary Alice was not invited for a meal, but she was offered a piece of pecan pie with butter pecan ice cream on top. Pecan-flavored coffee was also available. Mary Alice had a small piece of pie and a glass of water, as she usually did. After a brief visit, the three cousins gave Mary Alice their gifts and Evelyn's gift.

"You know what they are," Evelyn said. "You can just open them later."

Mary Alice presented her gifts to the only family she had left in all the world. The four women opened their gifts at the same time. The gifts were all the same—angels. Each angel, about eight inches high, was dressed in red and white quilted fabric. Each angel's dress had a star pattern on the front.

One cousin said, "Oh, look, a cute little angel!"

Another commented, "An old-fashioned Christmas angel."

Evelyn screamed, "Oh my Lord! You've cut up the Christmas quilt!"

"What?" shouted the third cousin. "I wanted that quilt, and you cut it up?"

Mary Alice should not have been surprised by their reaction. "Aunt Evelyn," she said. "I know you told me to throw it away. You said you never wanted to see it again, but I wanted each of you to have a part of the Christmas quilt. It did, after all, belong to me. Just as wise King Solomon ordered that a baby be cut in two because two mothers were arguing over who was the rightful parent, I thought that cutting the Christmas quilt would end the conflict within our family. Think of these angels as Christmas angels bringing the message of Christmas, 'Peace on Earth,' especially to our family."

The daughters of Evelyn Bauknight wondered why their mother had said she never wanted to

see the quilt again. Evelyn gave her own version of the story, blaming Mary Alice, of course. Then Mary Alice told the story about Queen Esther. She told all that she had learned about quilts and the Underground Railroad. She concluded, "So the quilt that our family has always called the Christmas quilt was actually a North Star quilt. The star that is on each angel is a symbol of hope and encouragement to people seeking freedom."

"What happened to the star with the bullet hole in it?" asked Evelyn.

"That panel of the quilt was framed with an explanation that I wrote," said Mary Alice. "It will be displayed in the Bamberg County Museum at the old McCall homeplace."

"And what about the rest of the quilt? Surely more could be salvaged than these few angels," Evelyn wondered.

"Yes, more was salvaged, and I have complied with your wishes. You'll probably never see it again. Your Christmas angels made from the quilt will be the only keepsakes any of us will ever have."

With that declaration, it was time for Mary Alice to leave.

* * *

On Christmas morning Mary Alice had one thing on her mind. She got up early, read her devotion, and ate a light breakfast, a pecan cinnamon roll and Lemon Lift tea. She had one more Christmas gift to deliver, the refurbished half of the Christmas quilt. She had written out the story of Queen Esther, the McCall family, and the history of the quilt. This remaining part of Queen Esther's handiwork was remarkably well preserved. Jo's quilting friend had done a beautiful job repairing and restoring the quilt, binding the cut edges with pieces of the original fabric. Mary Alice gently stroked the fabric, admiring the craftsmanship one last time. Each red and white star had been stitched with a prayer for hope and for freedom. Feeling satisfied, she wrapped the quilt with a note attached.

Mary Alice delivered the gift to a home she had never before visited. The young family was expecting her. Mary Alice was given their name by an adoption agency. The agency did the requisite background check on Mary Alice. "I want the name of the family who adopts a baby closest to Christmas," she had requested. They were a little like the Holy Family, she thought, welcoming a child born out of wedlock at Christmastime.

At the home she met the adoptive parents. They had wanted a child for more than seven years. Their new little daughter was a biracial child named Emily. Mary Alice gave the family the gift. "It is a very special quilt, an antique actually, made years ago by a kind woman. I know she would be delighted for a precious child like Emily to have this. It is just the right size for a baby quilt." The young mother opened the gift and marveled at the quilt. She wrapped her new baby daughter in the beautiful quilt and handed little Emily to Mary Alice. Mary Alice cuddled the child close to her cheek, delighting in the sweet soft newborn, as the young mother read the card. "Emily, you are a special child. God has a plan for your life." It was signed, "An adopted friend."

In her own home later on Christmas Day, Mary Alice opened the four gifts from Evelyn and her cousins, four boxes all wrapped in the same paper. Mary Alice had guessed correctly: four boxes of pecans. All unshelled.

She had one more gift to open. It was a box wrapped beautifully with paper that she had admired at the Old Market in Charleston. The tag read,

DO NOT OPEN 'TIL CHRISTMAS

The box was stuffed with sheets of red and white tissue paper. Inside she found a copy of the book *Hidden in Plain View*. She also found her very own quilted Christmas angel made from the Christmas quilt. Jo had her quilt salvage person make an additional angel. Jo had selected the most beautiful of the five quilted angels as a keepsake especially for her friend, Mary Alice.

Mary Alice again admired the delicate stitching done so long ago by Queen Esther, a kind and courageous woman who found her place in the world as a messenger of hope and freedom. Jo had attached a note on the back of the angel, which read:

> *To Mary Alice:*
> *You are an angel of peace;*
> *You are a star of hope.*
> *You have the heart of a quilt maker.*
> *You know how to take the scraps and pieces of life's shambles*
> *and transform them into symbols of hope and peace.*
> *Blessed Christmas.*

/

cedar tree

"God sure did know what he was doing when he made this place," Ed whispered.

The Last Christmas Tree

The morning dawned cold and gray in the southern Blue Ridge Mountains. Freezing drizzle had fallen throughout the night. Ed King finished the last of his coffee. He put the empty mug in the kitchen sink, took a heavy, worn corduroy coat from the brass hook at the back door, and stepped out onto the back porch. Low clouds obscured Ed's view of the mountains to the north. It was Epiphany, by tradition the day when kings from the East followed a star to Bethlehem to greet a new king. To Ed King, who knew nothing about Epiphany, it was just a cold January sixth.

Ed hated cold weather. Pulling the old coat on over a newer flannel shirt, he checked the pockets and found his briar pipe, tobacco, and matches. He packed tobacco into the bowl of the pipe as he walked, his boots crunching through the ice-covered grass to the barn. He lit the pipe with a single match, returning the matches and pouch of tobacco to his pocket.

Taking several puffs on the pipe, Ed unlocked the icy padlock on the barn door and entered his private domain. The front section of the barn had been converted into a workshop. Along one wall, power tools were hung on pegboard. A radial arm saw and a lathe occupied about a third of the wall. Cabinets stretched to the far corner of the shop, their small drawers containing nails, screws, and fasteners of every variety.

Along the opposite wall were tall storage cabinets with a collection of rods and reels lined up in special racks. Tackle boxes, each filled with an assortment of specialized lures, had their places on the top shelf. Nets, creels, and bait boxes were neatly stored at one end. All of the fishing equipment was kept behind closed doors as a protection from the inevitable sawdust.

A table saw was prominent in the center of the room. A workbench took most of the back wall except for the locked door that entered the back of the barn. Above the workbench was a wide assortment of hand tools hung on pegboard, the silhouette of each tool outlined in blue paint. In Ed King's orderly workshop, there was a place for everything, and everything was in its place.

In the front corner of the workshop was a small wood-burning stove. Mounted on the wall above the stove was a glass case displaying a collection of antique fishing lures. On a shelf near the stove were a pipe rack with five old pipes, all well-used, a humidor of Ed's favorite tobacco, and a small, framed picture of Ed's wife, Mary.

In the opposite front corner of the workshop was a staircase that ascended to an open loft that was used for storage. Ed climbed the stairs and found a plastic box freshly labeled

CHRISTMAS TREE ORNAMENTS

He had put the box back in the loft on the day after Christmas. This year Mary had insisted that he take the Christmas tree down earlier than usual and put all of the decorations away. Now, Ed needed to retrieve one item from the box, a small Christmas ornament that he tucked in the left pocket of his plaid shirt.

His mission accomplished, Ed closed the box and descended the stairs. He opened one of the cabinets containing fishing tackle and found a nearly empty spool of ten pound fishing line. He put the fishing line in the right pocket of his flannel shirt. He relit his pipe, dropped the spent match into the wood stove, and left the workshop. He securely locked the door behind him, snapping closed the ice-cold padlock with his bare hands.

Enjoying his pipe, Ed walked around to the back of the barn. The unfinished back section was about twice as large as the workshop. Ed's father and grandfather had used the barn for horses, mules, and cows, but now it served as a garage and a lumber shed. In the old hayloft Ed stored fine hardwood lumber—cherry, walnut, and oak—which he used to make furniture.

The original dirt floor was covered with a layer of granite gravel. Split oak firewood was kept dry in one of the four old stalls. In another were stored odds and ends of moulding and finished lumber. In a third stall scraps of plywood and paneling were kept. The fourth held framing material, 2-by-4s, 2-by-6s, and assorted wider pieces. Though the rear of the barn was more rustic than the workshop, it was tidy nonetheless.

Ed's vintage Ford pickup truck, a boat trailer, and a handmade johnboat took up most of the remaining area. A steel garbage can secured sunflower seed from pilfering by mice. Taking a scoop of the black seed, Ed went around the corner of the barn to fill a birdfeeder suspended from the limb of a Red Maple tree in the backyard. Both the tree and the feeder were draped with icicles. Immediately, a pair of chickadees flew down to dine.

Ed had positioned the birdfeeder so that his wife Mary could see it from her chair in the den, as well as from the bedroom and the kitchen. That view of the maple tree, the birds at the feeder, and the mountains beyond had been one of Mary's few pleasures in the last several months.

Ed tromped through the frozen grass back to the barn. As he returned the scoop to the steel container, he noticed above it the large plywood sign he had made and suspended from a rusty nail on the barn wall.

ED KING'S CHRISTMAS TREES
PICK OUT A TREE
WE'LL CUT IT FOR YOU
REASONABLE PRICES

The sign had been hanging on a fencepost out by the road since the week before Thanksgiving. Ed had returned it to the barn on Christmas Eve. He wondered if he would ever use it again.

The johnboat and trailer were already hitched to the pickup truck. Several cinder blocks, a coil of nylon rope, and five Christmas trees had been loaded in the truck the night before. Ed checked his pocket watch: 7 a.m., time for breakfast. He started the truck, relighting his pipe as the engine warmed.

The truck followed the long, twisting gravel driveway down to the road. On either side Christmas trees glistened with ice on sloped fields. Ed grew Scotch pines and white pines on his farm. He had tried a few Fraser firs, but they did not do well. They grew best higher up, above three thousand feet. Here in the foothills, on the land he had inherited from his family, the pines thrived. Tending Christmas trees was hard work year-round. The seedlings had to be planted in the cold of winter. Spraying with pesticides was necessary several times during the year. Then the trees had to be pruned and shaped each year to make them look like Christmas trees. It took twelve years for a seedling to grow to a size suitable for a Christmas tree. Even so, the trees had provided a good retirement income for Ed and Mary.

At the end of his gravel road, Ed turned the truck left onto the paved road. It was four winding miles to town. While the countryside looked like a winter wonderland, the road was clear. So far, the asphalt had retained enough heat from a warm December to keep ice from forming. As he made his way into town, Ed stopped to collect a few more ice-laden Christmas trees that had been left by the roadside. He recognized that most of them had been grown on his farm. He picked up three from the Reynolds' place. By the time he got to Debbie's Diner, he had filled the truck bed and the johnboat with discarded trees.

"Whatcha' gonna have today, Mr. Ed?" Debbie asked, popping her chewing gum.

"Debbie, I'll have two fried eggs. Make one of them tough as rubber and the other one so runny that I can't eat it with a fork. I'll have three pieces of bacon burned to a crisp on one end and raw on the other end. Grits with lotsa lumps, biscuits burned on the bottom and uncooked in the middle, and a cup of coffee, lukewarm with curdled cream."

"Ed King, whatcha' talking about? I can't fix no breakfast like that!"

"I don't know why not. You fixed me one just like that yesterday morning."

"Hush your mouth! You always goin' on about somethin'."

Billy Watkins, who had just come in, overheard the conversation. Billy ran a local service station, one of the few that still actually offered service.

"How are you, Ed?"

"Fine, Billy. Have a seat."

Billy pulled up a chair as Debbie shouted from behind the counter.

"Whatcha' gonna have, Billy?"

"Same as Ed, only burn my bacon on both ends and leave it raw in the middle."

"Y'all better quit messin' with me," Debbie shouted over her shoulder.

Turning back to Ed, Billy said, "I hear they're calling for a wintry mix today. Looks to me like we already have it."

"I don't care much for winter weather," Ed said.

"It's good for the trees, isn't it?"

"I suppose so. They don't do well in the heat, especially if it's dry. I lost a lot of them in that drought two years ago. I expect winter weather helps the service station business."

"Some. We get a lot of tire chain work. People worry about their antifreeze. And we do our fair share of jump starts."

Debbie brought breakfast. "This is the best I could do. Enjoy."

"Thank you, Debbie," said Ed. "It looks just as good as yesterday."

"Awright now."

Billy asked, "What are you doing with all of those trees on the sixth of January? Are you taking them to the Lutheran church? I hear they're having another big bonfire this year."

"No way!" Ed said emphatically. "Why do they burn all those trees anyway?"

"Preacher Kuhn was by the station yesterday. I asked him about that. He said it was to celebrate the coming of the wise men to see Jesus."

Ed smirked, "It's a pretty foolish way to celebrate the wise men, if you ask me. The fellows over at the fire station think it's downright stupid, too, especially since the Lutherans nearly set the old Methodist church on fire three years back."

"Whatcha gonna do with them trees?" asked Debbie.

"I'm having an after-Christmas sale, two for the price of one, used trees only."

Billy and Debbie laughed. Debbie added, "Ed King, you won't do."

Ed and Billy finished their breakfast. Billy remarked that his golden retriever had a nice litter of pups after Christmas. He planned to sell them, but if Ed wanted one, he could have the pick of the litter. It was a kind gesture, and Ed said he would think about it.

After talking about the weather, burning Christmas trees, dogs, and making a few jokes, they didn't have much to say to each other. The thing they were both thinking was left unspoken. Ed paid the tab for both of them, tipped Debbie, and asked if he could have a coffee to go.

Back in his truck, he waited for the defroster to clear the windshield of ice. He packed his pipe with fresh tobacco. As he smoked and sipped his coffee, he realized that the lighthearted banter at

Debbie's Diner might well be the last conversation he would have with another person for the rest of the day.

Ed drove down the main street of his small town. He stopped at the only red light in town, at an intersection referred to by townsfolk as Holy Corners. The traffic light was only necessary on Sunday mornings. Puffing on his pipe, waiting for the light, Ed looked at four churches, each on a corner of the intersection. He had assigned unflattering names to each of the churches.

The Lutheran church had been Mary's church. It had kept her very busy. Ed called it Our Lady of Perpetual Motion.

The Methodist church had a new pastor at least every four years and sometimes more frequently than that. Ed called it Our Lady of Perpetual Turnover. He looked at the church sign with the Methodist symbol, a cross with flames coming from the bottom. He remembered that three years ago, after the Lutheran bonfire had almost set the old Methodist building on fire, he had thought about changing the name to Our Lady of the Flames.

The Presbyterian church was the most traditional. The congregation rarely accepted anything new or creative. Ed called it Our Lady of Perpetual Boredom.

The Episcopal church had suffered an unfortunate indiscretion among the clergy. The priest and the minister of music had run off together. Though few members were surprised, the entire church was upset, as were the wives of the two ministers. Ed called it Our Lady of Perpetual Scandal.

Ed remembered that in years past, before the great influx of summer tourists and the year-round retirees, only the Methodist and the Presbyterian churches stood at this crossroad. Many of the working people of the town had belonged to the Methodist church or to the Baptist church, which was on the outskirts of town. The upper crust had belonged to the Presbyterian church.

In those days there were neither Lutherans nor Episcopalians in these mountains. They were flatlanders who only came to the Blue Ridge to see the leaves change colors in the fall, but once the tourist trade flourished and the retirement communities developed, the Episcopalians and the Lutherans came to stay.

Mary had been so happy to be able to go to a Lutheran church again. When they had moved to the homeplace forty-eight years ago, Mary had settled into the Methodist church. But when the Lutheran church was built, Mary gladly returned to the church of her youth.

The light turned green. Ed drove through the Holy Corners intersection. As he did he noticed the sign in front of the Lutheran church.

EPIPHANY SERVICE TONIGHT
JANUARY 6
THE FESTIVAL OF LIGHTS
HUGE BONFIRE
BRING YOUR CHRISTMAS TREES

The pastor of the Lutheran church, Rev. Calhoun Kuhn, was relatively new to town. Ed had thought Calhoun Kuhn was a perfectly good name, reflecting both the good pastor's South Carolina heritage as well as his Lutheran roots deep in the Dutch Fork area. Still, Kuhn, no matter how it was spelled, was a difficult name to be stuck with in the Southern mountains. There were just too many good raccoon and coon dog jokes. One thing Ed liked was that the pastor himself made jokes about his own name. A man who can laugh at himself has a good perspective on life, Ed thought. Most of the members of Rev. Kuhn's church simply called him Pastor Cal, as Mary did.

Pastor Cal had been a real friend to Mary and Ed in recent weeks. Ed had been thinking that if he ever did go to church again, he would go to the Lutheran church. One thing he knew for certain, he would never attend a Christmas tree burning. Besides, in this weather, the whole thing might be called off.

Just beyond the town limits, Ed passed the Baptist church, the church in which he had been baptized. He went back a few times after he returned from the war in Germany. But since he had graduated from Appalachian State Teachers College, he had not been to church anywhere, and that was more than forty-eight years ago. The last time he attended the Baptist church was for his dad's funeral.

It was good, he thought, that the Baptist church was not on Holy Corners. The Baptists didn't really have much to do with other denominations. They didn't even take part in the community Thanksgiving service. As he drove past, his unflattering name for the church came to mind, Our Lady of Perpetual Guilt.

Ed drove the truck, pulling the trailer across the bridge over Silent Creek. Beyond the bridge Ed passed the old high school where he had spent his entire teaching career. He had been the baseball coach, a football coach, a math teacher, and the shop teacher at the school. Following the war, Ed enrolled at App State on the G. I. Bill, long before the college became a university. He played football and baseball. He met Mary. She was a junior when he was a freshman, though he was one year older than she was.

When he graduated with a degree and a teaching certificate, they were married at the Lutheran church in Gastonia, North Carolina, Mary's hometown. They moved to his family farm, which he had inherited, and which became their mountain home for more than forty-eight years. Ed taught at the high school for thirty-four years. When the schools were consolidated, Ed retired and started a cabinet-making business in the barn. He had already started a Christmas tree farm in the pastureland several years before that.

Ed continued driving down the mountain road toward Lake Jericho. The freezing drizzle changed to sleet, so Ed slowed down. December had been unusually warm. Pearl Harbor Day brought an unseasonable thunderstorm, a sure sign that there would be a frost in May, according to the folk wisdom of the southern Appalachian Mountains. The wooly worms were right again. According to

the caterpillars' coloration, a warm beginning of winter would give way to a cold mid-winter. Spring would come late to the mountains because Easter would be late.

The temperatures had been warm enough that the pink geraniums on the Kings' front porch had survived until two days after Christmas. Pink geraniums were Mary's favorite flowers, and Ed had done all he could to keep them alive. He had moved them in and out of the house several times when the thermometer dipped below freezing in October and November. In December he brought them inside only once.

January was another story. By New Year's Eve winter had come to stay. Temperatures had been below freezing every night and not much above freezing during the day. Ed hated cold weather. Though he was a big burly man, he remembered a winter when he thought he would never be warm again. Ed was flying bombing raids over Germany with the Army Air Corps. He was the bombardier on a B-17, the fabled airplane also known as the Flying Fortress. After fourteen successful missions, his plane had a problem on the fifteenth. Over Berlin he had attempted to release the six thousand-pound payload as usual, but for some reason the automatic release malfunctioned, and the bombs did not drop. Ed left his seat, and, with the bomb bay doors opened, he walked the narrow catwalk and manually released the bombs. Walking a twelve-inch beam twenty thousand feet in the air through an open bomb bay was an act of uncommon courage. Ed shrugged it off, saying, "When you're nineteen years old, you'll do anything."

The big airplane carrying all that extra weight had fallen behind and had become detached from the rest of the squadron. German fighters shot down the plane, and the crew bailed out. Prevailing winds carried their parachutes just across the Swiss border where they landed in the snow. They wore only their flight suits and had no boots with them, as was usual for bomber crews. After two days and one very cold night in a makeshift snow cave, they finally found refuge in a Swiss dairy barn. Two of the nine crew members suffered hypothermia. Two more had to have toes amputated due to frostbite. Ed had disliked cold weather ever since.

Mary, on the other hand, always enjoyed the winter months. "Snow is like a beautiful white comforter covering the tired earth, inviting it to rest," Mary would say.

"When I was in Switzerland, there was nothing comforting about it," Ed would retort.

Mary enjoyed watching the snow fall, especially when the snowflakes were big and fluffy. "Snowflakes," she would say, "are angel tears." If anyone knew anything about angel tears, it was Mary.

Ed turned the truck onto a state forest service road and rumbled toward the lake. In a secluded spot near the shoreline, Ed maneuvered the truck, backing the trailer toward the water. With the Ford parked, he moved the Christmas trees out of the johnboat and loosened the frozen straps holding it to the trailer. He moved his boat to the water's edge. Cinder blocks from the pickup were distributed evenly on the bottom of the boat. Christmas trees were bound all around with rope to compress them. Icy, dead limbs cracked and splintered as Ed tightened the rope. He was able to stack all of the trees he had gathered into the johnboat. He arranged them carefully, balancing the load. He had room in the johnboat for just one more tree.

The last Christmas tree slid across the bed of the pickup. Frozen icicles broke in Ed's bare hands as he loaded the tree into the bow of the johnboat. The silver plastic icicles that had decorated the tree now stuck to his corduroy coat and to his plaid flannel shirt. He brushed them away. While putting away the Christmas decorations, he had saved as many of the silver streamers as he could, but there was no use taking these few back home. The decorations had all been packed in the attic a week earlier. Ed struck a match with his cold fingers, lit his pipe, and pushed the boat into the morning fog of Lake Jericho.

Under the weight of cinder blocks and trees heavy with ice from an all-night drizzle, the dark green boat rode low in the water. Still, Ed trusted his boat. He had built it in his own workshop five winters before. He had gotten the design from a store-bought metal boat he had seen on a fishing trip to the Outer Banks. To make it easier to paddle from both sides of the boat, Ed had designed the stern narrower than the one on the model. The morning was cold and quiet; the water was still. Ed could hear only the falling sleet and his paddle rippling the calm water as he followed the shoreline to the mouth of Silent Creek.

This would be the perfect spot. Either the Forestry Service or the timber company owned all of the land on this side of the lake. There were no lake houses. Only wilderness camping was allowed, and only in one designated area. Ed knew that no one would see him this morning. A raucous crow, carrying his complaint into the fog, left his perch in a bare oak tree near the water's edge. Even in the summer, Ed thought, his secret would be safe.

Ed took two hard strokes on each side of the boat and glided into the cove ahead. He searched his pocket for his trusty knife, a Boker Tree Brand. For Christmas Mary had given him a new Old Timer pocketknife with three blades. It was in the box in his top dresser drawer. He was not ready to use it. He might not ever use it.

The Boker had been his favorite for several years. He had spent Christmas Eve putting an edge on it. The larger blade had a broken tip, but even that came in handy when a screw had to be tightened. The small blade was what he needed now to remove the tiny green cedar needles that pierced his left palm like splinters. His hands had been so numb when he loaded the cedar into the boat, he had not noticed the needles. After he had removed a few, Ed continued to paddle. He craned to peer around the pile of evergreens in the bow until he regained the shoreline as his guide.

The fog was beginning to lift now. Through the mist the evergreens along the bank stood in sharp contrast to the trees lying in the johnboat. The cedars and pines along the shore, draped as they were in ice, looked like a Christmas card, but the trees that had been cut to decorate homes for Christmas were dead. The cut pines were already brown. The firs retained their green but were dead all the same.

Ed's load included only three firs—Fraser firs from the high mountains. All three had come from the Reynolds' place. Mrs. Reynolds decorated to the hilt every year and threw parties all through the holidays. Some said it was the only time of year that Stewart Reynolds could smile, since he owned the only mortuary in the county. The joke around town was that when the funeral business was good, as it almost always was, Stewart's countenance was appropriately sorrowful. *If it took three high-dollar Christmas trees from the high mountains to make Stewart grin*, Ed thought, *then it was worth it.*

Ed had seen a lot of Stewart recently. Stewart had helped him make most of the decisions about Mary's funeral. The Reynolds Funeral Home was the only one in the county, and there was not a finer man than Stewart Reynolds. Mary had requested a graveside service with a modest wooden casket. "A person's funeral ought to be in keeping with their life," Stewart had said.

Mary's service was simple and sweet, just as she had been. As he remembered Mary's funeral, Ed thought he might cry, but he did not. He had not cried since Mary's death, nine days before.

As the boat neared the mouth of Silent Creek, Ed became aware of the water level. The red clay border around the bank was only a few inches wide on the steepest slopes, so the lake was close to maximum level. Nine feet of water would be about right. All the trees measured eight feet or less except the big fir that was hanging over the bow of the johnboat. Mrs. Reynolds had used it in a foyer that had a ceiling fourteen feet high. Nine feet of water would be perfect if he tied two cinder blocks to the middle of the big tree to anchor it on the lake bottom.

About twenty feet out from the bank, there was a steep drop-off into deeper water. The depth of the shallows was no more than three feet when the water level was up. The water was seven to ten feet deep at the end of the ledge, which Ed had discovered last summer. It was then that he made his plans for this spot. He tied a length of rope and a cinder block to the first tree. He pushed the tree into the water and threw the cinder block away from the boat. The boat rocked and the tree sank from sight, trunk first, into the deeper water.

This was another burial, Ed thought. Like a gangster destroying the evidence of a grisly murder, concealing the victim's body, concrete blocks and all, he pushed the dead trees from the boat, one at a time.

The trees had served the purpose for which they had been planted. Ed had found them lying by the roadside like fallen soldiers. He was at least giving them the honor of a burial. It was one way to soothe his grief for the trees he had tended for twelve years. One by one, Ed dropped the trees overboard into the chilly waters of Lake Jericho. He knew why Stewart Reynolds didn't smile much. Burying the dead was nothing to smile about.

The last Christmas tree was the cedar that Ed had intentionally saved until last. It was different from the others. He had cut it himself from a fencerow on the farm. A bird, after a meal of cedar berries, had perched on the barbed wire and planted the cedar. The tree had grown naturally into its traditional Christmas shape, so Ed had not had to shear it, shape it, and spray it like the others. He had always preferred a cedar Christmas tree, not only because he liked the smell, but also because it was the kind of tree he had enjoyed as a boy.

One year Mary had wanted a bought tree. She purchased a Canadian spruce trimmed to the right shape. It turned brown before Christmas, and Ed vowed to have a cedar from then on. Even after he started the tree farm, he always had a cedar for Christmas.

A cedar Christmas tree was almost as important to Ed as the pink angel on top of the tree had been to Mary. The pink angel was a gift to Mary at a baby shower the December just before their little daughter was born. Their child was expected in February, but the tiny girl was born two days before Christmas. She was their only child. She had lived for only a few hours. In those days even the hospital in Asheville had no neonatal unit. Back then, though, at least in the mountains, babies were almost always born at home. Their daughter had been born in their bedroom. The doctor said the tiny child had just come too soon.

Ed remembered holding his tiny child. She was perfectly formed but no bigger than the palm of his hand. Ed had already planed and sanded enough walnut lumber preparing to build a crib for their new baby. After the little girl died, the grieving daddy stayed up all night long in the workshop building a walnut casket the size of a shoebox. She was buried on Christmas Eve in the cemetery on the top of Little Mountain.

In keeping with her Lutheran tradition, Mary had wanted their child to be baptized. Just before Christmas, the Methodist minister had gone out of town to visit relatives. By the time he returned, the baby had died. Mary told him how sad she was that their little girl had not been baptized before her death. At the funeral the pastor said the most comforting thing to them. Placing one hand on Ed's shoulder and the other hand on Mary's arm, he explained that their daughter had been baptized with their tears. Then he prayed using the words of Christ from the baptismal blessing: "Let the little children come to me, do not hinder them: for to such belongs the kingdom of God."

Ed reached inside his corduroy jacket and felt his left shirt pocket. The pink angel had been on top of their cedar Christmas tree every year since their little girl died. Mary said the pink angel was important because it reminded her that her baby was with God. The angel on top of the tree made Christmas bearable for Mary in the same way a cedar tree made Christmas special to Ed. He tied on the cinder block and fingered the branches of the cedar. He crushed some needles between his fingers and sniffed the aroma. No wonder the Cherokees considered cedar to be a sacred wood.

The morning was darker now as light sleet mixed with snow. Beneath the calm water, the tree-tops were barely visible. Ed packed fresh tobacco in his pipe. *This will be a great fishing spot*, he thought. *And no one else will know.* The trees, he knew, would make cover for bream and crappie. Bass would come to spawn in the shallows between the ledge and the bank. March and April for

bass; after the full moon in May, the bream would bed; crappie would take cover here through the summer. He found his knife and removed a few more needles from his palms. Leaning back in the boat, he smoked and watched blue jays as they pestered a squirrel in a sweet gum tree. The sky, the water, the trees, the birds; "God sure did know what he was doing when He made this place," he whispered.

After he discovered the ledge, Ed had wanted Mary to see this spot. He had only been to Lake Jericho once all of last summer. He had told Mary about the ledge and his plan. Mary didn't like to eat fish. She didn't cook fish. She didn't catch fish. But she would have gladly taken a book and enjoyed the boat ride and Ed's company. He really wanted to bring her to this spot, but she was never able to come with him. She was just too sick.

On Christmas night she had told him to start collecting trees for his fish bed. The day after Christmas, she had sounded urgent, "Ed, fix that fish bed you've been planning. You're gonna enjoy it next summer." Ed had gathered a few of the trees that very day. The next day Mary went into a coma. The following day, two days after Christmas, Mary died.

Ed looked at his pipe. Mary's illness and death seemed so unfair. Though she rarely said so, Mary had always wanted him to give up smoking. For her to die the way she did, when he was the one who had smoked all of his life, seemed so wrong. He knocked the ashes from his pipe. The burning tobacco hissed in the water. Tears almost came to his eyes.

Ed picked a few more needles from the cedar and ground them in his hands. He stood and balanced the boat. Gently he rolled the cedar tree into the water. A few more plastic icicles floated away. He threw the cinder block away from the boat into slightly more shallow water. He watched the cedar disappear beneath the water. More plastic icicles floated to the surface and swirled in a pattern above the tree. Ed watched until the water cleared, and he could see all the trees in their watery grave. Only a single sprig of green stood above the surface of the water—the top of the cedar.

Heavier sleet started to fall again. A kingfisher stole a shad from the shallows. It was January sixth, the day when trees were brought to the Lutheran churchyard for a huge bonfire. The year before, they had burned twenty or more Christmas trees. The entire volunteer fire department was on hand to control the blaze. Most of the trees had been grown on Ed's farm and planted in the dead of winter twelve years before. "What a waste," he said aloud. Down on the coast they used Christmas trees to hold sand dunes in place. Even burial in sand was better than cremation, at least for Christmas trees. How much better to build a fish bed, to let the fish find a home in the discarded trees.

Sleet changed to snow and started sticking on the branches of trees along the bank. The thin red line of clay along the shore was still too warm for much accumulation, but everything else was turning white. "Mary would have loved this place," he whispered. Ed watched the snow falling gently. *Snowflakes are angel tears*, he remembered, and a few of his own tears finally came.

It had been a hard year. Events had moved so rapidly. In early February Mary's doctor found the large spot on the x-ray. On Valentines' Day Ed and Mary celebrated their forty-eighth wedding anniversary. A week later she had surgery. The report was not good. Chemotherapy was brutal. Mary was terribly sick. She lost all of her hair. Together they decided to stop the treatments.

By Easter she seemed better, but she was very weak. Ed could not bear to leave her. In June she seemed to rally, and she encouraged Ed to go fishing. He did, but only one time. It was then that he found the ledge near the mouth of Silent Creek. By July Mary was low again. By September they were told the malignancy had spread.

By Thanksgiving Ed had started building a casket, as Mary had requested. It was a simple wooden casket made from white oak and lined with red cedar. Ed built it in the workshop. Mary never saw it, though she must surely have known what Ed was making. She teased him, saying he was doing something special for Christmas. In a way, he was.

Mary insisted on putting up a Christmas tree earlier than usual, so Ed cut the cedar from the fencerow. Christmas week was their last week together. She died the night of December twenty-seventh, the same night the pink geraniums on the front porch died from a killing frost. Ed was by Mary's side. He just plain forgot to bring the potted plants inside.

To Ed it seemed appropriate for the pink geraniums to die on the same night as Mary. Pastor Cal had even commented on it at Mary's funeral. He also said that, in some ways, it was a blessing that Mary died so quickly. *Maybe so*, Ed thought, though most of the time he didn't feel that way.

Mary had requested a graveside service. Ed was sure it was so he would not have to go into a church. It was a blessing that the funeral was on the last warm day of December. It would have been much more difficult for Ed to have Mary's service on a bitterly cold day.

In Mary's obituary Ed had asked that in lieu of flowers, contributions be made to the benevolent fund of the Lutheran church. He had told Pastor Cal any donations were to be used to keep people warm during the winter. Too bad, he thought, that the thermal energy from the bonfire could not somehow be used to provide heat for people who were cold.

As the snow fell, Ed thought of Mary's grave next to that of their little girl in the cemetery on top of Little Mountain. He knew that Mary was not there. She was somewhere beyond the low gray clouds, somewhere beyond the pale Blue Ridge Mountains. But Ed had watched as her tired, worn body, placed in a casket he had made of oak and cedar, was lowered into the ground. There was something peaceful about thinking of Mary as sleeping beneath the soft white comforter of snow that now blanketed her grave.

A pair of mourning doves flew up from the bank near the creek mouth. Snow was heavier now. "Mary..." he said, unable to say more. Sitting alone in his johnboat in a cove on Lake Jericho at the mouth of Silent Creek with fluffy white angel tears falling all around him, Ed King wept.

After a while, a cardinal chirped in a holly tree on the shore. Ed moved the johnboat over beside the green twig sticking up from the water, the top of the cedar tree, the last Christmas tree he and Mary had together. He took the nearly empty spool of fishing line from the right pocket of his shirt. He cut a piece with his knife. From his left shirt pocket over his heart, he removed the pink angel he had taken from the box in the loft of his workshop earlier that morning. In his hands he held the simple Christmas ornament that had graced their Christmas tree for so many years. He thought about what it had meant to his beloved wife. He thought of Mary and their little baby girl, together at last. To the top of the cedar tree, barely showing above the cold water of Lake Jericho, Ed King tied the pink angel.

Acknowledgements

I am thankful for the members of Morningside Baptist Church. Ten years ago they graciously embarked with me on this adventure in worship. The Christmas stories have become an annual tradition and a cherished part of our Advent celebration. The church family has encouraged me to write these stories. They have prayed for me as I crafted them. Family and friends have listened with kind patience as I told the stories aloud even as these tales were being formed in my own mind. Some have gone far beyond encouragement to making places, spaces, and tools available to me as I wrote. Many have offered helpful suggestions that have made the stories better.

I appreciate the confidence of Betsy Teter and the Hub City Writers Project board. Their acceptance of the proposal to publish the stories and their willingness to include June's illustrations bears witness to Hub City's devotion to its mission to cultivate local writers and artists. Betsy Teter is remarkable in her considerable ability and her dogged determination to develop the creative facet of our unique community. Spartanburg and the Hub City Writers Project are blessed to have her leadership. The sign on her door reads *The Hub City Writers Project World Headquarters*. Her vision is global; her heart is inclusive. Betsy Teter is working hard to make the world a better place for us all.

Kathy Green, my ministry assistant, is simply the best. Not only is she a superior secretary managing my hectic schedule, but she also has the literary knowledge befitting her master's degree in English. She read and edited every story, line by line, year by year, as they were being formed. Kathy is also a good friend and colleague who has worked willingly and collaborated honestly with me on this project.

Deno Trakas read and marked every story, never with a heavy hand. He is a gifted teacher who knows how to craft a good short story, and he is a skilled writer of engaging fiction. Deno made helpful suggestions about each story, gently teaching me along the way. The revised stories are much better than the original versions because of Deno. I have learned from him and, I hope, I have become a better writer.

I am grateful beyond measure for my wife, Clare. She is the love of my life and my companion in all things. Clare has listened to me tell these stories over and over before a word was ever printed on paper. And she has been with me as I struggled to put words on the page. She asked the penetrating questions that sharpened the tales into readable narratives. She has a keen editorial eye and has been willing to argue with me about changes and modifications. Most of all, she has put up with my absentminded preoccupation as I wrote. In joy and in sorrow, for better or worse, we share almost everything except toothbrushes and umbrellas. I am blessed.

Comfort and Joy would not have been possible without the generosity of Hub City donors. I am especially indebted to those benefactors who supported the project from the beginning by underwriting the initial production costs of the book. Each donor as well as everyone who purchased a book helped Hub City. I am most grateful and encourage all of you to continue supporting the creative endeavors of the Hub City Writers Project. Thank you all.

Finally, thanks to you, treasured reader. Without you, my stories would be meaningless. Words written but unread are nothing more than straw in the wind. I am grateful to all of you who read these stories. I hope that one or more will be your favorite and will linger in your memory Christmas after Christmas, year after year.

—Faithfully,
Kirk H. Neely